Creating Context in Andean Cultures

Oxford Studies in Anthropological Linguistics
William Bright, General Editor

CREATING CONTEXT IN ANDEAN CULTURES

Edited by

Rosaleen Howard-Malverde

New York   Oxford
Oxford University Press
1997

Oxford University Press

Oxford   New York
Athens   Auckland   Bangkok   Bogota   Bombay   Buenos Aires
Calcutta   Cape Town   Dar es Salaam   Delhi   Florence   Hong Kong
Istanbul   Karachi   Kuala Lumpur   Madras   Madrid   Melbourne
Mexico City   Nairobi   Paris   Singapore   Taipei   Tokyo   Toronto

and associated companies in
Berlin   Ibadan

Chapter 4, "The Art of Ethnic Militancy: Theatre and Indigenous Consciousness in Colombia" by Joanne Rappaport is
reprinted from *Cumbe Reborn: An Andean Ethnography of History*, Joanne Rappaport, copyright © 1994 by permission
of the University of Chicago Press.

Chapter 11, "On the Margin: Letter Exchange Among Andean Non-Literates" by Sarah Lund is reprinted from
Exploring the Written: Anthropology and the Multiplicity of Writing, ed. E. Archetti, copyright © 1994 by permission
of the Scandinavian University Press, Oslo.

Creating context in Andean cultures / edited by Rosaleen Howard-Malverde.
p. cm. — (Oxford studies in anthropological linguistics : 6)
Includes bibliographical references.
ISBN 0-19-509789-0; ISBN 0-19-510914-7 (pbk.)
1. Quechua language—Discourse analysis.   2. Quechua language
—Semantics.   3. Culture—Andes Region—Semiotic models.
4. Discourse analysis, Narrative—Andes Region.   5. Anthropological
linguistics—Andes Region.   6. Semantics—Andes Region.
7. Criticism, Textual—Andes Region.   I. Howard-Malverde, Rosaleen.
II. Series.
PM6303.C74   1997
498'.323—dc20   95-42967

1   3   5   7   9   8   6   4   2

Printed in the United States of America
on acid-free paper

In memory of
Eleudoro Gabriel Blas

Preface and Acknowledgments

Over the years, in the course of fieldwork in different parts of the Andes, many Quechua-speaking storytellers have shared with me their understandings of the complex social and historical setting within which their cultures have evolved. Through the narration of oral tradition, as well as the other media of expression discussed in this book, Andean peoples interpret and sometimes challenge the conditions in which they live, creating culture anew with each generation of speakers. This book is dedicated to the memory of one of those storytellers.

Ten of the papers in this volume were delivered to the conference on "Textuality in Amerindian Cultures: Production, Reception, Strategies," convened by myself and William Rowe and held in May 1991 under the joint auspices of the Centre for Latin American Cultural Studies of King's College London, and the Institute of Latin American Studies of the University of London. The paper by Willem Adelaar was given at a workshop on "Language, Discourse and Society in the Andes" held at the Institute of Latin American Studies of the University of London in February 1990. The paper by Denise Arnold was presented at an anthropology workshop on "Gender Relations, Work and Proprietorship among the Indigenous Peoples of South America," convened by Joanna Overing, also at the Institute of Latin American Studies, University of London, in December 1990.

The conference on "Textuality in Amerindian Cultures: Production, Reception, Strategies" was funded by the British Academy and The Nuffield Foundation, in addition to the host institutions; grateful thanks for their support are due to all these bodies. Thanks also to the Institute of Latin American Studies of the University of Liverpool, who met the translation costs of the papers by Lienhard and Millones. I should like to acknowledge the contributions of those who took part in the conference who are not represented in this volume, whose papers and participation in the roundtable on Sunday morning were invaluable to the debate: Hernán Aguilar, Margit Gutmann, Silvia Hirsch, Billie Jean Isbell, Peter Masson, Rodrigo Montoya, Joanna Overing, and Susanna Rostas. A special thanks to William Rowe, who has been involved with this project from the outset; I am grateful to him; to William Bright, OSAL editor-in-chief; and to Rodolfo Malverde, for their comments on a draft version of the introduction. Acknowledgments are due to the editorial staff at OUP for their expert advice. Thanks also to my father, Ben Howard, who, in late night conversations over the phone, helped me think through the ideas involved in the terms *textuality* and *context* and made me see the importance of having an active verb form in the title of the book. Tristan Platt gave much appreciated encouragement, and his comments on the text/context distinction were especially useful. Thanks most of all to the contributors, for their patience and diligence in seeing their papers through to the final versions presented here.

Liverpool   R.H.-M.
March 1995

CONTENTS

CONTRIBUTORS

Willem F. H. Adelaar
Department of Comparative Linguistics, University of Leiden

Catherine J. Allen
Department of Anthropology, George Washington University

Denise Arnold
Instituto de Lengua y Cultura Aymara, La Paz, and University of London

Sabine Dedenbach-Salazar Sáenz
Seminar für Völkerkunde, University of Bonn

Penny Dransart
Department of Archaeology, University of Wales, Lampeter

Penelope Harvey
Department of Social Anthropology, University of Manchester

Rosaleen Howard-Malverde
Institute of Latin American Studies, University of Liverpool

Martin Lienhard
Romanisches Seminar, University of Zurich

Luis Millones
Seminario Interdisciplinario de Estudios Andinos, Lima

Tristan Platt
Institute of Amerindian Studies, Department of Social Anthropology, University of St Andrews

Joanne Rappaport
Department of Sociology and Anthropology, University of Maryland

Sarah Lund
Department and Museum of Social Anthropology, University of Oslo

A Note on Orthography

The different contributors to this volume have not opted for a uniform style of representation in writing for the Quechua and Aymara languages. Variation depends in part on whether or not a phonemic transcription is being offered. There exist official alphabets for both languages, used in Peru and Bolivia particularly for language planning purposes. However, where authors have made other orthographic choices, the editor has respected these.

Creating Context in
Andean Cultures

ROSALEEN HOWARD-MALVERDE

Introduction

*Between Text and Context in the
Evocation of Culture*

At its inception, the 1991 conference on "Textuality in Amerindian Cultures" (see preface) proposed to examine diverse forms of cultural expression in indigenous Latin America, with a particular focus on the textualising processes and textlike attributes that such expression displays. The notion of text was taken in its very broadest sense: thus the *text* of *textiles*—two words with a common root in Latin *texere* meaning 'to weave'—could be as valid an object of our interests as the alphabetic script of the seventeenth-century Huarochirí manuscript or the oral discourse of speech makers and dramatists in modern day Peru and Colombia. The mutual influence between speech and writing is shown to be crucial in a number of the chapters and forms a recurrent feature of the volume. The metaphorical use of the concept of text as a paradigm for the description of other areas of cultural practice proved to be more problematical; this is a matter I discuss in more detail here, while some of the contributors also address the issue in relation to particular ethnographic cases.

In this introduction I shall explore some of the diverse ways in which concepts such as discourse, text, context, textuality, texture, and narrative have been used in recent approaches to the study of culture, be it verbally manifested or otherwise. These remarks are intended to clarify some of the terms of the debate from my personal point of view; in addition, each author represented here has his or her own usages which may further expand the discussion. In this way, the book presents a diversity of viewpoints around a set of issues currently topical within the disciplines of social anthropology and anthropological linguistics alike.

With regard to the concept of "text", in recognition of the different disciplinary traditions within which this concept is employed, I shall separate discussion of its primary, linguistic, sense, from discussion of the more metaphorical uses of "text" that have arisen in anthropology. This is not to suggest, however, that the contributions contained in the volume necessarily make such a stringent separation: many of the more anthropological papers make use of a rather linguistic notion of text (e.g., Harvey, Rappaport); Allen's chapter stresses that the Western notion of linguistic text is based on premises quite distinct from those at work in many Andean processes of textualisation; furthermore, in the Andes, the metaphor of "culture-as-text" may not necessarily be the construct of the ethnographer, but part of the indigenous conceptual system held by culture members themselves (e.g., Arnold, Platt).

The remainder of my essay will explore common threads between the chapters not picked up in the discussion of the linguistically derived terms and concepts. Thematic affinities will be shown across papers of different methodological orientations, from the more text-linguistic contributions (e.g., Adelaar, Dedenbach), to the literary-textual ones (e.g., Millones, Lienhard), to the ethnographic studies (e.g., Harvey, Rappaport, Allen, Dransart, Arnold, Lund, Platt).

Discourse and text as social process

The term *discourse* is applied in a variety of ways in linguistics, where it is taken to be an essentially verbal phenomenon manifested in either speech or writing.[1] Whether spoken or written, discourse is a communicative tool necessarily arising within a situation of utterance; in this sense, discourse is of the performative order of language use and is socially grounded. A related view of discourse as constantly reconstituting itself in the moment is to be found in Foucault's writings on the nature of discourse, in his words:

> We must be ready to receive every moment of discourse in its sudden irruption; in that punctuality in which it appears, and in that temporal dispersion that enables it to be repeated, known, forgotten, transformed, utterly erased, and hidden, far from all view, in the dust of books. Discourse must not be referred to the distant presence of the origin, but treated as and when it occurs. (1972: 25)

Foucault's observations pertain specifically to written discourses, such as the documents of history which, according to him, are "monumentalised" by conventional historiographical method. He advocates an approach that refuses to treat such documents as unassailable monuments, but seeks to analyse them by persistently asking the question, as he puts it, "what was being said in what was said"? (ibid., 28). The meanings of discourse are thus shown to be inextricably tied to the social and political conditions within which it is produced; the applicability of Foucault's approach to the analysis of oral—in addition to written—history, is something I have discussed elsewhere (Howard-Malverde 1990).

The groundedness of discourse is as true of the spoken medium as it is of the written one, although in the case of the latter the mode of reception is utterly different. The place and time of reception of the written text are removed from the place and time of its moment of production, so the naturally dialogic interaction that occurs in the oral medium is missing, or can only be artificially constructed by the interpretive activity of the reader (Ricoeur 1971). These observations may be borne in mind in relation to a number of the essays in the volume, where it is shown that oral and written modes of discourse are by no means always separate in practice. In light of the Andean evidence, there is scope for a revision of theories regarding the differential social roles and symbolic functions of literacy and orality in particular historical and cultural contexts: Lund, Lienhard, Allen, Arnold, and Platt make this revision part of their task. Also in connection with the "literacy-orality" discussion, Adelaar demonstrates the effects on discourse structure and linguistic form of the transposition of a traditionally oral language (Quechua) into the written medium.

It should also be mentioned, in relation to the meanings of "discourse", that Foucault's agenda provides the critical discourse analyst with tools to unmask the ways in which language is used to manipulate and control, especially in institutionalised domains such as the mass media, education, and religion (cf. Fairclough 1989). This leads us into a somewhat different area of analytical tradition, insofar as Foucault's conception of discourse is not strictly speaking linguistic. As Duranti and Goodwin point out, for Foucault discourse is a set of cultural practices and attitudes, a domain of knowledge that regulates social life (Duranti and Goodwin 1992: 30). Such cultural practices and attitudes frequently surface in language, although they are not confined to it. Thus, from a more anthropological perspective, discourse can mean something akin to ideology, and analysis of discourse can be conducive to an understanding of the dynamics of power relations in society and processes of social change (cf. Fairclough 1992; Street 1993: 15).

Following upon the above remarks about discourse, how shall we take the primary meaning of *text?* For Paul Ricoeur, when manifested in writing, discourse gives rise to the birth of text, which is held to be "any discourse fixed by writing" (Ricoeur 1991: 106ff.).[2] In this view, fixity is a most characteristic feature of text, and indeed, in commonplace usage, "text" bears connotations of an immutable script to which members of a society are constrained to adhere in their cultural beliefs and practices, as, for example, in the case of the constitutionalised "texts" that provide the basis for world religions and legal systems.

By contrast, William Hanks, in a useful review article, proposes a definition that orients us toward the idea of text as essentially social, and the notion of "fixity" thus recedes: "a communicative phenomenon located in the social matrix within which the discourse is produced and understood, towards which there is a social orientation, rendering text interpretable by a community of users" (Hanks 1989: 96).

Such a definition coincides with the views of text adopted by Lienhard, Adelaar and Dedenbach, according to which the literary and linguistic features of text are best apprehended and interpreted in light of the specific historical and social conditions of production within which it emerges.

Textuality, again to cite Hanks, can be taken as "the quality of coherence or connectivity that characterises text" (ibid.). Thus conceived, the concept of textuality stems from a prior concept of text in the terms just defined, and Hanks proceeds to a useful summary of the achievements of text-linguistics in identifying those aspects of linguistic form that help structure text and enable textuality. The use in text of deictics and orientational suffixes as analysed by Adelaar, and the patterning of evidential markers in discourse as Dedenbach describes, both pragmatic issues relating to the management of information, are excellent examples of the kind of text-linguistic feature that Hanks is referring to here.

In considering what text is, it is instructive also to think about what it is not. Hanks counterposes text to nontext in this respect: whereas text comprises a set of coherent symbols, the nontextual would consist in the random, unmotivated, juxtaposition of markings or objects, such as the senseless cacophony of a crowded street or scuff marks on a public wall (ibid., 96). In this respect we can appreciate the way in which the pebbles symbolically handled by the pilgrims in Allen's account are indeed components of text: the same pebbles on some other occasion, outside the pilgrimage, in the eyes of the goatherd casually passing by, might be meaningless, thoughtlessly kicked underfoot, a nontext in Hanks's terms.

I would argue then for an open and flexible notion of text along the lines that William Hanks suggests, whereby text is considered not merely as product but as process, a process that can be seen as a mode of social action whereby power is exercised, and human potential to bring about change in the world is fulfilled. Such a view of text emphasises the interpenetration of textual and extratextual factors, necessary for adequate interpretation; in Hanks's words: "The boundaries of text are best conceived as extremely permeable, incomplete, and only momentarily established" (ibid., 105). Such a view allows for the dissolving of the boundaries that separate the text from the world, boundaries that in their turn serve to maintain the illusion of the text's authority. This point connects with Ricoeur's conception of the interpretive process, to which I return later in this chapter.

Text in context, text as context

A dynamic and flexible notion of text requires a rethinking of the related concept of *context*. If the boundaries between the text and the world are conceived as permeable, it is hard wholly to sustain the traditional view of text as being located *in* a context, from which it can be disengaged for the purposes of analysis or, alternatively, to which it must be related to enable a fuller, contextualised, interpretation. In the customary view, context is taken to be something external to text, and the analysis of context in its own right is rarely included in the search for meaning. Clearly, context has an influence on the shape of text: the forms of discourse emergent in institutional settings, for example, can be related to a context that is "there" in the minds of participants to some extent, both prior and subsequent to interractions that take place within those settings. Nonetheless, there is an argument for revising the somewhat unidirectional conception of the text-context relationship as it has traditionally been held. While, on the one hand, context can rightly be said to be *constructive of* text, from another perspective, context can also be taken to be *constructed by* text in processes of interactivity. Thus conceptualised, context itself becomes a phenomenon shaped in social interaction. Text is then conceived not so much as *in* context, but rather as creative and *constitutive of* context, as Duranti and Goodwin propose: "Neither the physical nor the social setting for talk is something that is fixed, immutable and simply 'out there'. Instead these phenomena, and the very real constraints they provide, are dynamically and socially constituted by activities (talk included) of the participants which stand in a reflexive relationship to the context thus constituted" (Duranti and Goodwin 1992: 7).

A number of the papers in this volume (e.g., Harvey, Rappaport, Dransart, Allen, Platt) illustrate how texts and textualising practices are active agents in the shaping of experience and, effectively, the creation of context, whether this be by verbal or other symbolically expressive means.

Text as a model for the interpretation of culture

Recent studies have called into question the appropriateness of text as a model or metaphor for the description and interpretation of nonverbal forms of cultural expression (cf. Keesing 1987; Strathern 1987; Thompson 1990). The *culture-as-text* approach stems in particular from Clifford Geertz's inspired interpretations of social interaction observed during fieldwork in Morocco and Indonesia. Geertz describes his concept of culture as an essentially semiotic one, and elaborates his position in this much-cited passage from "Thick description": "Believing, with Max Weber, that man is an animal suspended in webs of significance he himself has spun, I take culture to be those webs, and the analysis of it to be therefore not an experimental science in search of law but an interpretive one in search of meaning" (Geertz 1973: 5).

The metaphor of culture as "webs of significance" calls to mind the linguistic interconnections between 'web', 'weave', 'text', and 'textile', which allow for the Aymara weavings discussed by Arnold (in this volume) to be as valid an object of present concern as the Huarochirí manuscript; later in the same article, Geertz makes use of the text, as opposed to textile, metaphor more specifically: "Doing ethnography is like trying to read...a manuscript—foreign, faded, full of ellipses, incoherencies, suspicious emendations, and tendentious commentaries, but written not in conventionalised graphs of sound but in transient examples of shaped behaviour" (ibid., 10). He further describes culture as an "acted document" (ibid.).

However, despite Geertz's quite explicit use of the textual metaphor in theory, a perusal of his method of ethnographic description and interpretation in practice—as with the complex episode of the Berber sheep-stealing raid in the same essay—reveals it to be less reifying and reductionist than recent critics of the model claim (e.g., Keesing 1987: 165; Thompson 1990: 134). For Geertz, the "text" of culture amounts to what he otherwise calls "social discourse", which may be conducted, as he puts it, "in multiple tongues and as much in action as in words" (1973: 18). The cross-cultural misunderstandings and conflicting political interests of the actors involved in the sheep-stealing episode are brilliantly unveiled by Geertz as part and parcel of his will to demonstrate how culture operates as text. The subtlety of his insights, and his skill in textualising events in the construction of his ethnographic account, lead to no reduction in meaning—quite the opposite. As I read Geertz's reading of the power game between the Jewish trader Cohen, the French commandant, and the Marmusha tribal sheikh, I am caught up in the excitement of the bluffs and tactical skirmishings, and intrigued by both the psychology and the cultural significance of it all. However, it seems to me that the text metaphor is somewhat superfluous to Geertz's ends. In light of the subsequent criticism to which his theory has fallen prey, Geertz can be said, in this case at least, to have got somewhat caught up in an interpretive web of his own making.

J. B. Thompson, for example, takes particular issue with Geertz's approach, arguing that the culture-as-text metaphor leads to the analyst eschewing problems of power and social conflict in the interpretation (Thompson 1990: 134). Thompson also sees the metaphor of text as likely to impose a monochrome interpretation upon situations of struggle in which multiple intentions and conflicting interpretations arise. My own reading of "Thick Description," as briefly expressed here, does not allow me fully to agree with Thompson on this point. Geertz's handling of the Moroccan data in my view skillfully lays bare the interstices of power relations in a colonial setting, as these are lived and experienced by human individuals of flesh and blood. Geertz's mistake, if any, is to overlabour a semiotic theory of culture that he neither particularly needs nor applies to the case study in point.

In reviewing the model of culture-as-text, Thompson also takes issue with Ricoeur, to whom we owe an important elaboration of the paradigm (Ricoeur 1991). He sees Ricoeur's definition of text—by dint of its "distantiating" quality as written discourse—as inadequate to engage with its own social conditions of production:

> To proceed in this way is to ignore the ways in which the text, or the analogue of the text, is embedded in social contexts within which, and by virtue of which, it is produced and received; it is to disregard the sense that it has for the very individuals involved in creating and consuming this object, the very individuals for whom this object is, in differing and perhaps divergent ways, a meaningful symbolic form. (Thompson 1990: 135)

This statement poses certain problems if juxtaposed with the interactive conception of the text/context relationship proposed earlier; the characterisation of text as object somewhat contravenes the spirit of such a conception. But my main point here is that Thompson's argument provides a rather one-sided view of Ricoeur's wider theory of the hermeneutic process, a theory that in fact allows for both the internal structure of the text to be exposed, *and* for the text to be related to its conditions of production; this two-way process—the hermeneutic arc, as Ricoeur describes it—crucially involves both explanation (text-internal) and understanding (text-external) in the interpretational equation (Ricoeur 1991: 119). Understanding is a crucial dimension of the activity of reception, in so far as it involves appropriation, which Ricoeur defines as a "struggle against cultural distance", a process, to cite him again, of "making one's *own* what was initially *alien*"; emphasis in the original). Elsewhere I have examined how just such a process of interpretive appropriation allows Quechua-speaking storytellers to use communally held oral traditions verbally to shape the conflict-ridden contexts of their individual lives (Howard-Malverde 1994). In this connection Ricoeur's thinking ties in with Hanks's characterisation of text as social process.[3]

In attempting to determine the appropriateness of the culture-as-text analogy, it is important to distinguish the perspective of the analyst from that of the cultural agent (the producer of culture). Clearly, the analyst's ethnographic enterprise leads to the textualisation of the observed. Here there is little to dispute, leaving aside for the moment the fact that there are ways and ways of writing ethnographies, some less disempowering than others with regard to the groups and individuals whose cultures are described.[4] What is at issue, rather, is whether the cultural practices being observed can suitably be characterised as textlike in their primary unmediated forms, before ever the ethnographer sets to work. Does not the metaphor of culture as text risk formalising the non-formalisable? Is it not too convenient to presume that social interaction is textlike in its patternings, when it comes to having to give a verbal account of the non-verbalised?

From culture-as-text to the evocation of culture

The idea of text cannot capture the experiential dimensions of socially and psychologically grounded human behaviour: be it ritually framed or otherwise, such interaction involves participants in strategies of positioning with regard to each other, a positioning process bound up with relations of power, and whose meaning emerges in its performative dimensions; the treatment of such processes as semiotic phenomena—which the text metaphor necessarily entails—cannot but obscure these socially situated meanings, positing an overly structuralist account, removed from the lived significance of cultural actions from the point of view of the actors involved.

If we are not to get caught up in the semiotic web as interpreters of culture, what approach must we then adopt? At this point, the analyst may take her cue from cultural agents themselves, by attempting to get at how they engage in the chain of reception, interpretation, and production of meaning. As Keesing (1987: 164) points out, members do not "read" the meaning-embodying symbols of their culture, but rather "evoke" them; that is to say, they engage with them and meaningfully reproduce them in an experiential way. Marilyn Strathern, in her comment on Keesing (Strathern 1987: 173), sees in this concept of *evocation* both a path to a more performative notion of culture, and a means to enabling a more dialogic encounter between the observer and the observed. The culture-as-text metaphor is radically overturned in Strathern's view, and along with it such text-derived notions as signification and reference: "Under the umbrella of post-modernism, representation itself has become questionable, discourse displaces text, alternities dissolve frames, and it becomes thoroughly appropriate that in symbolic anthropology the idea of evocation or elicitation should push aside signification and reference" (ibid.).

The implications of such a stance are far reaching, for they challenge the ethnographer to set herself free from the shackles of literacy, and look for new ways of producing cultural accounts—by elicitation, evocation, and dialogue—that stand to be less prepossessing than those produced by conventional textualising means. It might only be by such a route that the "Western" voice inscribed in so many ethnographies, and the voice of the indigenous subject, can ever conceivably meet.[5] Increasingly, anthropological narrative is ceding ground to the voices of the people; a commitment to such dialogue is surely imperative if the ethnographic enterprise is to be meaningful in the postcolonial world, and will bring about gradual and radical changes in the aims, objectives, and methods of anthropology in the years to come.[6]

All this being said, there is no doubt that Andean culture members themselves are prolific producers of text (be it spoken, written, woven, inscribed). Furthermore, indigenous Andean peoples have long incorporated the symbolism of Western writing into their theories of history. As Platt demonstrates, for example, the Macha shaman's Quechua discourse incorporates metaphors of alphabetic literacy and legalism as a means of cohering ideas about alternative sources of power: local autochtonous—the mountain gods, and national—the government and the state. To reject the culture-as-text analogy as an artifice of the ethnographer, might lead us to overlook certain features of symbolic practice actually produced by the people themselves. Other contributors to the volume will also have reason to investigate the usefulness of the model in application to particular cases (cf. Rappaport, Dransart, Allen).

From representation to performance

Strathern also refers to the concept of *representation*, the appropriateness of which has been recently questioned in social anthropological debate as well as within cultural studies. The problem with the idea of "representation" is that it suggests some objectified reality that pre-exists and stands outside the moment, then to be enacted before an audience who supposedly perceives it as an account of an external state of affairs. Thus, for the sake of argument, the Aymara herders in the llama corral (Dransart) or the goose-stepping paraders in the streets of Ocongate on Independence Day (Harvey) would be deemed to be "representing" perceived relationships between humans, animals, and landscape, or between local community and nation-state, rather than *living* these perceptions in the process of conducting rituals and ceremonies, as these authors make plain.

A performative conception of cultural process, by contrast, displaces the concept of representation—an analytical construct in the first place, and reality is conceived as constructed and emergent, an experiential process grounded in time and place, and in relation to the individuals and groups who, through their participation, position themselves in relation to one another and the wider social order. The following extract from Stuart Hall's discussion of the way in which cultural identities emerge in interaction illustrates this perspective:

> Perhaps instead of thinking of identity as an already accomplished fact, which the new cultural practices then represent, we should think, instead, of identity as a 'production' which is never complete, always in process, and always *constituted within, not outside, representation*. This view problematises the very authority and authenticity to which the term 'cultural identity' lays claim. (Hall 1993: 392; emphasis added)

There is obviously common ground between this emergent conception of cultural practice and the social interactive approaches to the text/context relationship emerging in linguistics, as outlined earlier.[7]

Enactment and the use of texture in visual performances

A performative conception of culture can be carried further if we introduce the related notion of *enactment*, for a number of reasons. Enactment is multifold in its levels of reference: it at once suggests involved participation by culture members (the "en-" prefix is the active component here), a playing out of experience (as in the theatrical sense of "act"), and an actualisation (whereby latent meanings are realised in relation to a here-and-now). Enactment enables us, yet again, to conceptualise text not so much as being *in* context, but rather to think of text *as* context. Rappaport's chapter provides an illustration of this approach: the politicisation of Cumbal youth is a process that emerges in the activity of doing theatre in Nariño; theatre here may be seen not merely as a medium for the representation of social and political circumstances, but as a means of empowering actors to interiorise, dramatically to interpret, and eventually to exert change upon those circumstances.[8]

The activity of interpretation referred to here is not the textualising procedure of the anthropologist, but a performative activity on the part of the agents of culture themselves. This interpretive activity may involve retellings of narratives, re-enactments of ceremonies, and so on. What is of interest in this process is the way in which the distinction between production and reception is blurred. In each performance, the particular shape of production echoes an aforegoing process of reception, of some previous performance in the past; at the same time, it contains the seeds of future performances to come, which in their turn will channel receptive responses and understandings into new instantiations, new productions. The process is a circular one of continuous and ongoing interpretation—Ricoeur's hermeneutic arc in living practice.

Theatre in a multilingual and pluricultural society—where linguistic codes are not necessarily shared between performers and audiences, or across different sectors of audiences—relies heavily on the visual for successful communication, on *texture* rather than text, as Rappaport puts it. We take texture to include expressive media such as dress, heraldry, visual icons, use of colour, sound, and body language, some or all of which enter into the literally theatrical enactments of the cases studied by Rappaport, but which also figure in the ceremonial practices relating to Peruvian Independence Day described by Harvey, and which perform a key symbolic function in the Aymara rituals, appropriately defined as "acts of remembrance", analysed by Dransart. In addition, the texturelike qualities of sound are well evoked in Platt's discussion of the shamanic séance, which takes place almost entirely in darkness.

"Enactment" also enables us to grasp what is happening as the pilgrims to Qoyllur Rit'i play out their aspirations and desires through the ritual handling of stone miniatures (Allen). The Quechua language itself offers support in favour of these links and cross-references, insofar as the verb *pukllay* can be taken to mean 'play' in the sense of 'act out'. "Pukllay" crops up across a number of contexts, suggestive of the full extent of its semantic range: as the word for the fight between the condor and the bull (Harvey), as the word the pilgrims use to describe their activities at Qoyllur Rit'i (Allen), and as part of the lexicon of theatre (Montoya 1993).[9]

Rethinking the theory of the linguistic sign

The conceptualisation of cultural expression as performance or enactment, as well as its application to the Andean examples considered in this volume, leads us to think about the construction of meaning as entailing a somewhat different relationship between signifier and signified from that commonly pertaining in twentieth-century Western linguistic theory. The Saussurean triangle of signification posits what could potentially be a non-hierarchical relationship between ideas, words, and the objects to which the words refer. Nonetheless, in certain logocentric traditions of the West, the linguistic sign tends to occupy the prior position, and words are taken to be signs for things, rather than vice versa.

A theory of meaning as process, if applied in the domain of symbolic anthropology, allows us to collapse the triangle and envision instead a synthesis of signifier and signified, in a signifying relationship whereby neither can be abstracted out from the other or be considered superordinate to the other. Kenneth Burke (1966) has demonstrated for the case of religious language that perceptual processes occurring as part of spiritual experience may imbue profane words with new, sacred, meanings. In this sense, he proposes that the signified (the object perceived and endowed with sacred power by the perceiver) becomes a sign for the signifier (profane words take on sacred meanings and can be put to new effect in discourse addressed to God).

Burke bases his discussion on language in Judeo-Christian tradition; however, similar processes seem to occur in Amerindian settings. For example, among the Aguaruna of Northern Peru, shamanic chants are learned by the ritual specialist through contemplation of objects in nature. Plants are the "owners" of healing songs and release their words into the consciousness of the shaman in response to ritual observances (Brown 1986). Bearing Burke's discussion in mind, were we now to reintroduce, for the sake of analysis, the notion of "standing for" into the synthetic signifier/signified relationship suggested in the preceding discussion, then, by maintaining our conception of meaning as process, we would be led to question, along with Burke, whether the signifier is necessarily always the sign for the signified or whether this relationship cannot be turned on its head in some cases, and the signified be seen as the sign for the signifier.

This strategy of inverting the accepted Western canon can be useful for understanding Andean ways of thinking, particularly in relation to cosmological beliefs: the papers of Allen, Dransart, and Lund provide evidence for this. Objects (stones, sites on the landscape, letters) are found to be meaningful tokens in their own right, endowed with message-embodying powers, which humans utilise for particular ends. This utilisation is part of a reciprocal interpretive process whereby, on the one hand, humans exert their agency on the external elements of the animate universe in order to control and bring about desired change in that universe and, on the other hand, elements of the animate universe exert their agency on the world of humans.

The two-way tension inherent in the signifying process that the ethnographic data suggests, seems all the more viable as a model for understanding ways of meaning in the Andes, when we consider that the Quechua language itself possesses a number of terms that are semantically complex in a related way. For example, the verb *unanchay* means both 'to make a sign' and 'to interpret a sign' (Gonçález Holguín 1952: 355). The verb *yachay* 'to know' provides a derived form *yachakuy* 'to become accustomed, to settle down', from which *yachakuchiy* can be further derived, meaning 'create, bring into being', which is commonly used to refer to acts of mythic creation in the Huarochirí texts (e.g., Taylor 1987a: 52). Knowledge at once brings the world into being and can be derived from observation of the world, as the features of the landscape embody the past and keep the oral tradition alive in the present.

Narrative and nation building

Another conceptual tool used by a number of the contributors is that of *narrative*. Narrative is a mode of storytelling that lends itself to the presentation of events in linear fashion and as such can act in a hegemonic capacity, imposing and sustaining one preferred version of events over and above all others. Thus, in the telling of history, narrative can create a sense of inevitability, a naturalising sense of the unquestionable in the given order of things. Narrative amounts to the discourse of history, whereas non-narrativity may better characterise the discourse of myth. In the latter case, spatio-temporal relations are non-linear and open to contestation; in the former, these relations tend to support a monolithic ideology of nationhood, couched in a linear concept of time, and are harder to deconstruct and rearrange.

Harvey's contribution to this volume demonstrates the tension between narrative and counternarrative (the state's version of history is contrasted with an indigenous expression of structural relations that invokes the pre-Hispanic past), and it touches on the effects of terrorist insurgency in Peru, which challenges all modes of narrative alike. Rappaport also makes use of the concept of narrative as she shows how indianist Cumbal playwrights construct a counterstate version of history in their attempts to rewrite the past.

The narration of history in any language raises issues with regard to the nature of sources of knowledge and the degree of veracity and authenticity that narrators attribute to these. In Quechua, such concerns are embedded in the grammar, in a series of sentence suffixes of epistemic modality ("evidential" or "testimonial" suffixes).[10] That epistemological concerns should be intrinsic in grammar suggests that "source of knowledge" is a deep-rooted conceptual category, the analysis of which is likely to prove fertile for demonstrating ties between language and culture. At the level of cultural analysis, Harvey's chapter suggests that this category is indeed operating in the conceptualisations of history that are ceremonially enacted in Ocongate on Independence Day. From the linguistic angle, Dedenbach's chapter shows how the use of evidentials in text is central to the construction of multiple points of view on the part of the narrator(s) of the Huarochirí myths.

The chapter by Millones also deals with the role of cultural expression in "nation-building", in particular the role of the Catholic Church in its mission to shape the New World in its own image, and Andean challenges to this. The uses to which the image of Saint Rose is put in her different cultural settings (as expressed in poetry and song) sheds light on the alternative modes of consciousness—Latin American, Peruvian national, local indigenous—that evolve, as religion is used to shape society.

A voice for indigenous peoples

I referred earlier to the challenge to develop a more dialogic approach in ethnographic research and writing. We need to keep separate the issue of whether and how our scholarly pursuits might contribute to empowerment and audibility for indigenous peoples from the ways in which Andean indigenous peoples themselves have striven to make their voices heard in the colonial setting, where cultural and linguistic barriers have persistently hampered them in the exercise of power. I here turn my attention to the latter.

The voice of indigenous peoples—as long as it is projected into the wider social arena where those who listen do not share the same position in the social structure, or the same experience of colonisation, as those who speak—will necessarily have to be shaped in order that the non-indigenous will understand the words. This process does not only require the acquisition of European linguistic codes but may also incur the adoption of values and concepts actually derived from the colonising group, a strategy of conceptual accommodation that arises from the need to acquire both communicative and merely linguistic competence across the ethnic divide. As usual, it is the subordinated group that makes the accommodating gesture in order to set up a framework for communication in the first place. This point is made by Lienhard in his discussion of the epistolary discourses that arise from indigenous attempts to coopt alphabetic literacy for the purposes of communication with successive colonial administrations.

Hybridisation as a strategy of accommodation and resistance

Spanish colonisation of the indigenous people of the Andes produced profound cleavages in existing structures at every level of human experience: in systems of communication, knowledge, religious belief, and social and political organisation, to name but a few. The strength of those who resist oppression and try to maintain integrity against all odds is a factor in explaining how five centuries of colonialist domination have not completely eradicated linguisitic and cultural diversity and creativity among Latin American peoples of indigenous origin. The very cleavages mentioned here have been moulded into spaces in which innovative forms of cultural expression are produced, acting as tools in the fight against total assimilation. *Hybridisation* is a phenomenon naturally generated at such interfaces, and many of the contributions to this volume deal with the problematic of what happens in this "space between". I shall explore how this is so.

To take linguistic practice as a starting point, in verbal discourse hybridity pertains at a number of levels: in the medium, the form, and the content of the message. Regarding the medium of the message, hybridity was at work early on in colonial indigenous texts that combined alphabetic script with visual images, such as the illustrated manuscript of Guaman Poma de Ayala. In this volume, several chapters deal with transpositions and articulations between one medium and another: Arnold provides evidence that weaving and writing perform complementary and interdependent functions among the Bolivian Aymara, each medium expressing differential relations of production of agricultural crops and knowledge, along gender lines.[11] Lund's study of the uses of literacy by non-literates in highland Peru illustrates how orality and writing may merge into a common set of mutually reinforcing practices in specific social-historical circumstances. With regard to hybridity of form: the excess of honorifics in the written Mesoamerican discourses studied by Lienhard exemplify the way oral habits of speech may intrude into fledgling styles of writing; the effect of incipient literacy on language form and use is also the theme of Adelaar's chapter. As far as content is concerned, the Huarochirí manuscript is an example of textual production emerging from a "place between" on this level, too: the Quechua narrator's conflict of loyalties toward two systems of religious belief is a feature discussed by both Adelaar and Dedenbach.

The emergence of hybrid forms of religious belief and practice is also dealt with in Luis Millones's paper, where the cult to Saint Rose is shown to have evolved into a specifically Andean form of devotion, in which it is compatibilised with other focuses of belief and constructs of history, involving both the cult to the earth and commemorative ceremonies that re-enact the capture and death of the Inka Atahuallpa.

The practices described by Rappaport and Harvey, emergent in theatrical and ceremonial space, respectively, are seen as modes of resistance to state-interested versions of history and social structure. In the case of the Cumbal dramatists (Rappaport), theatre provides the medium for a "re-invented" ethnicity that serves to reinforce identities at the interface between indigenous and national society. In the case of Harvey's study, a series of interlocking symbolic relationships are observed: between past and present, landscape and urban space, Quechua and Spanish, province and metropolis, non-Christian and Christian, and, most ambivalently, condor and bull. None of these is an oppositional relationship, but together they are a series of ambivalent intermeshings that produce hybrid discourses in cultural practice.

If landscape embodies counterhistory, as suggested by public ceremony in Ocongate, private rituals focused on pebbles, the product of that landscape, may also be interpreted in light of the concept of interface. The stones used in "play" by pilgrims to Qoyllur Rit'i, as described by Allen, are seen to be a means of communication with the upper and lower worlds by the human inhabitants of the world in between, the *kay pacha* of Andean cosmology.[12] The importance of stone(s) in Andean theories of space and time cannot be overemphasised: the lithomorphosis of the culture hero or heroine in myth has the effect of leaving a lasting trace of his or her past activities in the present, visible to the living eye for generations to come (cf. Duviols 1979); stone stands at the crossroads between past, present, and future, and between inner and outer worlds, and perfectly epitomises the merging of space and time in Andean thought.

In the wake of colonisation, cultural hybridisation may be the only means whereby an effective indigenous discourse of resistance can evolve: the "authentically indigenous" is an inescapable anachronism in such a setting, while the alternative to hybridisation is the engulfment of the indigenous by the hegemonic cultural forms and values of the colonising society. From this point of view, hybridisation generates a space for the formulation of new meanings, by combining re-use and transformation of the indigenous, with appropriation and adaptation of symbols originating with the dominant culture.[13]

Concluding remarks

The essays in this volume represent Andeanist scholarship within a number of fields—anthropology, linguistics, history, literature—and reflect the diverse scholarly traditions of a range of countries. Despite the diversity of approach, several recurring themes unite the chapters and make of the volume a coherent whole. This coherence arises in part from the geographical focus of the book: the Andean area, although physically extensive, and displaying linguistic and cultural heterogeneity still today, also enjoys a degree of common cultural history reaching back to pre-Hispanic times. Furthermore, European colonisation, while not a uniform experience for all the human groups involved, nonetheless drew indigenous Andean peoples into types of structural relations with the conquerors that can usefully be compared from group to group: relations of social, cultural, and linguistic domination, as well as ones of resistance and accommodation.[14]

The studies presented here focus on indigenous responses to the experience of colonisation, as revealed in diverse forms of cultural and linguistic expression ongoing today. Common themes include social identity; state-indian relations; the concept of nationhood from the indigenous perspective; political violence and its traumatic consequences; gender relations; the construction of knowledge and multiple theories of history; cosmological beliefs about different sources of power; and alternative media of communication, and the techniques and ideologies associated with these. In all, it is seen that language and culture are powerful instruments for creating contexts, and shaping identities within those contexts, in ways that challenge the official view. Culture, be it enacted verbally, in ritual, or by visual or other means, emerges in the Andean practices described in this book as an effective political tool.

I shall end by reflecting on one feature of Andean cosmology that has proven to be particularly dynamic and adaptable to circumstances through the ongoing process of colonisation: the apparently changing symbolic role of the condor. The condor can be said to be the embodiment of indigenous Andean identity and focus of cosmological beliefs par excellence. In many parts of the Southern Andes, where it most abounds, the condor is believed to be an ancestor god and one of the forms adopted by the mountain spirits when the latter are invoked by humans in ritual contexts (see Platt, this volume). In my own fieldwork, I have noticed the symbolic role of the condor in the indigenous fiestas of Northern Potosí, Bolivia: the fiesta sponsor's brother-in-law (*tullqa*)—a spouse-taker who forms the affinal link between two family groups—dons a feathered condor skeleton as a headdress and cavorts around the periphery of his wife's brother's fiesta-going group. This example lends itself to the interpretation of condor symbolism in terms of in-group kinship ideologies and local cosmovisions, which I cannot develop here.[15] However, the second and final chapters of this volume (Harvey and Platt) also accord a special place to the condor, and here, by contrast with the case I have just cited, what strikes the reader is that the symbolism attached to the condor is very much a product of the colonial process. In these accounts, the power of the condor is seen to extend not only over the autochtonous sphere (ancestor god; brother-in-law of a local patriline), but to incorporate elements of power deriving from the outside, mestizo, society. The condor of Ocongate (Harvey) is on a par with other visiting dignitaries representative of the state; the condor of Macha (Platt) is a lawyer-judge whose Quechua discourse is peppered with Spanish-derived legalisms and who masters alphabetic writing. I can advance a closing speculation here, in line with my previous remarks about hybridisation. While the condor is the paramount symbol of the Andean past and local autochtonous power, perhaps the key to its survival as a symbol for the future lies with its flexibility to adapt, and an ability to relate to the outside as well as to the world within, as new hybrid contexts are symbolically, as well as actually, created.

Notes

1. See Schiffrin 1994 for a survey of the many approaches to the study of discourse in pure and applied linguistics. I do not here discuss the autonomous linguistic notion of discourse as a unit of analysis above the level of the sentence, as my focus is strictly on discourse as a social, albeit verbalised, phenomenon. For extensive treatment of the concept of discourse as social practice, see Fairclough 1992.

2. Ricoeur's use of the term *discourse* can be contrasted with that of Emile Benveniste, also writing in French, for whom *discours* is necessarily spoken while, by contrast, *histoire* supplies the written order of language with its particular formal characteristics (Benveniste 1966).

3. For further discussion of Ricoeur's concept of text, see Harvey in this volume.

4. For a discussion of problems of power in social science research and the writing of culture, see, for example, Clifford and Marcus 1986 and Cameron et al. 1992.

5. I recognise that the definition of who or what is "Western" is highly problematic; I am here referring to the classical type of anthropological writing that emerged as part and parcel of the colonisation process in many parts of the world and which is becoming increasingly challenged today.

6. The spirit of this imperative is well captured in the innovative collection of essays in postcolonial criticism aptly entitled *De-scribing Empire. Post-Colonialism and Textuality* (Tiffin and Lawson 1994); cf. Arnold et al. 1992 for a further example of dialogic ethnography.

7. The intellectual debt of these perspectives to the theory of practice of Pierre Bourdieu, whether it be direct or indirect, also needs to be acknowledged (Bourdieu 1977).

8. Rodrigo Montoya's contribution to the conference, published elsewhere (Montoya 1993), describes the comparable use to which theatre is put among young militant theatre groups in Peru.

9. Montoya (ibid.) also points out the similarity in semantic range between Quechua *pukllay* and French *jouer*, in this connection.

10. Evidentiality is a feature of the grammatical systems of many languages, cf. Chafe and Nichols 1986; Howard-Malverde 1988; Dedenbach, this volume.

11. That Aymara exegeses of weaving make recourse to the language of ploughing is interesting in light of Walter Mignolo's recent observations regarding "connections between writing, weaving, agriculture, and distribution of labour according to gender", not only in Mesoamerica and the Andes but also in the Latin Middle Ages (Mignolo 1994: 296–297).

12. The notion of a conceptual "space between" that acts as a place of regeneration is an enticing one for Andean scholars, insofar as it can be related to a properly Andean construct, that of the *chawpi* in Quechua (Aymara *taypi*) or 'middle place', which has been examined in a number of studies of Andean cosmology and symbolism (e.g., Bouysse-Cassagne and Harris 1987).

13. The consequences of such a process are not without its perils, however; hybridisation can entail something of a double bind. This point has been explored in relation to the aboriginal

populations of Australia by Gareth Griffiths, who argues that as a result of his/her attempt to construct a discourse that will be listened to across the cultural divide, the aborigine is seen as "less authentic" by the white colonial society, and this very lack of authenticity provides yet another argument on the part of the whites for disallowing the legitimacy of the aborigine voice (Griffiths 1994). A comparable Latin American case of double bind is discussed in relation to the polificisation of the Tukano of lowland Colombia by Jean Jackson (1991). For a theoretical critique of the wider issues involved here, see Spivak 1993.

14. The Andean focus is with the exception of the chapter by Lienhard, which compares Andean, Mesoamerican, and Guaraní sources.

15. See Harris 1994 for an interpretation of condor symbolism in Northern Potosí in terms of gender ideologies.

TEXTUALISING HISTORIES AND IDENTITIES IN CULTURAL PERFORMANCES

PENELOPE HARVEY

Peruvian Independence Day

*Ritual, Memory, and the Erasure
of Narrative*

> Our society has become a narrated society in a threefold
> sense: it is defined by narratives, by quotations often, and
> by their interminable recitation.
>
> Michel de Certeau (1984: 52)

Peruvian Independence is commemorated annually on 28th July. Throughout the nation, this date is marked as significant by official ceremonies, speeches, parades, and other public displays of "patriotic civic consciousness". In many small Andean towns, these official ceremonies are followed by sporting events, and in some places by a bullfight, which is billed as the highlight and grand finale of the celebrations.

As might be expected, the official acts of commemoration pay particular attention to that moment in the nineteenth century when Peru was declared an independent state. The historical processes that link contemporary Peruvians to that moment and render it significant are made explicit in public discursive accounts. By contrast, the bullfight, an event that offers no explicit narrative or chronology of events, allows quite different connections to be drawn between past, present, and future. Most importantly, it offers a shift in focus away from the moment of independence to that of the encounter between the Hispanic and the indigenous worlds.[1] Thus, despite the fact that the bullfight is an integral part of the commemorative activities, it invites a reinterpretation of the accounts produced in the official ceremonies. Above all it stresses the presence of indigenous peoples in the contemporary nation state. It is an occasion that produces intense interaction and an image of fruitful cooperation between agents of the state, supernatural powers of the landscape, and local people.

However, while the public ceremonies and the bullfight provide contrasting focal points for the central commemorative event, I will argue that in many ways the effects of these rituals are complementary rather than contradictory. The indigenous presence is not an alternative, but an integral aspect of the Peruvian nation. Highly stylised and conventional accounts of the relationship between past and present are enacted in both parts of the extended Independence Day rituals which systematically convey a positive evaluation of the role of the state in contemporary Peru. In this respect it is not surprising that Shining Path, the guerrillas at war with the state in Peru, have consistently intervened in the commemorative ceremonies, bombing public installations and threatening, even murdering, state officials.[2] Their activities constitute a direct challenge to the ways in which the official ceremonies depict Peru as a nation of free citizens. Shining Path do not look to the past to motivate their actions. When they talk publicly, they focus on a very particular configuration of contemporary social relations, and their narrative is directed toward the future. For them, the significant historical event is the moment of the state's destruction.

This chapter is not directly concerned with these very dramatic and salient acts of contestation, but rather with the ways in which the annual commemorative activites are realised in the interpretative acts and bodily practices of those participating in them. It will be argued that latencies of memory, connecting past experiences with present concerns, motivate particular understandings of the activities in which people are engaged. As collective practice, commemorative rituals re-present the past, depicting and interpreting it, shaping it to particular social ends, yet, as embodied practice these rituals are also generated by the past, by the former experiences and assumptions of participants.[3] The relationship between history, memory, and ritual will thus be considered by looking at the ways in which events are brought into connection with each other and at how these connections, the articulation of past and present, constitute people's experience of history. The focus is on lived experience and owes much to Munn's discussion of how regionality is constituted in experience, as part of the lived world of the island of Gawa in Melanesia. She stresses the importance of looking at the "experiential syntheses that actors create in practices and the events that transpire in their terms" and that these syntheses occur "through microhistorical processes in which Gawans carry forward certain past events (spatio-temporal 'moments') and configure certain futures in their present experience" (Munn 1990: 2).

I take historical narrative as a parallel example of such a cultural synthesis. The official ceremonies of commemoration produce explicit narratives of Peruvian history, which depict a chronology of significant events generated through the agency of a number of notable and named figures whose actions guided the emergence of the modern state. The telling of this story in the ritual of commemoration produces a particular ordering of the past for conscious consideration. This kind of official history constitutes a very different mode of retrospective interpretation from what we usually understand by "memory". Indeed, given that the event lies outside contemporary experience, its memory has to be actively constructed in the ritual.

Two problems occur to me as I consider the possibility of working with this idea of the contrasting connective force of historical narrative and remembered experience in Peru. The first is that this particular distinction between history and memory is grounded in a very specific European tradition, with all the obvious limitations for a cross-cultural application.[4] The second is that the consideration of history and memory in these terms raises questions about the relationship between discursive and non-discursive practice, narratives that link past and present through the production of explicit connections, and fragmented, disconnected embodied memorisation which may or may not be put into words. A consideration of these divergent ways of remembering and recounting will be used to generate a critique of the ubiquitous use of textual metaphors in contemporary Western cultural theory.

History and memory

As thinkers in the nineteenth century began to explore the nature of the agency of the human subconscious, memory was represented in philosophical discussion as a privileged site of subjectivity that fascinated because of the creative power of its hidden side. In the emerging schools of psychoanalysis, conscious memory was apprehended as the subjective construction of past events, a coherent narrative sequence that coexisted with other possible but hidden meanings. This realm of the psychological other—the alternative, subconscious, forgotten versions of the past— could be triggered into consciousness by moments as apparently insignificant as Proust's tasting of the famous *petite madeleine* (Proust 1987: 48).

Memory occupied a totally different space of preoccupation from objectifiable history, the emerging discipline that sought to achieve an analytical distance from subjective memory and arrive at a truth undistorted by the complex unconscious concerns of individual psychology (Nora 1989: 5). History and memory as modes of retrospective interpretation in the European tradition thus carry the overtones of a distinction between objectivity and subjectivity, between general truth and individual experience.

It is now generally acknowledged that both history and memory are social constructions whose difference lies in their conditions of production and reproduction rather than in their truth value.[5] Within this framework it is usually assumed that memory furnishes the raw material from which history is abstracted. Such memories might be either verbal or written archives of past experience, but they exist as concrete articulations and are thus available for redefinition and interpretation. The agency of non-discursive memory, the forgotten experiences, the silences and spaces that animate the unconscious, is harder to assess but obviously lies at the heart of the psychoanalytic tradition and the theoretical application of this perspective in recent discussions of social history.[6]

Despite the cultural specificity of these abstractions, there are justifications for applying some distinction between history and memory, as ways of telling, to the Peruvian context. First, the commemorative event that I am discussing here is itself rooted in nineteenth-century European culture. The declaration of independence in 1821 referred to a political struggle between two groups of Hispanics and did not in any sense imply the end of European cultural influence, particularly at the level of state activities. If anything, these influences increased as the independent state sought to integrate the population in the service of the new political economy. History, as coherent authoritative narrative, is thus an important aspect of the state's symbolic production. Second, local concepts of narrative genre are also concerned with truth, accuracy, and narrative authority. The Quechua language distinguishes the recounting of subjective experience from events reported by others through the use of grammatical markers that enable a speaker to establish the greater or lesser distance entailed by direct, as opposed to indirect, knowledge. While these linguistic markers are frequently used to denote respect or deference, the reluctance to take responsibility for the facts of an account can also open up potential ambiguities as to the account's accuracy or impartiality. In this respect, the claim to truth or accuracy of narratives on the basis of personal experience is established in terms similar to those with which we are familiar.

There are, however, narratives that discuss events that occurred in other worlds, prior to the one in which people live today. These are the narratives of ancestor spirits, of Inkas, of fantastic animals. These stories also inform and order people's understanding of the past, but they are less concerned with the chronological sequencing of events that explicitly connects the past to the present. The notions of time implicit in these accounts are not primarily evolutionary, insofar as the contemporary world is said to have emerged suddenly from the radical and catastrophic transformation of former ways of being and is not presented as a result of the accumulation of past events. The ancestor spirits who lived in the age of the moon were displaced by the coming of the age of the sun, just as the Inkas were displaced by the Spaniards and the advent of Christianity.[7] Nevertheless, these categories of this world and other world narratives are not definitively distinguished. Ancestors and Inkas were displaced, but not destroyed. They are still significant and potentially active forces in contemporary social life. Inka history is taught in school, ancestor spirits appear to the living.[8]

Ultimately, the validity of any of these accounts depends on the extent to which the teller can get others to accept it. The articulation and sequencing of past events carries more or less authority, according to the circumstances of the telling. Both the official commemoration ceremonies and the bullfight provide coherent, optimistic, and stylised accounts of the relationship between past, present, and future. Furthermore, these accounts contextualise mundane memory. They are immediately recognisable in terms of various practices in which people are habitually involved. However, the authenticity of such accounts is not absolute, and, as this chapter will show, these privileged and overt connections are vulnerable to contestation in the interpretative process. This co-existence of privileged and alternative interpretations brings me back to the question of the relationship between discourse and experience and the appropriateness of the textual metaphor for the analysis of events of this kind.

Commemorative ritual as text

Much has been written about the ways in which cultural theorists have extended the metaphor of text to cultural practice in general, including the anthropological practice of doing ethnographic research. In these debates the work of Paul Ricoeur on meaningful action and the concept of text has emerged as a convenient point of reference.[9]

For Ricoeur, the essential features of text are associated with the processes of distantiation that objectify particular cultural activities and render them available for interpretation. A recent article by Moore (1989) traces very clearly the development of Ricoeur's treatment of the human subject in the tradition of hermeneutic phenomenology, from a concern with spoken discourse, to written texts, and finally to meaningful action. In all these cases, Ricoeur seeks to articulate a new relationship between sense and reference, system and performance, semantics and semiotics. If we take the case of discourse, these paired dimensions of meaning, which exist in a dialectical relationship to each other, embrace both the language system and the world outside to which language ultimately refers and in which discourse is realised. Ricoeur stresses that all discursive interaction is interpretative, as language is inherently polysemic: speakers thus have to reduce linguistic ambiguity through interpretation in order to communicate, but this polysemic quality of language also expands the possibilities of reference through metaphorical extension.

Despite these common features, Ricoeur is concerned to distinguish speech and writing on the basis of the autonomy of the written text from the conditions of its production. It is in this regard that he elaborates four forms of distantiation:

> The first form of distantiation concerns the fact that what writing preserves is the meaning of discourse in such a way as to transcend the passing moment of the instance of discourse itself. Thus the event of saying is surpassed by the meaning of what is said. . . . The second form of distantiation concerns the relationship between the intention of the author and the meaning of the text. . . . In written discourse the author's intention and the meaning of the text cease to coincide. . . . The third form of distantiation concerns the gap between the text and the conditions of its production. Unlike spoken discourse which is addressed to a hearer, the written text is addressed to an unknown audience, and, in theory, to anyone who can read. . . . The fourth form of distantiation designates the emancipation of the text from the limits of 'ostensive reference'. . . . A text does not refer to the situation of its production, but to the world. (Moore 1989: 94)[10]

Such a notion of text does not in itself provide the framework for the dynamic performative understandings that Ricoeur is seeking to establish. Structuralism operates with a similar model of text, which might indeed appear to encourage a disengagement from the world of social relations. It is the dialectic between polysemy and interpretation that continues to interest Ricoeur. Thus while readers will engage with the sense of the text (in the Lévi-Straussian sense) they will also look at what the text refers to, at how it relates to the world.

Finally, Ricoeur's theory of interpretation is extended to what he calls "meaningful action". Human actions are analogous to written texts in their plurivocality and insofar as they undergo the necessary process of objectification as set out in the four forms of distantiation. Meaningful action can be conceptualised as a text that discloses a world open to a variety of competing interpretations.

Ricoeur's notion of text has obvious attractions for post-structuralist anthropology with its stress on polyvocality and contested readings, the anti-essentialist approach to meaning and the possibility of a new synthesis of structuralist and performative approaches. However, there are certain potential problems that I will briefly outline before proceeding to a more detailed analysis of the particular commemorative event with which I am primarily concerned.

Moore's objections to Ricoeur centre on his failure fully to appreciate the implications of the fact that texts are produced in social relations and that the symbolic ambiguity on which both interpretation and creativity rely is the primary site for the assertion and contestation of social inequality. Social texts are not produced in a vacuum. They are produced for an audience with expectations and wishes that have determining effects on the kinds of texts that are produced and recognised as such. In this respect, the following analysis of the Independence Day rituals clearly demonstrates that, while interpretations of meaningful action are multiple and contested, they are motivated by material experience and mediated by the dynamics of social power which do not enable all participants to author or to read texts in the same way.

Moore's objections have been echoed in a slightly different form by those who point to the flattening effects of the textual metaphor, which fails to distinguish between knowledge and experience because of the assumption that meaningful action merely represents experience. Such an approach fails to look at the way in which action constitutes experience.[11] Even stylised practices such as rituals are not simply occasions for the expression of relationships but are rather the events in which these relationships are constituted. Ricoeur does recognise that, due to the intrinsic polysemy of communicative forms, interpretation simultaneously involves the contextualising processes that reduce meanings and the creative metaphoric extensions through which innovation occurs. Interpretation could thus simultaneously comprise a reductive act of contextualisation and the innovative extension of previous interpretative possibility.

The second set of objections to the textual model for social practice is concerned with the fact that such models are so firmly language based. The textual model relies on the metaphor of a message to be read and has no consideration for the non-expressive, non-representational aspects of social life. Criticisms of this kind acknowledge that anthropologists are deeply involved in textual practices, since our analytic work implies the objectification of social relations which thereby become susceptible to interpretation.[12]

My interest in the motivating force of memory is that it can embrace both discursive and non-discursive practice. A focus on memory enables us to consider the links between knowledge and experience and the simultaneity of interpretation and creativity. Representational acts are embodied practices which then exist as latent memories for the generation of future events. Thus mindful of the possible analytic separation of textual and non-textual practice, I will now look more closely at the role of memory in articulating knowledge and experience in the Independence Day rituals of Ocongate.

The official commemoration

The commemoration of nationhood is a phenomenon that dates back to the nineteenth century. As the new nations of the world emerged, a consciousness of their existence was instilled in their populations through symbolic practices that allowed people to imagine themselves as part of an extended community of citizens, an identity entailing new lines of demarcation between self and other. Symbols of nationhood, such as flags and anthems, were the concrete manifestations of the imagined communities which required that the myriad inequalities and differences that exist between people be forgotten in the project of abstracting that sense of sameness on which the nation's integrity depends.[13]

Independence Day in Peru is a national holiday. All public institutions are closed, and people's energies are redirected to the enactment of particular rituals that commemorate the emergence of the modern state. In Ocongate, an Andean village of some 1,500 people in southern Peru, people were required to paint their houses in the colours of the Peruvian flag—red and white. Any household which had not repainted those walls that constitute the public space of the village was liable to a fine, levied on the morning of the 28th. Town hall officials went round checking to see that the houses were painted, that the streets were clean, and that each house was hanging a Peruvian flag from its windows. The official programme of events for the 28th, publicised over loudspeakers in the market and in the central square, was the same year after year. On the night of the 27th, one of the hillsides that frame the village was lit up. One hundred old cans filled with kerosene-soaked rags were arranged to inscribe the words "viva el Perú" (long live Peru) across the dark slope. At 5.00 A.M. the following morning, the *guardia civil*, the civilian police, fired a 21-gun, or rather -pistol, salute. The houses and streets were inspected during the morning, and the main activity of the day began at about noon with the *desfile*, a parade or march past of certain sectors of the community, particularly the school children and state employees. This parade entered the village square to the applause of the gathered townspeople, accompanied by the school's brass band and records of military marches. As each group appeared, a town hall official, acting as animator of the event, announced their identity over the loudspeaker.

The goose-stepping marchers saluted the assembled authorities and then lined up facing the town hall. When all were gathered, the local police raised the Peruvian flag. With hats off and hand on heart, people accompanied the crackly record of the national anthem or stood looking suitably solemn until the moment came to shout "viva el Perú! viva!"

The schoolchildren then performed various "numbers"—folkloric dances or poetic recitations—and both the mayor and the district governor made speeches. Finally, there was a general invitation to drink a toast in the town hall and to bear witness to the minutes of the foregoing activities. These minutes were prepared in advance by the secretary to the town hall, who meticulously copied them out from the minutes of the previous year, carefully reproducing this official account of the day's significance to the village.

The mayor made another short speech, called on the secretary to read the minutes, and then proposed the toast. Again, all these proceedings were broadcast over the loudspeaker attached to the balcony of the town hall. All present stood and raised their glasses, and then one by one filed up to the mayor's desk to sign the minutes. After a few glasses of sweet "champagne", the local authorities produced a case of beer and talk turned to local concerns and particularly to the forthcoming bullfight that was to be celebrated on the following day.

It is not difficult to see how participation in the ritual practices described here might invoke a particular historical consciousness that both validates the present existence of the state and provides tacit support for its future projects. Painting the houses and hanging out the flags involves considerable time and some expense. The walls are first whitewashed, then edged with red and some people paint flags or words as further embellishment. The flags that each household must display have to be large and sewn in cloth. Those who try to get away with sewing red and white plastic are fined for disrespect. A statement of national identity is thus literally inscribed on the most intimate social space in the village, the individual family dwellings. Furthermore, it is inscribed indelibly. The flags come down after the festival, but the red and white houses and their national slogans remain as permanent testimony to the existence of the nation.

The communal singing of the anthem, the public raising of the flag, the signing of the minutes, and the parades themselves also create an image of unity and discipline. They are ritual actions that in the moment of their enactment constitute those present as a collectivity and also link them to all the other villages and cities in the nation who are performing the same acts at the same time. In these aspects of the ritual, the state is produced as a concrete entity. This national unity is invoked in the words of the anthem and of the speeches. Thus people sing—and here I paraphrase the national anthem without the strange grammatical distortions that the music requires:

> We are free, may we always be so. The sun's rays will die before we renounce our solemn vow which the fatherland has raised to eternity. Through the ages the oppressed Peruvian dragged the chain of a cruel servitude, through the ages he wept in silence, in humiliated servility basely did he raise a sacred cry. We are free, may we always be so . . . . [14]

Similarly, an extract from an official speech made in 1987, but typical of many I have heard on such occasions, reads as follows:

> The central commission of festivities for the 166th anniversary of national independence has given me the responsibility of speaking these words, to offer you in my name and in that of the commission, this commemorative declaration, on the very day that we celebrate once more the historic date of our independence from the Spanish yoke. In my capacity as first political authority of the district of Ocongate, I offer the following words. It simply remains for me to offer a moment of reflection so that in this way we can determine to continue working for the integral development of our district. As Peruvians, who love Peru so much, we will contribute to the development of the country, beginning with our own district. [15]

In this speech, the district governor exhorts people to unity appealing to their shared love of the nation. Other speeches traced the chronology of events more explicitly and in the very particular style of public oratory associated with literacy and prestigious hispanic knowledge. The authority of the following account is constructed through the use of this style and its copious citing of names, dates, and figures, as well as the use of direct quotation:

> In that year of 1821, on this very date, national independence was proclaimed in the city of the kings, today Lima, capital of Peru. San Martín entered Lima on 12th July 1821, accompanied by a small escort. He was received by the Marquis Montemira, colonial governor of the city, and on 14th July he sent a message to the court in which he invited them to proclaim independence, in a full assembly of the court, under the presidency of the Count of San Isidro, permanent officials, titled by Castille, members of the ecclesiastical council, military orders, and the notable residents of the city. More than 3,400 of them signed with full flourish the Act of Independence in a solemn ceremony on 28th July, amidst popular jubilation on the platform in the main square of San Martín. Independence was proclaimed with these celebrated words: "From this moment Peru is free and independent by the general will of all the people and through God-given justice".[16]

The speeches concentrate on the common past of all Peruvians just as the national anthem articulates their common freedom. The parades represent the state as an effective source of power. The order in which people file through the village square implies a particular categorisation of the population into groups which all refer in some way to the agency of this power. The main body of the parades throughout the nation is composed of schoolchildren, all dressed in the same grey and white uniforms and carrying notebooks. In Ocongate, they were followed by the adult literacy classes whose presence further affirmed the state's connections with certain forms of knowledge. After them came the local authorities, the forces of order and administration in the district, the people through whom government money and food aid is channelled, the people who impose a standard of morality through the sanction of the courts, and the police force. After them the workers from the health post, then the breadsellers, parading as a group in white overalls, indicating the imposition of health controls. Finally the PAIT (*Programa de Apoyo al Ingreso Temporal*, or Seasonal Income Support Programme) workers, employed by the state on government projects as part of their policy to bring work and wages to rural areas. The identification of these groups was directed by the words of the town hall animator:

> In these moments the women of the association of bread-bakers of Ocongate are marching by, the truly hardworking women who with their efforts feed the village. . . . The directors who work in our primary education centre are also coming with their hearts bursting and overflowing with joy and filled with patriotism they march in a martial fashion past the official stand. . . . Dear public, we are seeing how the children from the private school of the education centre of Cunicunka are participating in this patriotic festival and are performing their triumphal civic patriotic march past, etc.[17]

These various groups cohere as an army, an image which they themselves are well aware of. The schoolchildren are drilled for several weeks by the police force, even the kindergarten kids make wobbly attempts at the goose-step, and some of the schoolchildren, boys and girls, carry wooden machine guns as part of their festive attire.

The dominant or intended vision of Peruvian history as invoked in this official ceremony is an extremely optimistic one. The state is represented as a liberating institution that provides work, food, health, wages, order, discipline, and coherence. Democracy is emphasised as the people make a series of statements about their sense of themselves as part of this wider community. The state thus consists of its citizens and constitutes their freedom. Furthermore, it is important to emphasise that it is through the ritual that everyone in the village is experientially involved in constructing this image of the state. Even if they do not march, they at least paint their homes and put up the flag, and thus provide the physical setting that lends meaning to the parades.

This act of commemoration thus operates on two levels. In one sense, it concerns a distant past which nobody present experienced. The rituals present this event to subjective experience in terms that depict the state as a force of effective and desirable historical agency. The state requires people to participate in a series of actions that might retrospectively constitute a collective reminiscence, through a symbolic state-ment of national unity, of the original act of the declaration of independence. People are thus forced to collaborate in the telling of a particular version of their past, the glorious emergence of the Peruvian Republic. However, a further step is needed to connect this creative act of liberation to the contemporary presence of the state.

An event cannot be meaningfully commemorated unless it in some way resonates with the subjective experience of those involved in its commemoration. It is thus important to note that, although the original event lies outside the experience of any of those present, the terms of its remembrance, the symbolic elements of the ritual, resonate with the daily lived experience of all those taking part. The displays of patriotic and civic sentiment on the occasion of Independence Day are simply a large scale orchestration of smaller utterances of this kind made throughout the year. I have mentioned how the painted houses provide a permanent if fading link between one year's celebration and the next. Every day, at noon and at midnight, the Peruvian national anthem is broadcast over all radio stations. Every Sunday in the larger cities, schools take turns in parading in the square and saluting the national flag. It is most particularly in the schools that these nationalist sentiments are fostered. Here the ritual is enacted on a small scale every Monday morning throughout the nation, and it is in this social space that children are taught about the importance of the independence of Peru, an event that is not remembered in the oral tradition of the region. The continual repetition of these symbolic practices in the everyday lives of the people of villages such as Ocongate enables the state to use an event as distant and removed from contemporary experience as the signing of a document by a Colombian army general in 1821 to motivate national consciousness and to have the kind of emotive impact on people's lives that I have described. In the act of watching and interpreting the groupings of the parade, people are directed to connect experiences and to remember the ways in which the state is active in their region. Schoolchildren are connected to the state's investment in the future, the PAIT workers with employment and wages, the local authorities with order and administration.

The ritual creates a context of consensus and authority. The commemorated event is presented as self-evidently significant and the particular narrative of the past through which it is presented naturalises the continuing presence and social agency of the state. It could be argued that this event merely reproduces the effect of a centralised education system. The difference, however, between the Independence Day presentation and the history lessons in schools is that the former uses the experiential and consensual nature of the ritual to conceal the contingent and partial nature of the particular connections that its narrative implies.

Before I go on to look at how commemoration rituals can also lead to a questioning of the narratives that are presented in them, I wish finally to emphasise the symbolic power of these rituals by examining how the state has used them to inaugurate important policy shifts and changes in the practice of government. New governments are always sworn in on 28th July. During their term of office, this is also a day that has frequently been chosen to announce quite dramatic measures that will affect the lives of all Peruvian citizens, and which usually belie the notion of a democratic state in which policies supposedly emerge as the negotiated outcome of discussions with all sectors of the population. Thus, President Alan García announced on 28th July 1985 that Peru was not going to repay the national debt according to the terms of the International Monetary Fund; two years later, again on 28th July 1987, he nationalised the banks. The year 1990 saw the swearing-in of President Alberto Fujimori, who was elected to protect the peasant and shanty town populations from the stringent monetarist policies of his rival, Mario Vargas Llosa, and who promptly announced an economic package of undreamt-of severity that terrified the poor and middle classes alike. I mention these recent political events to stress that the Independence Day rituals invoke a sense of continuity that can be used to legitimate future innovation. The sense of continuity is linked to the power of the state itself, its importance as the central institution of government whose offices can be occupied by changing individuals, each claiming that they will realise the potential of state administration and provide effective government for their nation.

However, contemporary Peru is wracked by civil war as the army attempts to protect the very existence of the state itself against the challenge of various armed guerrilla groups. The pervasive awareness of a split between state and civil society indicates that consensus is by no means the inevitable outcome of these rituals, although their symbolic power is such that guerrilla groups find it necessary to intervene in them directly.

At this point I want to look at the more detailed ethnography of how the narratives that emerge in the rituals of commemoration are contested in the interpretative processes. We are dealing here with a gap between representation and experience. Memories are subjective abstractions of human experience. To remember a particular past is to forget another. Thus, while the state can attempt to control the representation of its past and thus validate its actions in the present, the past experience of those involved in the rituals will also be brought to bear on their interpretations. I have shown how many aspects of people's daily lives might be activated in this sense to provide the interpretation that effectively constitutes state power; nevertheless, they also provide a dimension of interpretation that the state cannot control. Thus, the enactment of the Independence Day parades across the nation does not imply a homogeneous understanding of, or response to, these ritual practices. The attempt on the part of the state to construct an objective history through these rituals is both made possible and challenged by the ways in which subjective reminiscence intervenes in the process of interpretation.

The parades give a good example of this process. While the parades provide a very positive image of state agency in the locality, this particular representation of the community of Ocongate is also very problematic. Many of those who live in the district are not represented at all in this apparent cross-section of citizens. Peasants, shopkeepers, traders, families, political parties, and migrants are nowhere grouped and named as such. Yet these are all extremely important social categories in the daily lives of the people in this area. Furthermore, the work groups that are represented in the parades are as likely to invoke feelings of exclusion as feelings of support for the positive agency of the state. The workers on the PAIT scheme, for example, were widely thought to have been recruited along nepotistic lines of favouritism, whereby local officials looked after their own to the exclusion of the majority of local people. The breadsellers dressed in white also provoked memories of the struggle that occurred between these workers and the local authorities. The latter tried—unsuccessfully, as it happens—to enforce standards of hygiene that were seen as totally arbitrary by the women concerned. They saw the obligation to wear white overalls as a step toward trying to control their work practices, and their resistance to the move was effective. As a result, they now only wear the overalls for the Independence Day parade. Similar alternative interpretations exist for all the possible positive messages that the represented groups carry: there are those who have never been to school, who left illiterate, and who do not speak Spanish; there are those who were made ill at the medical post or whose relatives died from lack of skilled attention; there are those who have been harassed by state employees, maybe even fined that morning for not having the right flag; there are those who are extremely poor and who do not have food for their families. For many, the state narratives are so irrelevant to their daily experience that they stay away from the celebrations. Others make fun of them, even when forced to attend. Goose-stepping can easily become a kick in the bottom for the person in front of you (Gose 1986).[18]

The official ceremony affirms a particular history of the Peruvian state, backed up by the consensus of experiential participation in the rituals. Villagers enact an image of the state of which they are themselves a part, a state which provides essential services, a state which is disciplined and united. The real problem for the Peruvian state is that this image, despite the power of its symbolic affirmation, simply does not ring true. Furthermore, this contradiction with other areas of lived experience finds an accessible mode of articulation in alternative understandings of the agency of state power, kept alive in the oral accounts and ritual practices that present the state and the locality as distinctive entities. In these accounts, local people depict state power as outside power, unpredictable and difficult to access. It is associated with the conquering forces of Spanish-speaking foreigners, destroyers of local autonomy through the incursion of abusive institutions, particularly the army and the police, and with the implementation of arbitrary and destructive economic policies characterised by neglect of local needs, particularly in terms of schools, medical provision, roads, water, and electricity; finally it is seen as corrupt, where state officials look after their own and take from others for their own ends.

The clearest or most articulated counter-statement made by the people of Ocongate to the official history of the Peruvian state occurred in the bullfight, the most popular part of the commemoration ceremonies. While many villagers stay away from the official rituals, nearly everyone attends the bullfight; furthermore, people come from the most distant settlements of the district. As part of the overall commemorative event, the bullfight makes constant reference to, and therefore comments on, the official history of the state. It remembers and re-presents that part of the ritual that preceded it, and that constitutes the immediate conditions of its production. In doing so it does not erase this history, but rather renarrates and re-emplots events. The connections that are drawn in the bullfight produce a different, but not necessarily incompatible, history from that narrated on the previous day.

The bullfight

The Ocongate bullfight differs in many respects from the Spanish bullfight. There are no professional bullfighters, and the bulls are not harmed in any way. Ideally, a condor should be brought down from the highlands above the village to "play" with the bull in the village square.[19] The bullfight is organised by the officials of the town hall who need the collaboration of the owners of the bulls and of the specialists in catching condors. These people live outside the village in small isolated hamlets in the *puna*, high above the valleys.

Some several weeks prior to the bullfight, representatives of the Town Hall travel out of the village to request the assistance of these puna dwellers, and they make every effort to diminish the potential social difference that their status as village authorities might evoke. They have to demonstrate that they are able and willing to welcome the bull owners and their families as honoured guests to the village on the day of the bullfight, and they thus offer gifts of food, drink, tobacco, and coca and show friendship and affection by drinking and chewing coca with them in their houses.

The bulls that are brought down for the bullfight usually belong to several individuals who collaborate with each other along lines of kinship and *compadrazgo*, under the guidance of the senior male of the family. Two or three days prior to the bullfight, they begin to round up the animals and, together with a group of contracted horsemen, the *laceadores*, they begin the journey down to the village. As they approach the village, they are joined by young men who are sent out on the day before the bullfight to assist in the final stages of the roundup.

Catching the condor is a more lonely task. The catcher sets off up to two weeks before the bullfight, and laying a trap up by the snowline of the high mountains in the district waits patiently, requesting the mountain spirits to allow the condor to come down to the village and "play" with the bulls.

In the village itself preparations are also organised along lines of kinship and compadrazgo. Sponsoring authorities begin to prepare the food and drink and to hire musicians. On the eve of the bullfight they go round to every house in the village requesting small gifts, such as articles of clothing or plastic goods, which can be given to the bullfighters and bull owners. Finally the village square is closed off with wooden poles to form the "ring" in which the bullfight will take place.

The owners of the bulls and their families arrive in town on the day of the bullfight itself, the women and senior men usually arriving in a lorry which is sent to collect them. The condor is prepared for the event. It drinks substantial amounts of wine and the tips of its wings are tied. In the assembling crowd, puna dwellers in their homespun *bayeta* clothing jostle with villagers in Western dress for a good view, cramming themselves behind the wooden barriers, onto balconies and lorries. The owners of the bulls are invited up onto the balcony of the Town Hall from where they watch, squeezed in with the musicians and with friends and relatives of the village authorities.

The bulls are released into the square one at a time, although two or more sometimes get out at once. Those men who wish to show their skill and daring demonstrate their passes, using ponchos or even jackets and hats as capes. When the bull tires or refuses to "play", the laceadores rope it back into the corral or *pozo*, and another one is pulled into the square. There is usually less action during the first half of the bullfight as the bullfighters need to get slightly drunk to build up the necessary courage to go in and fight. Many men and occasionally a young woman will go in to face a small harmless looking animal, but few will risk their lives with heavy fierce bulls or with an agile cow who knows to go for the body and not for the cape. A meal is served halfway through the event and throughout the day the authorities have to keep the owners, the laceadores, and the bullfighters supplied with drink. The condor is released drunk into the square and faces the bull alongside the bullfighters, supposedly using its wings as capes.

At the end of the day the bulls are released to find their way back to the high pastures. The condor is set free on the following morning during a final farewell ceremony for both the condor and the owners of the bulls. With ribbons attached to its wings it walks slowly up the mountain side. When it catches sight of Ausangate, the dominant snow peak in the region, it is supposed to take flight. If it circles the village, people know that it has enjoyed itself and may return to play another year.

The connections between past and present that the bullfight invokes are quite different from those emphasised in the ceremonies of the previous day. The bullfight appeals quite openly to a source of power that exists outside the realm of the state, and which resides in the landscape of the locality. This landscape is inhabited by a pantheon of supernatural forces, among whom are the *apu* and *awki* spirits that inhabit the hills and mountains, and the Pachamama or *tierrakuna*, the earth powers present in pastures, roads, paths, fields, and houses. The interaction of these spirits with human beings is problematic. It is necessary for the regeneration of the local community, yet it is also dangerous, as the powers are unpredictable and essentially outside human control. The daily experience of the ambiguous nature of these powers has generated a similarly ambiguous sense of the nature of the connection between their present existence and the past events which displaced them from the centre of the human universe. Were they defeated by the Spanish powers at the time of conquest? Were they irrevocably weakened by the neglect that religious repression entailed? Has the Christian god in fact rendered them redundant? Are they still available for effective intervention in contemporary society? There are no clear answers to these questions. However, there is the sense that the local population must do all it can to maintain effective communication with these forces, because the state does not offer a viable alternative source of regenerative power in and of itself. Much local ritual practice thus works to combine the possibilities offered by state and landscape, and the Independence Day rituals are no exception.

As was the case in the official ceremonies, the ritual practices of the bullfight ostensibly present a very optimistic version of the history and agency of outside power. The forces of the landscape are depicted as powerful and alive, as available and well disposed toward the community, and as respected and honoured by the state through their officials. These positive images are created in the whole process of preparation and enactment of the bullfight.

Both the condor and the bulls dwell in and belong to a powerful non-human landscape. The bull has long been associated in mythology with wild, non-human power, and the condor, so wild to the human, is the domestic chicken of the apu hill spirits. These animals are strong; they cannot be forced down to the village. Their presence must be requested, their journey facilitated by their supernatural owners. Those responsible for rounding up the bulls and herding them down to the village engage in complex ritual activities involving divination with coca leaves, inspection of cow dung, major offerings to the hill spirits before the journey begins, and smaller offerings of coca and alcohol during the journey and in the corral in the village where the bulls are kept. The catching of the condor involves a similar attention to the hill spirits, offerings, divination, and, once the condor is caught, careful attention and respect. Both the owners of the bulls and the herders continue these magical practices in the village as they attempt to encourage and support their bulls. The owners, for example, throw hot peppers, alcohol, and oranges from the Town Hall balcony to make their animals more fierce through the contagious magic of "hot" substances, and the herders offer alcohol to the bulls to establish a relationship of support. Bullfighters say that the owners interpret injury and death as a good omen and that they believe the spilling of blood in the bullfight constitutes an offering to the earth spirits, and can thus ensure a good harvest and good fortune. The bullfighters also have their "secrets". They, too, make offerings to the hill spirits for protection and have magic amulets which they keep on them during the fight to protect themselves.

There are many more ways, apart from this direct appeal to the powers of the landscape, in which the practices associated with the bullfight constitute a statement of an indigenous identity that asserts a continuity with a non-Hispanic past. Work practices are based on traditional reciprocal labour patterns that stress kinship ties; the bull owners dress in their most elaborate homespun clothes, a statement that is reinforced by the traditional music and dances performed as part of the event. These practices must also be understood in terms of the very different symbolic statements made in the same physical space on the previous day—through the marching parades of schoolchildren, the brass bands, and the records of military music. The Town Hall, for example, is converted from the space in which elaborate speeches were made in florid Spanish to the scene of a wild party of unrestrained drunkenness and where all talk is in Quechua.

Nevertheless, this symbolic reversal does not negate the power of the state. For a start, it is the state authorities who organise and sponsor the bullfight. The bulls themselves not only represent untamed wildness but are also a substantial source of material wealth, a wealth that confers status on their owners in the value system supported and upheld by the capitalist market. The bulls are owned by people as well as by the apus, and the owners of the bulls are well aware of this status when they are welcomed into the village by the elected state officials. A similar symbolic ambiguity surrounds the condor. Unlike the bulls, the condor has no single human owner; as a protected species, condors are in fact the property of the state, and people talk openly about the condor belonging to the state. This status is reflected in the way they behave toward it. The respect accorded the condor is analogous to that extended to a powerful visitor from the city, a respected outsider with the sensibilities of an urban Hispanic world. The condor has refined tastes and does not eat and drink to excess, behaviours that would be seen as cultural imperatives for adequate attendance on indigenous dignitaries. One of the village authorities informed me that the condor should really only mix with high-status officials in the village: "I've been noticing that anybody can hold onto the condor nowadays, even get their photo taken with it, but it didn't use to be like that. Before it was very sacred, the only people who were authorised to hold onto the condor were the mayor and the governor, nobody else".[20]

Nevertheless, however much the town authorities would like to claim the condor as their own, they cannot actually gain access to the bird without the help of the specialists and ultimately the hill spirits. The important point to emphasise here is that neither the bulls nor the condor can be associated unambiguously with either an indigenous or a Hispanic tradition. The bullfight distinguishes these "traditions" by contrasting the powers of the landscape with those of state institutions. However, the ritual itself also brings these two possibilities together to constitute a more totalising environment. In the bullfight, the power of the landscape is paramount, but it is linked to that of the state—not in opposition, but in a complementary relationship offering a positive statement about the collaborative possibilities of indigenous and state power.[21]

Thus the bull and the condor in the village square can embody the power of the landscape, contained within the village but not reduced or diminished by such containment. The danger and strength of outside power is experienced in the bullfight as real and tangible. The power of the landscape cannot be defeated in the confrontation between bull, condor, and human. Human beings enter into a social interaction with the outside powers. The interaction involves a confrontation between the bull owners and the bullfighters, but more important than the confrontation is the intensity of the interaction. A failed bullfight does not result from injury or death, but occurs when the bulls show no interest in the "game", and interaction is thus refused. One man expressed it to me thus:

> In the bullfight we sometimes see what we want to see: Will the bull play or not, or will it perhaps catch somebody? And sometimes in some bullfights we see the bull catch someone, sometimes even kill them. These things happen in the bullfight, and this is what makes people enthusiastic. That is why Ocongate is alive with its bullfight. Before, Ocongate was an insignificant place; now it's a better place with its bullfight.[22]

Thus, although the ritual practices of the bullfight are not explicitly discursive, and unlike the official ceremonies of the previous day do not provide a continuous commentary of intended meaning, they do nevertheless allow the construction of a particular set of connections between present and past events. They invoke a non-Hispanic world, a source of creative power that establishes a continuity that stretches back beyond the event of independence, which acknowledges the existence of the state, but stresses its incorporation into an enduring indigenous tradition. It is in this sense that the bullfight could be said to renarrate the events of the previous day and to establish different connections with the past, to the extent that the event of independence itself is rendered insignificant. The significant axis of history is redefined as the moment of encounter between indigenous power and the state.

However, as with the official commemoration of independence, the ritual practices of the bullfight also generate contradictions between the representation of the past from the perspective of the present and the memories of past experience that subvert this performative control. If we consider much of the ritual practice of the bullfight, there is considerable emphasis placed on preventative, placatory, and exhortatory measures. Interaction with the powers of the landscape is extremely problematic and by no means entirely under the control of the local population.

The offerings and the magic performed by all those who plan any direct interaction with the bulls and the condor are not necessarily effective, and people are aware that their lives are at risk. This risk should be understood in the wider context of the general preoccupation about the reluctance of the powers of the landscape to communicate with human beings. I was told that these powers never talk to people directly. Might not this silence also imply that they do not listen, just as the state has consistently not listened to the petitions and requests that have been sent from the village? Those who participate in these events most directly know from past experience that the ideal of producing an intense interaction with these powers in the ritual context might be achieved at the cost of their own lives. They remember the deaths of others; their scars remind them of their own vulnerability.

These memories of pain and fear also motivate the interpretations of the families of those who face the bulls. While the general atmosphere of the bullfight is one of animated festivity, there are also many spectators whose attention is focused on a spouse, parent, or sibling, ready to prevent them from entering the square if necessary. It is common to see women and even children, shouting, crying, or running into the square to drag away a man fired with an alcohol-induced bravado.

The bullfight is also pervaded with an air of uncertainty. People never know until the last minute whether the bulls will be brought down from the pastures, whether the condor will be caught. Sometimes they elude capture, and sometimes when the bulls arrive in the village they will not "play". In my experience, the condor never "plays". I have never seen it use its wings as capes, nor does it fly to greet the spirit of the snow mountain Ausangate with its ribbons flowing behind it. It usually got somewhat knocked around in the square, having been made too drunk to defend itself, and was fairly quickly removed to a place of safety. On the following day in the farewell ceremony, it walked slowly up the hillside, stopping only to pull off the coloured ribbons until it was a mere speck on the horizon, presumably waiting for the hangover to wear off before it flew back to the place it had come from.

In these circumstances, it is not surprising that there is often a sense of failure surrounding the bullfight. It is never as good as it should be. There is nostalgia for past bullfights, the ones where everything did turn out just as it should. It is interesting here to consider Rosaldo's discussion of nostalgia, in which he comments that nostalgia is an emotion usually evoked in an attempt to establish one's innocence while talking about what one has destroyed (Rosaldo 1989). Rosaldo was referring to ex-patriot colonialists, but his insight is relevant here, especially in the context of the Independence Day commemoration which celebrates local involvement in a modern state that has only a cosmetic interest in the notion of an indigenous past. The fascination of taking pictures of themselves holding the tip of the condor's wing might be part of the same phenomenon: preserving the memory of an unusual and possibly unrepeatable event in the concrete form of the visual image.

Finally, the bullfight also reveals the fragility of the local community as an integrated social unit. In the official commemoration ceremonies, this fragility is demonstrated by people's absence, their failure to participate in the events of the day. In the bullfight, the fragility is dramatic and confrontational and directly related to the importance of drinking in all rituals that address the supernatural powers of the landscape. In the bullfight, drinking creates a local community—the owners of the bulls drink with the authorities of the Town Hall, the bulls and the condor are offered drink, and frequent offerings are poured on the earth or flicked into the air for the hill spirits. The interaction between the humans and the bulls is intensified as people dare to enter the square. However, the drunkenness also highlights the rifts in the human community and belies the unity that the ritual practices construct. Fights frequently break out, particularly between the bullfighters and the owners of the bulls. I have argued elsewhere that, in Ocongate, drinking ideally serves an integrative function; it should generate social cohesion and ensure social reproduction through the integration of human beings both among themselves and with supernatural powers (Harvey 1987, 1991, 1994). Such groups are actively created in the initial stages of drinking and then celebrated and expressed in the later stages of drunkenness. However, the abstractions required to achieve this sense of group or sameness are problematic. The process is never completely under the control of either drinkers or non-drinking participants, as people operate with conflicting models of the group that is being formed. Thus, drinking often appears to achieve or enforce a particular interpretation of community at the cost of social relations. Because drunkenness is about creating community from the available relationships in people's social experience, it is also a time when the fragmentary nature of "society" is revealed. This fragmentation is revealed precisely as people are frustrated in their constructive aims and as they voice their understandings of the contradictions on which the fictions of social cohesion and community are built. These frustrations are highly visible in the hostilities and local tensions that are often brought into the open by drunks on the occasion of events such as the bullfight.

It can thus be seen that while the bullfight provides an alternative history and one that is potentially more empowering to the local community than that of the previous day, this version is itself constantly undermined in practice by the subjective reminiscences of the participants in the ritual.

Conclusion

The commemoration of Independence Day in Peru engages people in both textual and non-textual practices. As public events, both the official celebrations and the bullfight produce connections between the past and the present. However, the articulated historical knowledge or consciousness which emerges from textual practice is mediated by the creative recuperations of the past that individual memories afford. These memories, based in concrete material experience, both enable the recognition of the intended symbolic content of the text and simultaneously work against its implications.

The hegemonic history of the official ceremonies attempts to establish the declaration of independence in 1821 as the significant moment in the historical process that defines contemporary Peruvian identity. This was the moment which granted the freedom that all Peruvians supposedly share today, and which founded the overarching institution of the nation to which all are tied with strong emotive bonds. The narratives that depict the importance of this moment of liberation thus contrast the positive agency of the modern state with the negative oppression of the Spanish colonial regime. The authority of this narrative lies in the way in which it is produced in a ritual of such public and widespread consensus. The massive participation in the telling of this account, along with the implicit collaboration in its continual retelling in the everyday reaffirmation of its symbolic elements, creates a powerful experiential synthesis that, as Munn suggests, not only carries past events into the present but configures certain futures. It is in awareness of this that state officials attempt to legitimate radical political change by introducing innovation in the context of this powerful statement of continuity.

I would argue that it is also in this awareness that the Maoist guerrilla group, Shining Path, expends such considerable effort on the disruption of the Independence Day celebrations. Shining Path has consistently disrupted these events, placing bombs and murdering local state officials. Indeed, the memories of these attacks are now sufficient for Independence Day celebrations themselves to invoke the experience of terror and disruption that Shining Path seeks to instill in the population. People notice it if nothing happens. Such emotions strongly undermine the narrative that tells how the modern state perpetuates the freedoms established for all Peruvians by the liberator San Martín. You do not have to sympathise with Shining Path to experience the contradiction between the words of the national anthem and the banning of all public ceremonies and parades. Shining Path subverts the memory of state symbolism in local consciousness and thus begins to appropriate the public images of state control. They practice a politics of erasure and of retextualisation. On the one hand, they produce new innovative, confrontational narratives as they wipe out the patriotic writings on the houses and replace them with revolutionary slogans or rearrange the kerosene lanterns to inscribe their own symbolic repertoire on the hillsides. On the other hand, they may simply produce spaces and absences that disrupt the continuity of the official narratives. Instead of drawing innovative connections between past and present, they work to sever the connections that the state has produced.[23]

At particular historical junctures, such as that of contemporary Peru, the challenge to official memory can thus be extremely violent and explicit. The inability of the contemporary Peruvian state to deliver in the terms of its own historical projections has led to a situation in which counter-memory no longer simply comments on official memory but begins actively to eradicate it.

This challenge to the state is dramatic and highly confrontational. It is also very public and pervasive. The alternative accounts more commonly generated in Ocongate are less subversive. As I have discussed, the redefinition of the significant axis of history which the ritual practices of the bullfight produce, can and does co-exist with an account of state history that accepts its legitimate continuity, although it doubts its efficacy. In this account, I have produced the bullfight as a public text, drawing connections and making explicit the links that enable this interpretation. In classic anthropological style, I have moved between what is explained and what is taken for granted, the explicit and the implicit, attempting to make visible that which an outsider might not expect to see. However, I do not want to over-emphasise the salience of this interpretation. Strathern has recently reminded us that our concept of culture compels us to make culture explicit to ourselves and leads to our privileging of the representational (textual) aspects of social practice (Strathern 1992: xvii). In this vein, anthropology operates to disclose, order, and contextualise the practices of others, to reduce the ambiguity of polysemy, and to produce a coherent and plausible text. My argument here is not that such a text might not be recognised by the people of Ocongate, nor that its effects are negligible. They, too, have a concept of culture as performative, representational practice. However, we should also be mindful of Taussig's warnings as to the nervousness of our systems: he points out how order, stability, and structure also operate through normative disorder, through secrecy, silence, and paranoia (Taussig 1992). The force of disorder is not a state monopoly. Disarticulated subjective reminiscences can challenge hegemonic histories. Many of these alternative interpretations of the significance of past events are never made public, never move from the space of (inarticulate) memory to the articulate abstraction of an alternative historical narrative.[24] Textual models cannot account for this dimension of social life, the memories that disarticulate text from experience.

The state undoubtedly produces a text on 28th July in the commemoration ceremonies. The bullfight and the activities of Shining Path both erase and partially renarrate the terms of this account. However, while it may appear that beyond these forceful public statements there are as many meanings as there are interpretative acts, we should not be satisfied with pluralist models that fail to distinguish the agency of the state from that of a drunken peasant. If we consider the role of memory in interpretation, it is possible to appreciate the simultaneity of normative contextualisation and disruptive creativity as people's material experience enables them to recognise, but also to disarticulate, themselves from the texts which they themselves produce.

ACKNOWLEDGMENTS   Earlier drafts of this chapter were presented to the Department of Anthropology at the School of Oriental and African Studies, London, in 1990; in 1991, to the Department of Anthropology at the University of Manchester; and to the symposium on Textuality in Amerindian Cultures held by the Centre for Latin American Cultural Studies, London. I am grateful to the participants of these seminars for their comments and suggestions. I am grateful also to Peter Getzels and his assistant Benigno Díaz for their collaboration in the recording of interviews on the nature and meaning of the bullfight which were carried out as part of a film project on the Ocongate bullfight (see Getzels et al. 1990).

Notes

1. In the light of the polemic over the use of the term "encounter" to describe the nature of the contact between native Americans and Europeans in 1492, it is worth pointing out that my use of the term here is deliberate and refers to the explicit avoidance of the use of the term "conquest". As will be explained, local narratives are ambiguous about whether the Spaniards did or did not conquer/defeat indigenous powers.

2. The fieldwork on which this account is based was carried out between 1983 and 1988, a time of intense guerrilla and army activity in the central and southern Peruvian Andes, although during that period the village of Ocongate was not the site of any such confrontations.

3. See Terdiman 1989 and Ingold 1994.

4. Thomas Laqueur has written a fascinating article on memory and naming in the Great War which looks at the adoption of new techniques of memory in the mid-twentieth century. His general point is to stress the historical specificity of commemorative practice (Laqueur 1994).

5. See for example Tonkin et al. 1989, Hastrup 1992, and Gillis 1994.

6. See for example Theweleit 1989 and Taussig 1990, 1992.

7. There is a widespread oral tradition in the Andean region which tells of the three ages of mankind: the age of God the Father, the age of God the Son, and the age of the Holy Spirit (Gow and Condori 1982, Nuñez del Prado 1970, Ossio 1973, Urbano 1980, Wachtel 1977). People presently live in the age of God the Son. This Christian millenarian chronology meshed with Andean millenarian beliefs summed up in the notion of *pachakuti* (the world turned upside down) which refers to the Inka belief that contemporary worlds are inevitably overturned to make way for new world orders, the transformation occurring through the forces of nature (Gow 1976, Ortíz 1973, Ossio 1973, Wachtel 1977). The sense of ambiguity in local narratives concerning the historical source of civilisation reflects these separate traditions. At times the narratives are quite explicit that the coming of the Age of the Sun coincided with the emergence of the Inka state; at other times the dawn of civilisation is associated with the advent of Christianity. In this latter case, the association between Christianity and Spanish rule is left implicit, as is the implication that the Inkas were therefore living in pre-civilised times.

8. See for example Allen 1988 and Harvey 1987.

9. See Keesing 1987, Fernandez 1985, and Moore 1989. A key article by Ricoeur in this respect was Ricoeur 1971.

10. Moore is summarising Ricoeur's concept of distantiation as set out in Ricoeur (1981: 134–203).

11. For elaboration of this point, see Friedman 1987.

12. According to Wagner (1981: 8–10), this is all we can do as anthropologists, and this is what differentiates our practice from that of those we describe. In a somewhat different way, Bloch (1991) has also argued that much of what anthropology is trying to understand is precisely

this non-articulated, non-lingustic knowledge, what is commonly designated as the taken for granted or common sense.

13. For further discussion of these issues, see Anderson 1983, Segal 1988, Spivak 1988, Fox 1990, Segal and Handler 1992, and Lofgren 1993.

14. The Peruvian National Anthem:

> Somos libres, seámoslo siempre, seámoslo siempre
> Antes niegue sus luces, sus luces el sol
> Que faltemos al veto solemne,
> Que la patria al eterno elevó.
>
> Largo tiempo el peruano oprimido la ominosa cadena arrastró,
> condenado a una cruel servidumbre.
> Largo tiempo, largo tiempo,
> Largo tiempo en silencio gimió,
> Mas apenas el grito sagrado.
>
> La humillada serviz levantó,
> Serviz levantó.
> Somos libres, seámoslo siempre . . .

15. The original words of this speech were as follows:

Es un cargo de parte de la Comisión Central de festejos del 166° Aniversario de la Independencia Nacional; hace que mi persona se dirija la palabra para ofrecerles a nombre mío y el de la Comisión la presente manifestación conmemorativa, justamente por cumplirse un año mas la histórica fecha de nuestra Independencia del yugo española. En mi condición de la primera autoridad política del distrito de Ocongate a más de mi palabra ofrecimiento. No me queda sino a un momento de reflexión para que mediante ello nos propongamos seguir trabajando por el desarrollo integral de nuestro distrito. Como peruanos que amamos tanto el Perú contribuiremos al desarrollo del país, empezando desde nuestro distrito. (Transcription by Janett Vengoa de Orós)

16. This speech was made by a resident of Ocongate in 1987:

Aquel año de 1821 como en esta fecha fue proclamada la Independencia Nacional en la ciudad de los reyes, hoy es Lima capital del Perú. Hasta que San Martín entró en Lima el 12 de julio de 1821 acompañado por una pequeña escolta, lo que fue recibido por el marqués Montemira gobernador colonial de la ciudad para que el 14 de julio envió al Cabildo una comunicación por la cual le invitaba a proclamar la independencia reunida en el Cabildo bajo la presidencia del conde de San Isidro, regidores perpétues, títulos de Castilla los miembros del Cabildo eclesiástico, los órdenes militares y los vecinos notables de la ciudad y luego rubricaron en la acta de la Independencia con más de 3,400 en un acto solemne el día 28 de julio en medio de júbilo popular sobre el tabladillo en la plaza mayor San Martín proclama la Independencia con las celebres palabras: "Desde este momento el Perú es libre e independiente por la voluntad general de los pueblos y por justicia que Dios defiende. (Transcription by Janett Vengoa de Orós)

17. The following words were broadcast over the town hall's loudspeaker into the square:

En estos momentos está haciendo su paso las señoras de la asociación de panaderas de Ocongate, verdaderas señoras trabajadoras que con su esfuerzo alimenta al pueblo. . . . Los directores que trabajan en nuestro centro educativo inicial vienen también con el corazón enchido y lleno de alegría y llena de patriotismo hacen paso marcialmente marchando al frente de la tribuna oficial. . . . Amable concurrencia estamos viendo como los niños de la escuela particular del centro educativo de Cunicunka, participan en esta fiesta patriótica. Así de esta manera está haciendo su paso cívico patriótico triunfal, etc. (Transcription by Janett Vengoa de Orós)

18. Gose's account of the Independence Day parades in Apurímac emphasises the way in which the "didactic and expository approach to performance", which the parades and speeches require, contrast with other expressive performative genres, which are in fact usually taken more seriously (1986: 172–73).

19. The English term "bullfight" is somewhat misleading as it overemphasises the confrontational aspects of the encounter between bulls, men, and condors. In Quechua the term is *turu pukllay*, in Spanish *corrida*. The Quechua term describes the activity as play (*turu* 'bull', *pukllay* 'to play'), and this concept is reinforced in the ways that people talk about the bullfight. A condor catcher remarked in 1988: "The old condor is also going to go as a player. Old condor, you are going to play well in the square of Ocongate, you are going to cape well with the bulls" ("El viejo condor también va a llegar de jugador. Condor viejo, pues vas a jugar en la plaza de Ocongate bien vas a capear bien a los toros"). This concept of play is taken up in the idea that bulls, condors, and men are supposed to enjoy their encounter and return to play again in subsequent years.

20. This conversation was recorded in 1988: "Ahora más bien he visto ya cualquier persona agarra y hasta fotos se hacen tomar, pero antes no era así. Antes era muy sagrado, los únicos que eran autorizados para agarrar al condor eran el alcalde y el gobernador nada más" (Transcription by Janett Vengoa de Orós).

21. It should be noted that this interpretation of the Ocongate bullfight diverges in important ways from other interpretations of Andean bullfights which depict the encounter as a confrontation between the indigenous and the Hispanic, the bull standing as an image of Spanish power and domination. Such accounts, popularised in films such as Luis Figueroa's classic "Yawar Fiesta", or Paul Yule's "Our God the Condor", refer primarily to the Yawar Fiesta (Blood Festival), in which the condor is tied to the back of the bull and the bull is eventually killed. The Yawar Fiesta is also the theme of the novel of the same name by José María Arguedas (Arguedas 1941). My criticisms of these analyses are elaborated in Harvey 1992 and illustrated in "The Condor and the Bull" (Getzels et al., 1990). Even taking into account the ethnographic differences between the Yawar Fiesta and the Ocongate bullfight, I am critical of the tendency in these films and novels to fix symbolic values into simple oppositions such as bull/condor, Hispanic/indigenous, and of the tendency in Andean ethnography to conflate the indigenous or non-Hispanic with the Andean. At this point, I would also stress the strong differences between the contemporary Ocongate bullfight and the Spanish-style bullfights which also take place in Peruvian cities. Analyses of these latter confrontations, whether they focus on gender and honour or social class, tend to rely on the fact that the bull is killed. See Douglas (1984) for an overview of such analyses.

22. These comments were made by the man who had caught the condor in 1988:

En la corrida a veces vemos lo que queremos ver, si juega o no juega el toro, o si tal vez lo pesca a la gente, y como a veces vemos en algunas corridas que lo pesca a la gente también el toro, y hasta a veces lo mata, esas cosas pues pasan en la corrida, con eso se calienta el pueblo, por eso pues Ocongate vive siempre con la corrida, antes Ocongate era insignificante y ahora es un mejor pueblo con su corrida.

23. See Taussig 1992 for further elaboration on the workings of terror through processes of fragmentation and the generation of absence and disconnection.

24. It is interesting in this respect that the words of the drunks, who are most likely to produce public discursive countermemories, are themselves forgotten as the social norms that allow for their articulation also require that they are not received as significant (see Harvey 1991).

Luis Millones

Saint Rose through the Eyes of Her Devotees

From Flower of Lima to Mother of Carhuamayo

Born in Lima, Isabel Flores de Oliva was the most important of all the saints to emerge from the Viceroyalty of Peru. Her period (from the end of the sixteenth century to the second half of the seventeenth) is notable for its bumper crop of holy men and women (Saint Toribio of Mogrovejo, 1538–1606; Saint Martin of Porras, 1579–1639; Saint John Macías, 1585–1645; Saint Francis Solano, 1549–1602; Pedro Urraca, 1583–1657; Francisco Camacho, 1629–1698; Nicolás Ayllón ?–1677; Francisco de San Antonio, 1593–1677; Ursula de Cristo, 1629–1666; and others). Not all of the aforementioned attained canonisation: some remained as blessèds; others failed even to get that far. Even so, the number of persons who felt singled out by God, and achieved official recognition for it, is considerable. But besides this official list, there was another route to acceptance which did not necessarily coincide with the church's verdict in any given case—namely, the popular fervour that viewed the holy persons in question as a means of access to the divinity.

In those years there began to develop a group of spatial centres of power and communication, around which there grew up a mixed population composed of indigenous people uprooted from their communities (through fleeing from taxation or as a result of the *reducciones*), freed or escaped blacks, mestizos, and poor whites. With the establishment of the mining circuit which fed the colonial economy, the relations of the viceregal capital with Potosí and Huancavelica converted Lima into an administrative focal point, serving as a magnet for people from the whole Andean area. This heterogeneous population was to be the setting for the actions of many of the above-mentioned saints, and their attributes and biographies took shape in this setting, side by side with the official version prepared by the prelates of the church. In some instances, despite attaining canonisation, certain saints (e.g., Torobio de Mogrovejo or Juan Macías) steadily lost their popular following and ended up as mere names in the rolls of the saints; in other cases, holy persons have been constantly reinterpreted, acquiring a status and an enduring appeal far beyond whatever rank the decisions of the church conferred on them.

The situation described changes dramatically when the cult of a saint takes root in areas with a high proportion of indigenous peoples. In such places, Catholicism was only one element of a whole spectrum of belief, ranging between intense acceptance on the one hand and militant rejection on the other. In these places, the veneration of the saints was filtered through systems of regional and local belief, which adapted the teachings of the missionaries to their own logic and context. As a result, the "urban" hierarchy of the saints became ever more distorted as the community established its own order of precedence, in disregard of the decisions of the church. Even those saints who had become "patrons" of the community or were established as part of its immediate pantheon had to modify their attributes, symbols, and hagiography so as to be incorporated into the common history—an oral history, obviously—of the social group that took them to its bosom.

If we stick to the official version, the life of Saint Rose (1586–1617) was divided between her great charitable works for the poorest sectors of society and the severe physical self-chastisement that she practised as part of her quest for heavenly glory and the capacity to intercede for the souls of sinners. Her beatification and canonisation were achieved in a record time for the period (1668 and 1671). In 1669 she was already patroness of the Viceroyalty of Peru, and by the following year her sainthood extended through all America and the Philippines (Millones 1989: 891–905).

The popularity of Rose seems to have very ancient roots, directly related to her charitable works, already alluded to, and which she devoted especially to the patients in the charity hospitals. On her death, the "plebe colonial" came together en masse to say farewell to their benefactress. The crush as people tried to get close to her, touch her, and take her garments as relics was so great that her body had to be rescued by the viceregal guard. The Dominican order assumed this popular interest as its own and hastened the process that ended with her consecration as a saint. Rose, however, was never more than a tertiary (i.e., lay) member of the order, and never entered a convent, despite having worn the habits of both the Franciscans and the Dominicans at different stages of her life.

Her cult had immediate repercussions in Lima, where two churches were built in her honour (Santa Rosa de los Padres and Santa Rosa de las Madres). Her name reached beyond the confines of the church: even before her canonisation, all manner of places—streets, squares, towns, and cities—were dedicated to her. Today there is no Latin American country where Rose is not known: candles with prayers to her are sold on the U.S.–Mexico border; her image is borne in processions in Manila; and there are centres of pilgrimage in places such as Pelequén (Rancagua, Chile) or Quives (Lima, Peru).

This multiple perception of the saint is not an unknown phenomenon in the Catholic Church. Even in countries with a more homogeneous social base than the

Andean states, there are marked differences between the popular forms of cult and those which appeal to the middle or upper classes. When we add, to the variable of class, the factors of ethnicity and the passage of time, the spectrum of types of veneration to which sacred figures are subject becomes much wider.

Still more complex phenomena lurk behind these diverse perceptions of the saints. It could be postulated, for example, that contemporary urban veneration of Saint Rose has more to do with the evangelical policies of the Dominican order, and that the saint, as she is envisioned in rural areas with a largely indian population, draws together a whole series of processes of religious superimposition and interpretation.

By way of elaboration, consider the stress that the Dominican order placed on the need for a holy figure to replace Our Lady of the Rosary as a maternal force. When writing about Rose, the Dominican biographers reiterated time and again their joy on discovering that there was now an American saint, born, moreover, in the capital of the viceroyalty. It is no accident, therefore, that it should be Our Lady of the Rosary who, in Rose's accounts of her frequent visions, gives her son in marriage to Rose.

This hand-over of responsibilities does not form part of the "sacred history" of the Peruvian sierra. As can be seen in the verses that her faithful dedicate to her, the saint seems to be linked more strongly to the local environment. Mountains, streams, fauna, and flora rejoice at the mention of her name and seek to ensure the blessings of heaven that they achieve through Rose's intercession. Having been incorporated into the local pantheon, she ceased to be the exclusive property of Lima, and became—with or without ecclesiastical approval—the patroness of the people, responsible from then on for the well-being of her charges.

Let us consider, in the light of all this, the work of two poets. Luis Antonio Oviedo y Herrera, count of La Granja, was born in Madrid in 1636 and educated at Salamanca. A member of the social circle of the Marquess of Castell-Dos-Rius, viceroy of Peru in the Academia de Palacio, he wrote in 1707 (or 1708) a very long poem, "The Life of Saint Rose", in royal octaves (Oviedo 1867: III; Sánchez 1950–51: 139). The poem recreates in verse the official story of Isabel Flores de Oliva and sets forth all the stereotypes in terms of which society in the viceroyalty thought of the non-Catholic world, eulogising in its turn the colonial Arcadia which was seventeenth-century Lima.

Pío Campos Chávez was a contemporary poet, writer, and musician from the central highlands. Born in Carhuamayo, his career was at its peak in the 1970s, when he directed and composed the majority of the verses, dramatisations, and songs that were performed in the festivals of his town. He began, but never completed, his religious studies, but he made up for his lack of formal education with curiosity and intelligence. He succeeded Herminio Ricaldi, who had been the innovator of the popular festivals of the central highlands. His early death put an end to an already significant and prodigious output.

The American identity of Saint Rose in the poet's muse

Let us begin with Oviedo's Rose. The colonial author begins by explaining his reasons for writing the book and, to this end, places the sacrifices of Rose in the context in which woman can attain glory—namely, in the struggle against her sinful nature.

Oviedo, entirely in accordance with the thought of the period, goes on to explain why, on this occasion, the purpose of his writing is not the celebration of military glories:

> I do not sing the deeds, the victories
> Of an immortal male, warrior champion,
> Nor famous memories of high renown,
> Sculpted by steel in bronze and marble;
> I sing the glories of a sacred heroine
> Who was born a Rose that she might bring the dawn
> And with deepest heart of true humility
> Triumphed over Lucifer, herself, the world.

(Oviedo 1867: 1)

Further on he refers to Lima:

> To the Tormes and the Henares, which in Spain
> Are mirrors of one and the other science,
> Rimac, which bathes its learned Areopagos,
> Cedes not in antiquity nor in eminence:
> There is to its children no art or science,
> But they take it with ease unto their bosom;
> As lively comprehend the minds that study,
> So, with ingenuity, they better what they learn.
>
> More than fifty churches on her bank
> The Rimac sees, where art and grandeur both
> Give form to the religion of Castille;
> Increasing the richness of their fervor
> With equal splendour at the one time shine
> The altar and ecclesiastical purity:
> Their learned desire is archive of the faith,
> And each holy man a living temple.
>
> Two thousand or more from every order drawn
> Busy themselves in sacred ministeries;
> Almost their equal in number and perfection
> There flourish monasteries of virgins:
> Other saintly folk, not formally encloistered,
> Abide yet by their own strict discipline,
> And join in chorus with her who is triumphant
> In this militant new Jerusalem.

(8–9)

Comfortably established in the City of the Kings, where he would remain until his death, the count compares his colonial paradise with the Old World that he left behind him, and with pre-Columbian indigenous society:

The abysses of errors and deceptions
Threatened to o'erwhelm the ship of the church;
Africa and Asia, equally afflicted,
Were inundated with floods of sects;
Great flocks from the supreme shepherd
The wolves of Europe they robbed,
And thus was necessary a new world
In which to plant the renewal of our faith.

(Oviedo 1867: 16)

The author sketches a portrait of Catholic Europe, ruling out consideration of the other continents, which he supposes lost to the cause of the faith. But he is anxious also for Europe because of the Protestant Reformation that, "like a pack of wolves", is stealing away the flock that had previously belonged to his church. One must turn, then, to America as the setting in which to found a world freed from sin and from the mistakes of history. He begins his account of the continent by describing its inhabitants and religions:

Made blind by ancient ritual, they rendered
Adoration to the prince of Avernus,
To worship at false idols and altars alike,
The base alternate error inflamed them:
The three siren furies of the Cocytus,
Peopled in the Indies another Hell,
So that evils unpardonable
Might crown blame with blame.

(ibid.)

The first task of the Catholic faith, then, is to purify this great stage, peopled with idolaters despite its magnificence, so that it may itself take root there and compete on equal terms with the mother country. The birth of Isabel Flores de Oliva, the future saint, answers that need for a miracle:

Pouring out aromas, putting forth sweet odours,
Revealing nectar in wallflowers,
Like daybreak between snowy splendours
Or dawn between crimson banks of cloud,
Rose was born in April, month of flowers,
And in Lima, whose orange blossom turned to rubies;
It being impossible to be born in Heaven,
She was born in Lima—the next greatest honour.

(Oviedo 1867: 19)

This is not the place for an analysis of Oviedo's verses. What I wish to point out here is the way in which he expresses a profoundly Latin American consciousness, despite his having been born in Spain. From his perspective, Rosa is the culmination of a process of civilisation which makes it possible to achieve in America a perfection that was never attainable in Europe. His text also reveals an utter fascination with the Peruvian capital, in which he enjoyed great personal success. As he puts it: it being impossible for Rose to be born in Heaven, she was born in Lima.

Rose and Pachamama in *serrano* evocations of the sacred

While Oviedo is preoccupied by the date of Rose's birth, Pío Campos is concerned with the current civic/religious festivity, on 30th August. This date was settled upon by a minor alteration of the real date of her death (24th August) for reasons of organisation of the ecclesiastical calendar. One could speculate, also, that Oviedo felt the need to present Rose as the dawn of a history which was just beginning to be written. His reference to April and the European spring (which does not correspond to the Andean cycle of seasons) seeks to reinforce this sense of beginning which tinges all his verses. As we shall see, this is not what concerns Campos:

LET US REMEMBER

> Let us be cheery,
> Let us sing, then,
> Let us remember
> Little Saint Rose.
>
> Thirtieth of August, feast of the people,
> when the hearts of all are cheered.
> Thirtieth of August, feast of the people,
> when one day my devotion was born.
>
> On which you share her feelings
> like the wind in the reeds
> in her beautiful lakes.
>
> Let us be cheery . . . etc.
>
> Thirtieth of August . . . etc.
>
> It is the tradition of Carhuamayo
> to drink of its fair ancestry
> which its fathers left to it. . . .
>
> Let us be cheery . . . etc.
>
> Thirtieth of August . . . etc.

In the central highlands, the saint is the presiding spirit of one of the most important festivities of the region. In Carhuamayo (department of Junín), the celebration lasts nearly two weeks and involves a continuous round of processions, church services, dances, and dramatic performances. During the commemoration of Rose of Lima that I attended in 1984, the drama portraying the death of the Inka Atahuallpa was performed, although there is both oral and written evidence that other works—such as the "Ollantay" and "Túpac Amaru II"—have also been staged on this occasion. Nevertheless, in August, Rose and the last Inka coincide perfectly because both of their cults are strongly linked to the earth.

On the one hand, Rose with babe in arms appears to personify Mother Earth, and it is in this aspect that she is prayed to and celebrated. August is the ideal month for this, as it includes the time of first ploughing, and in turning over the soil one moves her body, with the attendant possibility of displeasing her. The death of Atahuallpa seems to be transformed into a ritual of appeasement, whereby the sacrifice of the chosen person ensures the favour of the gods so that life may be renewed. It is worth noting, moreover, that during the fiesta the body of the executed monarch disappears immediately. This alludes to the historical fact that Atahuallpa's corpse was removed from its Christian tomb and probably taken to Quito or to one of the snow-capped mountains near Cajamarca. Interpreted more symbolically, when no evidence of his death is to be found, the Inka enters the supernatural universe, ready to be reborn when his people have need of him.

This way of perceiving death removes the element of mourning from the ceremony and reminds us that, for the indigenous population, the concept of final destiny in heaven or hell of Catholic doctrine, are inapplicable; in fact, dying simply means entering another level of existence (Millones 1985: 51–58; 1992).

MY HOPE

Carhuamayo, you grow huge
in the harshness of thunder and wind,
where the hail and the pampas
roar by day and night.

Chinchaycocha made you a pearl,
and your children a beautiful town;
we will follow with firmness
the way of progress.

We work with vigour,
and tradition strengthens us,
disdaining strange fancies;
we remember the Inkas
exalting immense faith;
we venerate Saint Rose.

In contrast to Lima, Carhuamayo boasts of its ability to tolerate the harshness of its situation, 4,200 meters above sea level in the *puna*. Chinchaycocha is the lake on whose banks stands the town and its six thousand or more inhabitants, with their strong herding tradition. Their capacity for hard work, as they tell us themselves, is a legacy from the Inkas, and is an important motif in the civic celebrations. Next, the bard emphasises the rural beauty of his region and offers dominion over the environment in tribute at the feet of the saint:

O LITTLE SAINT ROSE (LONG LIVE MY TOWN)

Long live my land,
beautiful Carhuamayo,
Covered with *ichus*, flowers, and *quihuash*.

With its dear lakes,
just like your eyes,
their waters are the colour of my sky.

O little Saint Rosie,
patroness of my town,
you are the guardian of our hopes and dreams.

Thirtieth of August,
I sing to you
with the soul, from the heart,
that you may give to me
your sacred devotion.

The identification of Rose with Carhuamayo goes beyond the Christian blessing that is received from heaven. As can be seen from the preceding verses, the saint is incorporated into the lavishly depicted landscape. This is not due to any naturalistic zeal; in making her "patroness", the poet identifies this friendly terrain with the saint herself, whose eyes are "the image" of the "dear lakes" so characteristic of Carhuamayo. This relationship is made clearly explicit in a *wayno* by Campos, which tells us once and for all, in its closing lines, what is implicit all throughout the celebrations: Saint Rose personifies Mother Earth, or Pachamama, in whose lap the people find shelter.

Carhuamayo, pretty and beloved land,
in your breast our hopes take on new life;
I respond with my mind and my arms
to make you a happy and a great town.

As long as I have the breath of new life,
Carhuamayo, I will increase your greatness;
I'll plough a furrow for those who come after,
because your name is so noble and so sacred.

Now your children are workers and drivers,
artisans and intellectuals,
who bring you fame and honour.

Saint Rose, tender and beloved mother,
light up for me the fate which I have chosen;
let neither distance nor time separate us,
for I live beneath the shelter of your cloak.

Conclusion

How are we to explain the transformation of a colonial mystic into one of the favourite images of popular Andean religion? Here, there are two possible leads to explore. On the one hand, August is the month when the earth is "turned over"—that is, prepared for sowing. It is a dry time, before the arrival of the rains in November. This action of turning over the soil for farming has serious ideological implications in the Andes. In delving into the soil, dangerous channels of contact with the inner world (*uku pacha*) are opened up, and it is possible thus to offend the ancestors ('old ones', *machu* or *gentiles*) who may cause harm to the community as a whole or individually to anyone they think has failed to show them respect. The ritual, then, is intensified by the need to maintain a balance between the relationship with the supernatural and the fact that it is vital to prepare the earth in the hope of a good period of rains for the next farming season. This makes August a difficult and dangerous month, and therefore ideal for the Catholic saints whose feast days fall around that time to assume the necessary native attributes to enable the reworking of their cult.

The second trail is a historical one. Saint Rose lived in Quives during her adolescence. She arrived at the age of eleven and was confirmed in the chapel of the town by Saint Toribio of Mogrovejo. But Quives already had a long memory of relationship with the sacred. The *curacas* (native chiefs) had warded off with spells the ambitions of their highland neighbours (the Cantas) and their coastal ones (the Colliques). Their lands were well known for a variety of coca (*Erythroxylon novagranatense* var. *truxillense*), highly valued in all corners of the Andes. In the end, the Inka, from his base in Cusco, crushed the Quives and their rivals and took possession of the coca-growing areas. The people of Quives were not daunted by this, and they even tried to "poison" the "Son of the Sun", which brought down fresh reprisals upon them (Rostworowski 1988: 178–179). Years later, under Spanish administration, the natives of Quives still maintained a reputation for sorcery, which gave rise to the colonial refrain "Esquive vivir en Quive" 'avoid living in Quive[s]' (Palma 1983: 46–47). It was there that Gaspar Flores secured an appointment as superintendent of mines for the area, and brought his family with him. He was in charge of the local indian workmen who wrested the silver from the ore, prior to its despatch to Lima. In this improvised town, which was basically a mining encampment, lived the large Flores Oliva family; among the youngest was Isabel, later to become Saint Rose of Lima.

It should come as no surprise, then, to find that the contemporary fiesta contains within itself manifestations of both the Christian tradition and the indian worldview, interpenetrating yet mutually incompatible, to the accompaniment of processions, bands, firework displays, and sexual licence. In the colourful diversity of these two universes, conjoined yet contrasting, the whole culture of the Andes is contained. The way that these worldviews are expressed in fiesta does not conceal the conflict, but makes of it the foundation of a commitment to living together that we are only just beginning to discover.

ACKNOWLEDGMENTS   Translated from the Spanish by Christy MacHale. The ethnographic information on Carhuamayo comes from fieldwork undertaken between August and September 1984. The songs by Pío Campos were photocopied in manuscript form from the Campos family archive in 1984 as well, by permission of the songwriter's son, Dominique Campos.

JOANNE RAPPAPORT

The Art of Ethnic Militancy

Theatre and Indigenous Consciousness in Colombia

In June of every year, the state-sponsored commemoration of the "Day of the Peasant" is celebrated throughout the Colombian countryside, accompanied by the flowery discourse of local officeholders, the cacophony of small-town bands, the aroma of grilled beef furnished by politicians in search of votes, and the distribution of seedlings to forest-eroded mountain slopes. In highland Nariño, the celebration has been renamed the "Day of the Indian". While the municipal mayor delivers his speech in the town plaza, the band erupts into raucous song, the senator flies in from Bogotá, and trees are exchanged for votes, the communities for whom the celebration is intended stage their own festivities in their community house or in the public space of repossessed lands. Shielded from the gaze of local mestizos, community leaders deliver their own speeches, and the public is treated to dramatic presentations and the music of rural bands. The art of these ethnic militants recalls the exploits of their colonial chiefs, the horrors of conquest, and the achievements of the modern land-claims movement. Visual image and verbal cliché prompt the audience to reflect on the rhetoric of the contemporary native rights movement on the one hand and the narratives of community historians on the other.

Cumbales and neighbouring Muellamueses use song and drama to assert an indigenous nationalism that at once reinforces their commitment to the construction of a distinct ethnic identity, while it acknowledges their membership in the broader Colombian nation. On the one hand, militant art emphasises cultural specificity through recourse to a history conveyed through texture, and obtained through the dense combination of sound, movement, image, and story, as opposed to a single-channel narrative. Texture is achieved through the choice of themes and cast of characters, the design of costumes, and the use of language. On the other hand, implicit in their artistic production is a recognition that indigenous historical experience intersects with that of other Colombians. The shared nature of the past compels native people to clarify what it means to be at once Pasto and Colombian, a task that the artists accomplish through appeals to a national indigenous political discourse.

This chapter will examine the conflicting poles of attraction exerted by national and ethnic identities as they are manifested in politically inspired artistic creation in the communities of Gran Cumbal and Muellamués, Nariño. These high-altitude Andean villages, which lie along the Colombia–Ecuador border, are *resguardos*, communally owned indigenous territories administered by semi-autonomous political authorities.[1] Under Colombian indigenous legislation (Colombia 1983), resguardo lands are legitimised by colonial-era titles granted by the king of Spain.[2] Notwithstanding indigenous appeals to colonial authority, many of the lands encompassed by such documents have fallen into the hands of local non-native landlords. As a result, indigenous people generally inhabit the mountain slopes, surrounded by mestizo-owned cattle ranches located in the valley bottoms; many resguardo members are forced to seek their livelihoods as day workers on haciendas or as domestic employees in nearby cities. While the land base controlled by the community has diminished considerably since the colonial period, the native population has grown, forcing land-poor communities to pursue a variety of legal and extralegal methods for reclaiming their lands. Repeated failures to regain territory through the courts led indigenous leaders of the early 1970s to embark on a militant programme of land claims that has included the peaceful occupation of those ranches that lie within resguardo boundaries, as well as the revitalisation of native culture and historical consciousness (Rappaport 1994). This new-found militancy has caused communities to re-read their colonial resguardo titles of which they acquired certified copies on repeated occasions since the turn of the century. Their creation of ethnic art can be understood as an attempt to convey this knowledge to the population at large.

Artistic representation and history

Selective reconstructions of the past

Dramatic presentation and musical composition are not new to the Nariño highlands. Dramatic spectacle has been an integral part of the celebration of Christian feasts since the colonial period: Holy Week and Advent processions include re-enactments of biblical scenes, while biblical tableaux are prepared for Epiphany, and Spanish-language nativity plays punctuate the Christmas season.[3]

Contemporary theatre and musical presentations are, in contrast, frequently secular in nature, performed for neighbours in rural schoolhouses or for broader cross-sections of the population at large community meetings; some of the more politically active sectors of Panán have introduced secular, historical theatre into Epiphany carnival. Recognised by the community as official community organisations, these artistic groups are frequently short-lived. Nevertheless, they play a central role in integrating young people and women into political life, providing a chance for those not directly involved in the all-male and highly politicised resguardo council to participate in the political process. Members of theatre groups usually attend most council meetings, joining grass-roots public works organisations. In other words, they are an avenue for the insertion of young people into community affairs. It is thus no accident that a few years down the line, some of the young male actors have become council members: their theatre experience groomed them for political office.

In communities in which *memoristas*, or community historians, are generally older men who were once active in community affairs, music and drama also serve as vehicles for more youthful forms of historical interpretation.[4] Thus, it is no accident that Los Cumbes, a Cumbal drama group, identified itself as memoristas on the title page of its scripts:

> HISTORIA DEL GRUPO ARTISTICO LOS CUMBES, representantes de esta gran historia que surge de una gente muy joven como es EL GRUPO ARTISTICO LOS CUMBES, quienes memorizaron este gran evento. . . .
>
> [HISTORY OF THE ARTISTIC GROUP LOS CUMBES, representatives of this great history that arises out of very young people, as is THE ARTISTIC GROUP LOS CUMBES, who memorised this great event. . . .]

Artistic performance thus creates a space in which historical knowledge can be interpreted by alternative sectors and shared with a broad public. The past that artists present is a selective construction, based in part on the scanty historical documentation that native Cumbales have had access to, and in part on the actors' and singers' personal experience. More than narrative portrayals of particular historical milestones, artistic interpretations of the past serve as mnemonics, references to other more complete stories (Cohen 1985, Rappaport 1990).

The selective reconstruction of the past is most useful in the present, providing people with a model of reality to strive for. Among the Pastos, the contents of this model are to a large extent grounded in the distant past, offering a glimpse of what indigenous autonomy might look like once the community wins its struggle. This model is centred around the historical event that has most traumatically affected native Colombians: the Spanish invasion. Let us look at the plays presented at the 1988 celebration of the Day of the Indian in Muellamués. Four of the six plays presented treat conquest themes, portraying Spanish authorities—such as, for example, the local landowner, Erazo—who swindle native lords, sometimes local chiefs, but also figures from Colombian national folklore, such as Nutibara and La Gaitana. Of the two other presentations, the re-enactment of a traditional marriage ceremony is a theme common to Nariñense theatre groups. The Muellamués rendition is particularly interesting because of the title of the play:

> Vereda Riveras presenta los novios con sus tradiciones y costumbres indígenas, con nuestra autoridad y su ley especial que nos protege, Ley 89 de 1890. ¡Viva el día del indígena!

[Vereda Riveras presents a marriage with its indigenous traditions and customs, with our authorities and their special law that protects us, Law 89 of 1890. Long live the Day of the Indian!]

Here the theatre group linked its depiction of traditional marriage customs with support of the resguardo council, perhaps prodding the audience to remember that in the earlier part of the century resguardo councils were charged with the moral education of the community and frequently obligated courting couples to get married. But even this portrayal of recent history is intimately connected to the memory of the Spanish invasion. The title incorporates a slogan in favour of defence of resguardo legislation, which is frequently confused by Cumbales with their colonial-era titles; even though this particular play treats a relatively recent theme, its creators have situated it within the broader framework of the conquest and colonial periods.

The selectivity of these presentations is due in part to the paucity of available historical documentation. Incursions into regional archives are inspired by the need in the course of land claims for copies of colonial-era briefs. Given that these documents provide useful, albeit abbreviated, information on colonial political actors, conquest plays that draw upon them concentrate almost exclusively on naming conquest-era hereditary chiefs and colonial-period Spaniards.

It is possible to distinguish some of the other sources from which the historical interpretations of these dramas are drawn. The funeral of Nutibara, for example, opens with the pre-conquest burial of a hereditary chief, his body covered with gold jewelry. The image was taken from a poster advertising a museum exhibit of pre-Columbian goldwork; the poster hangs in many council offices.[5]

In a fascinating analysis of a sixteenth-century *relación* describing the conquest of Querétaro, Mexico, Serge Gruzinski (1985: 40) demonstrates that its Otomí authors used costumes and dances from colonial festivals as templates for describing pre-Columbian armies. The Muellamués theatrical version of the traditional wedding similarly employs ritual as a source of historical evidence. Other dramatic portrayals of weddings highlight the process of negotiation between the families of the bride and groom and the accompanying exchange of cooked food. The Muellamués play depicts the wedding ceremony itself, complete with priest and mass. This is reminiscent of farcical re-enactments of weddings that take place at the Sacada de la Vieja (Removal of the Old Woman), a secular ritual performed at the completion of house construction, in which the woodland spirit (the "Old Woman") hidden in the beams is removed from the house.

History and ethnic typologies

Insistence upon the conquest-era roots of contemporary indigenous experience is a product of more than the paucity of historical data. It also reflects the authors' acceptance of the ethnic typologies of the dominant society, in which native peoples are relegated to the historical past (Fabian 1983, Dorris 1987). Similarly, militant theatre situates native communities in distant locations, especially in the tropical lowlands. For example, Cumbal theatre presents shamans wearing headdresses from the Putumayo, but since they omit any acknowledgment of the origins of the costume, the actors imply that the curer is from Cumbal. In "The Story of an Indigenous Slave from Gran Cumbal, Having Arrived at the House of Two Bad-humoured Foreigners", a Los Cumbes actor states that the power of native peoples originates in the jungle:

> Tu no sabías que nosotros los indios, tenemos nuestro estudio por medio de la telepatía o de las brizas que cubren los cuatro vientos de la Amazonía colombiana.
>
> [You didn't know that we native people got our learning through telepathy or from the breezes that cover the four winds of the Colombian Amazon.]

The practice of using geographic displacement to define "otherness" also characterises traditional Nariñense ritual and dance. The Jambo dancers of Panán, for instance, represent the people of Mayasquer, on the warmer slopes of the cordillera overlooking the Pacific lowlands; the word *jambo* is a common variant of *yumbo*, a term used in highland Ecuador to signify the lowland outsider (Salomon 1981, Poole 1990). Many of the actors in contemporary nativity plays carry baskets made in Mayasquer, as if to equate terrestrial distance with the temporal remoteness of Christ's birth.

But in the popular Colombian imagination, native people are increasingly associated with the production of ethnic art, a stereotype used over and over by Nariñense actors. Equally influential in this image is the fact that the only available evidence of the pre-Columbian past is found in ceramic artifacts. The Muellamués version of the conquest shows people peacefully going about their everyday lives, painting small statues of birds. Similarly, one of Los Cumbes's plays, in which miserable sharecroppers overthrow a greedy and exploitative landlord, is entitled "The History of Our Native Handicrafts from Our Gran Cumbal".

Rewriting History

In *How Societies Remember*, Paul Connerton (1989) suggests that ritual constitutes the most powerful source of historical knowledge in most societies. Commemorative ceremonies in particular serve as vehicles for historical interpretation, insofar as they not only remind participants of events, but *re-present* them, thereby lending an instrumentality to history by shifting its locus from the past to the metaphysical present. Once history is inscribed, not on paper, but in bodily activity, that claim upon the past is strengthened. According to Connerton, commemorative ceremonies "do not simply imply continuity with the past but explicitly claim such continuity . . . by ritually re-enacting a narrative of events" (ibid. 45). Penelope Harvey (in this volume) notes that such ceremony does more than "re-enact a narrative of events", but re-emplots them, thus in effect subverting the purpose of remembering the original narrative. Commemorative ceremony, far from honouring the past, becomes a tool for resistance in the present. As we shall see, this is precisely the purpose of ceremony in highland Nariño.

Resguardo council ceremony effectively re-lives the past through the voicing of the same words that were used in the colonial period to grant land rights to native authorities. It is thus no accident that these ceremonies are frequently re-enacted in militant theatre. But re-presenting history implies more than the repetition of events of the past: in Nariñense drama it also signifies the concomitant *correcting* of history. Muellamués portrayals of the conquest depict early battles in which native people are always the victors. Los Cumbes sets its characters in the timeless past, living in grinding servitude to large landowners, but the natives always win in these plays, which close with slogans of the contemporary land-claims movement. The moment of triumph of the native forces against Spaniards or landlords is always greeted by cheers from the audience. The correcting of history is a cathartic experience.

But even if history is corrected by dramatic forms of establishing connections to a heroic indigenous past, the triumphs of conquest-era chiefs are situated in a European historical framework. For instance, Vereda Comunidad in Muellamués named its play the "Pasión y Muerte de Nuestra Raza", a very clear reference to the life of Christ. The roots of this Christian framework originate in the theatre of the past. Traditional drama was always religious in nature, teaching universal Christian history to the native South American faithful. Holy Week processions, for example, were essentially a series of biblical tableaux in which people impersonated biblical characters, moving across the countryside in a chronologically organised pageant of Judeo-Christian tradition.[6] I observed a truncated version of the elaborate processions of the past in Panán in 1987, including a host of tableaux, only one of which was locally inspired: the council with its banner, trailing behind the cross of Christianity and the souls of humanity. In this procession, native history is absorbed within the framework of the universal.[7]

Although militant theatre employs Christian metaphors, the presentation of secular plays is also situated within a specifically Andean vision of the past in which historical chronology is reconstituted to conform to the organisation of topographic space. Indigenous communities of highland Nariño are organised in a series of parallel bands of territory, which I will call sections, ordered in a hierarchy. Events of the past are conceptually arrayed within this territorial structure (Rappaport 1988, 1994). The Muellamués commemoration of the Day of the Indian, for example, is celebrated with a series of plays presented by sections, although at the performance I witnessed they were not presented in hierarchical order. The history of Cumbal theatre groups is frequently extremely localised, situating historical chiefs in specific sections. Such local histories are loosely organised according to the section hierarchy, where historical figures and sections are represented by their most common surnames.

The power of images

Cacique Cumbe

The history embedded in Pasto drama and song is not revealed through narrative, but through images that move people to remember the past and also to act upon it. The power of images finds its origins in the present, in concrete activity; Pierre Nora (1984: xix) contrasts this active and malleable past with history by calling it memory.[8] I am not speaking here of history in the chronological sense, but of the forging of a connection with the past by re-creating it in the present, a process that, as has already been noted, Connerton (1989) maintains is most powerfully expressed through ritual.

The experience of the past that derives from ceremony is inchoate, vague, and open-ended, unlike the more circumscribed reactions evoked by narrative; I will distinguish through the use of the term *texture* that non-discursive experience which is less likely to be interpreted coherently, but which is infinitely more powerful than narrative.

Texture and its component images lie at the heart of national identity. Vague, abbreviated, and sometimes stereotyped, they supply the foundations for a sense of nationality (Melo 1989). In Cumbal and Muellamués, many such symbols are culled from readings of resguardo titles. Little is known about the meaning of or the historical referents associated with these images because they are only scantily described in the documents. Nevertheless, or perhaps precisely for this reason, they move people to action. The power of such symbols was expressed to me in the following story about the repossession of the Llano de Piedras, the first of a series of militant land claims actions in Cumbal. Confronted by repression, people invoked the name of Chief Cumbe to justify their actions:

> La policía les decía, "A Ustedes, ¿quién les dice vamos a recuperar?" o "¿Cuál es él que empieza? Uno ha de ser". Entonces que decían, "No, a nosotros nadie nos avisa. No sé. Ni se conoce a la gente que baja. Vamos a la tierra, pero no se sabe quién. Es que a nosotros nos relumbra el cacique. Vamos a la tierra y todo el mundo se levanta. Relumbra en el sueño el cacique". (Bernardita Chirán, Vereda Cuaical)

> [The police would say to them, "Who tells you to repossess the land?" or "Who is it that goes first? It has to be someone". Then they would say, "No, no one tells us. I don't know. You don't even know the people who are going. We go to the land, but don't know who (sends us). It's that the chief lights our way. We're going to the land and everyone gets up. The chief lights the way in dreams".] (Bernardita Chirán, Vereda Cuaical)

Cumbe's name is borrowed for countless music and theatre groups, which frequently call themselves by some variant of "Los Cumbes" and the chief is invoked, time and again in plays and in music. He does not appear in any colonial-era documents. The power of his image derives from the link between past and present that is established through the use of a name that so closely approximates the name of the resguardo.

The invoking of the referent-less image of Cumbe conforms to traditional Andean forms of representation. In the pre-Columbian Andes the significance of visual images depended on oral exegesis (Cummins 1988). Similarly, Cumbe's name serves as a stimulus for the recall of events to be remembered and interpreted by the listeners.

Photographic images, according to Susan Sontag (1977: 18–19), are only made meaningful to the viewing public when they are articulated within a previously constituted ideology. Similarly, Cumbe is meaningful to the Cumbales only within the context of the ideology of their movement, whose programme developed only after native historians began to interpret indigenous history for community members. The young memorista playwrights and songwriters recast history in images framed by contemporary ethnic ideology. Their framework, aptly conveyed by the use of political

rhetoric in dramatic dialogue, is most thoroughly experienced by the actors themselves, for whom theatre constitutes a form of political education. The young
memoristas develop a familiarity with political ideology and with resguardo history
as they prepare and learn their lines. What they ultimately create, though, are images
that the audience must situate within its own framework.

Visual images are essential to historical representation as it is expressed through
militant theatre. On one level, they are all that the audience receives in the course of
these dramatic productions, given that the untrained voices of the actors rarely project
enough to be heard by the public. But on a more fundamental level, in Andean culture,
knowledge is acquired through the act of seeing. The active quality of seeing is
expressed in colonial-era Quechua prayers and in contemporary women's songs, in
which divine knowledge is acquired through sight (Harrison 1989); among the
Colombian Páez, seeing is integral to political ritual and mythology related to the
legitimisation of land tenure (Rappaport 1985).

The texture of the past

What the audience sees in these dramatic presentations is a series of static images
whose meaning is conveyed through texture. In a study of the symbolism of community among African-American migrants to Washington, D.C., Brett Williams describes the re-creation of rural Carolina culture in the metropolis as it is manifested in
foodways and in gardening. She emphasises that Carolina customs convey a sense of
texture, of "dense, vivid, woven, detailed narratives, relationships, and experiences",
which take on meaning as they are relived through expressive forms that "rely
powerfully on repetition, improvisation, and the exploration of sometimes narrow
situations through many emotional, sensory, interpersonal, and reflective voices"
(1988: 47).

I would like to narrow Williams's notion of texture, removing narrative from its
component attributes, in order to convey the essentially visual and aural experience
of theatre in Nariño. The texture of Nariñense theatre is depicted most clearly in
costume and in the symbolic use of language, which is conveyed through the names
of characters and the languages they speak. Texture constitutes the principal vehicle
for recalling the history of everyday life, as opposed to political history, which is
frequently expressed through plots and through dialogue. Let us look first at costumes.

In Muellamués, pre-conquest people are frequently portrayed with tropical forest
attributes. Warriors are semi-naked, wearing grass skirts, feathers, and face paint;
chiefs wear tunics. Panán's *cacica* María Panana, appearing at the 1987 Carnival,
donned a modest but makeshift tunic, similar to those worn by theatrical chiefs. Almost
all pre-Columbian characters are decked out with "gold" jewelry, made from metallic
paper. Golden headbands hold in place the long hair that these characters exhibit.

Costumes conveying a sense of the more recent past, and sometimes even the
distant era of the chiefs, are generally constructed from the clothing that old people
still wear: double-weave ponchos and flannel trousers for men; homespun skirts and
shawls for women; everyone barefoot or shod with hemp sandals. Such garb is by no
means aboriginal in origin; it is worn by non-native peasants throughout the Andes.
Nevertheless, it has assumed a symbolic importance in the Nariñense indigenous

movement, representing indigenous culture as it used to be; the display of this clothing is interpreted as a form of cultural revitalisation.

Non-native characters sport stereotypical costumes that are almost a parody of mestizo dress. Priests are identified by their red capes, pith helmets, leather boots, and ties. Landlords and soldiers wear leather jackets; they are frequently identified by their sunglasses.

Clearly, theatrical costume is hardly historically authentic. Instead, it is meant to convey historicity through contemporary stereotype and cliché, as well as through the distancing of observer and historical subject. It is thus not so much the accuracy of the costume as the associations it elicits which are at stake here. Nariñense theatre differs in function from the historically accurate nostalgia of contemporary North American re-enactments of the past. It is not meant to arouse a sentimental appreciation of earlier lifeways; instead, it invokes history in order to activate militant sentiments in the present (Lowenthal 1985).

Costume provided the major vehicle for historical expression in processional theatre. Biblical characters did not do anything: they were simply represented by virtue of their clothing. This is obvious in the personal reminiscences of participants in the elaborate processions of the past, whose descriptions are essentially lists of costumes, arrayed in processional order. Raúl Fueltala of the resguardo of Panán always played King Saul in the Good Friday celebration in Chiles, taking his place in a procession of sixty to one hundred tableaux. He remembers the texture of the procession, especially the clothes he wore and the props he carried:

> Así, yo me tocó de ser el Rey. Entonces, claro, yo era a componer el caballo. El caballo era bien compuesto con capa, bien adornado desde los cascos forrados, con papel de ese amarillo, riendas, freno, la frente, todo, el galápago tapado con capa, brillando eso de estrellas, adornos. En eso iba pues, en Rey propio, pues eso sí, y yo iba vestido blanco con capa y con la espada y con un copón también de rey. Iba manejando mi caballo y con la espada y cogido el copón y con buena corona, todo. A mí me tocó atrás de los Centuriones. Los Centuriones iban adelante, cuando ya me gritaban por lista, "El Rey Saúl, siga!" Entonces, ahí tenía que seguir, y atrás de mi vuelta, los que les iba a tocar.

> [So I got to be the king. And, sure, I had to ready the horse. The horse was decorated with a cape, adorned even to his gilded hooves, with that yellow paper, the reins, the bit, his head, everything, the saddle covered with a cape that shone with stars and ornaments. The king himself, then, rode out, that's right, and I was dressed in white with a cape and with a sword and also with a king's goblet. I would steer my horse, with the sword and carrying the goblet and with a nice crown, everything. And I came after the centurions. The centurions would go ahead, and then they shouted out to me from the list, "King Saul, your turn!" Then, I would have to follow, and behind me, those who were next.]

This sense of the past is not organised according to a chronological series of events, obeying, instead, a sequence of images that are arrayed over topographic space, duplicating in commemorative ceremony the close relationship between time and space that pervades the native Nariñense historical memory.

Texture is also conveyed through the use of language in the plays. The Pasto language disappeared during the nineteenth century; the indigenous peoples of highland Nariño are all monolingual Spanish-speakers. Various methods of re-creating the aboriginal tongue are employed in theatre to convey what it meant to be a native person in the past, on the one hand, and the intention on the part of many young people to embark on the impossible task of linguistic revival, on the other. Indigenous names, some Pasto and some from far-flung regions of Colombia, convey a feeling of linguistic autonomy as characters appear on stage: Cruz Angela de los Cumbes, Cristián Sotavento, Sebastián Panán. In one of the Muellamués conquest plays, actors, probably return-migrants from Quito, speak Quechua while a narrator declares over the loudspeaker that the community has finally recovered the lost Pasto language.

Toward a national indigenous discourse

An examination of Colombian native manifestos led Michel de Certeau (1986) to declare that the discourse of indigenous organisations is marked by cultural and geographic specificity, and not by the construction of a common ideology and language. I would agree that indigenous militancy is not centralised, as the historical and geographic specificity of Nariñense plays eloquently demonstrates. Nevertheless, militant drama plays an important role in the creation of a national indigenous discourse, conveyed through texture and image, much like the costume and language already described.

Cumbe and Quintín Lame

The birth of a pan-native discourse is especially clear in the scripts written by Miguel Angel Alpala, director of Los Cumbes. These scripts are but imperfectly memorised by the actors, but the formulaic utterances they contain are remembered by all. Let us look at some of these formulas:

> Nosotros, los indígenas, mas aborrecidos de este gran "Cumbal" de los blancos españoles *que llegaron este día 12 de octubre de 1492 hasta las tierras llamadas Guananí, que hoy las llamamos Colombia.*

> [We, the natives, detested by that Gran "Cumbal" of the white Spaniards, *who arrived that October 12th, 1492, at the lands called Guananí, that today we call Colombia.*]

> *El hijo de un indígena se sentará en el trono de sabiduría,* para defender nuestra propia sangre, sangre que por largo tiempo *se ha estado ocultando por este vengativo feroz de nosotros.*

> [*A native son will sit on the throne of knowledge,* to defend our own blood, blood which for a long time *has been hidden by our fierce vengeance.*]

> *La prehistoria repercute lo de nuestros antepasados, sus asientos allá en esa colina donde está sepultada la casa de la divinidad, según la prehistoria de*

Bochica, quien por medio de signos o parábolas donde se constataba en los sublimes rayos del sol: cuando se presentaba por el oriente y así se consagraba las ceremonias de los dioses que adoraban nuestros antepasados. Pero los aventureros que llegaron el 12 de octubre de 1492 en nombre de la civilización hicieron blandir la cuchilla de la mano y la intención para quitarnos la vida de nosotros y esas grandes riquezas que nosotros teníamos heredado de nuestros caciques antepasados. Y de hoy en día nosotros, los Colombianos, estamos acompañados del valor, y *unidos como un concierto de águilas encolerizadas lograremos la defensa de nosotros* para que se nos haga justicia, y seamos amparados por las autoridades competentes de toda la nación, de toda Colombia, y para todos los colombianos.

[*Prehistory echoes our ancestors, their homes there on that hill where the house of the divinity is buried, according to the prehistory of Bochica, who through signs or parables found truth in the sublime rays of the sun: when it shone from the east and in this way they consecrated the ceremonies of the gods that our ancestors adored. But the adventurers who arrived on October 12th, 1492, in the name of civilisation*, brandished knives in their hands and the intention of robbing us of our lives and of those great riches which we had inherited from our ancestors, the chiefs. And today we, the Colombians, are accompanied by valour, and *united like a concert of angry eagles, we will achieve our defence*, so that we are done justice, and so that we are protected by the competent authorities of the whole nation, all of Colombia, and for all Colombians.]

Each of the phrases I have highlighted is a quotation from Manuel Quintín Lame's *Los pensamientos del indio que se educó dentro de las selvas colombianas* (Lame 1971). A Páez sharecropper who moved the native peoples of Cauca and Tolima to demand their rights to reclaim land, to have an autonomous political authority (the resguardo council), and to occupy an autonomous territory (the resguardo), Lame wrote his book in 1939, but it was not published until 1971, several years after his death. The treatise swiftly became a tool for political education in indigenous communities, including in Cumbal, where several copies circulate.[9] Let us look at how Lame's book operates as a model for dramatic dialogue in Cumbal:

1. *12th October 1492*: The playwright makes repeated reference to Columbus's arrival in America, although the Spaniards would not invade the Pasto region for some four decades. The insistence on 1492 echoes Lame, who repeatedly asserts that 1492 was a turning point in indigenous experience; Lame frequently opposes it to 1939, the year in which his book was completed, since he perceived the 447 years between 1492 and 1939 as marking the period of indigenous oppression, which would end with the appearance of his treatise. The playwright calls Colombia by an alternative name, "Guananí", the Bahamian island upon which Columbus made his first landfall. Similarly, aboriginal territorial autonomy is repeatedly referred to by Lame through the use of the same concept. Both Lame and playwright Miguel Angel Alpala use 1492 and the name Guananí as mnemonic devices: Lame, to recall the cataclysm of the Spanish invasion and the existence of a separate and autonomous indigenous experience; Alpala, to recall Lame.

2. *Reclaiming the throne*: Lame's treatise is profoundly messianic, proclaiming his role as saviour of Colombia's indigenous peoples, who would liberate native Colombians from the darkness of ignorance through the power of his knowledge; then justice would be done:

> Ese crimen está oculto, señores; pero esa justicia llegará, en que el indio colombiano recuperará su trono, etc., etc. (ibid. 21)

> [That crime is hidden, sirs; but that justice will come, when the Colombian native reclaims his throne, etc., etc.]

Similarly, the playwright makes reference to the coming millennium, when the aboriginal throne will be reclaimed, and native blood, long hidden, will once again be visible. Lame writes that his knowledge was acquired through nature, not through a formal education, likening his intelligence to the flight of birds:

> Este cóndor de mi pensamiento y esa águila de mi psicología indígena la que se engendró cuando pasó ese cóndor o cóndores como un concierto de golondrinas parleras que visitan las estaciones del tiempo. . . . (ibid. 65)

> [That condor of my mind and that eagle of my psychology, an indigenous psychology that was conceived when the condor or condors passed by, like a concert of swallows that visit the seasons. . . .]

The same flight of birds becomes a metaphor for knowledge and political awareness in the Los Cumbes's script where, "united like a concert of angry eagles, we will achieve our defence".

3. *Prehistory*: the lengthy passage in the play that situates the source of knowledge in prehistory—in particular in archaeological remains—and identifies the sun as a mouthpiece of this knowledge is also reminiscent of Lame's writings. *Los pensamientos* states that humanity learned its crafts—goldwork and stone-carving—from the sun (ibid. 24), making reference also to the Chibcha deity, Bochica. For Lame, history is encoded in the remains of this glorious past (ibid. 76).

All three themes—the cataclysm of 1492, the messianic future, and the roots of knowledge in the aboriginal past—are examples of a pragmatic sense of history, as it is articulated in metaphoric language, in potent images, that at once entreat indigenous theatregoers, in Connerton's words (1989: 45), to "re-present" their past within their present conditions and to appeal to their memory of the words of Quintín Lame to recall the demands of their movement.

It is indeed significant that native Nariñense theatre draws upon a printed source for its nationalist verbal images, for the written word has served as a vehicle for communication with the dominant society since the colonial period. In effect, written language can be understood as one of the points of intersection between native Colombians and the national society, one of the interpretive spaces in which we can begin to comprehend how these communities are, in fact, Colombian. Colombian law, which is itself encoded in written form, requires that resguardos supply documentary evidence of their existence in order to maintain their character as autonomous political and territorial units. Writing thus forces native Colombians to consult the past in order to justify the present.

Nevertheless, in the past two decades, written language has also become a vehicle for communication among native peoples themselves. *Unidad Indígena*, a national indigenous newspaper, is read and contributed to by the leadership of Nariñense resguardos. Communities routinely produce pamphlets and leaflets in the course of their struggle. As Anderson (1983) has suggested in his analysis of nationalism, the printed word generates a sensation of an "imagined community". Among native Colombians it inspires a feeling of the existence of an extensive population that participates simultaneously in membership in a broad indigenous community. Cumbal playwrights invoke the existence of this imagined community by drawing on Lame's published works for the metaphors they include in their plays.

Conclusion

If the purpose of militant drama is to expand the space of historical interpretation so that it includes sectors heretofore excluded from the analysis of the past, it is only partially successful. On the one hand, theatrical expression serves as a vehicle for the reconstitution on the artistic plane of a sense of community. This is achieved through a communal activity that makes personal reminiscences and memorista histories publicly meaningful. In theatre, historical mnemonics permit the collectivity to re-live past experience and, thus, to reappropriate it for use in the present (Shopes 1986). In this respect, militant theatre represents a democratisation of historical expression. Moreover, this new approach to historical interpretation is successful, inasmuch as it recasts in secular form the religious spectacle of the past that once provided people with a sense of universal history. But when we consider militant theatre against the backdrop of the history recounted by Cumbal's local historians, it is considerably less successful in its objectives. In comparison to memorista narratives, which themselves incorporate only a few historical referents, these plays display a conspicuous poverty of historical detail. The young actors seem to have neglected their homework, displaying little knowledge of the contents of pertinent documentation or the experiences recounted by memoristas.

The space of dramatic presentation might be better understood, though, as an opportunity for young people to learn *how to remember* history, as opposed to *what should be recalled*. Like local historians, militant dramatists insert historical referents into a framework describing experiences of the present or the recent past. While memoristas weave this background with threads originating in narratives of recent experience, actors evoke the quotidian and the recent through their portrayal of costume. The names of the native authorities of the titles are thus projected against a contemporary and experiential backdrop. Likewise, quotations from Lame are selected as familiar images that are deployed in a visual field built upon the clothing of recent memory.

Notwithstanding the amateurish historical analysis of the playwrights in comparison to that of the memoristas, it is precisely by emphasising recent experience to the detriment of historical explanation that militant actors constitute themselves as a new brand of historians. If their dramatic training leaves them with little in the way of historical data, it introduces them to the craft of the memorista, whom they learn to emulate. In time, some of the best of this youthful group will take up the mantle of the resguardo council, acquire a greater fluidity in interpreting the past, and eventually become memoristas in their own right. How they articulate their historical knowledge in the future, whether through oral narrative, newspaper articles, political rhetoric, song, or some other medium, will become evident in future years.

ACKNOWLEDGMENTS   The research upon which this paper is based was conducted in Cumbal, Nariño, and in various Colombian and Ecuadorian archives in 1986–87 under the sponsorship of the Council for the International Exchange of Scholars, the National Science Foundation, and the Social Science Research Council; in 1988, sponsored by the Fulbright Program of the U.S. Department of Education; in 1989, sponsored by the Wenner-Gren Foundation for Anthropological Research; and in 1990, sponsored by the University of Maryland, Baltimore County. Research was conducted under the supervision of the Cabildo Indígena de Cumbal. Luz Angélica Mamián Guzmán and Jesús Iván Villota Bravo of Pasto and Gilberto Helí Valenzuela Mites of Cumbal all assisted in the collection of oral histories. Cristóbal Landázuri and his associates at Marka, Instituto de Historia y Antropología Andina, collaborated in the collection of archival materials. The Grupo Artístico Los Cumbes of the Vereda Cuaical was kind enough to allow me to reproduce copies of their scripts.

Notes

1. *Resguardo* is a legal term for which I hesitate to provide an English gloss (like "reservation") to avoid misidentification of this specifically Colombian institution with very different kinds of entities in North America.

2. The eighteenth-century titles of Cumbal and Muellamués were registered in provincial notarial offices during the late nineteenth century: *Notaría Primera de Pasto* (NP/P), "Expediente sobre los linderos del Resguardo del Gran Cumbal", Escritura 228 de 1908; *Notaría Primera de Ipiales* (NP/I), "Título de resguardo de Muellamués", ff. 336–342, 14 de octubre de 1885. The boundaries enumerated in the title to Gran Cumbal encompass four modern resguardos: Cumbal, Chiles, Panán, and Mayasquer.

3. Theatrical presentations of the Three Magi, using Spanish scripts, were widespread in the Andes and can still be found in some regions (see, for example, Beyersdorff 1988). Until recently, such plays were performed in Cumbal and in Muellamués. In the early colonial period, sons of hereditary chiefs trained at special schools in Quito were inculcated with the Christian doctrine through participation in dramatic presentations. See Moreno Proaño (1979) cited in Hartmann and Oberem (1981).

4. *Memoristas* are people recognised by their communities as interpreters of history. Most of these people have been council members, many of them the children or grandchildren of important leaders. Their knowledge derives from oral histories passed down in their families, but is also supplemented by the reading of documents in the community archives, as well as historical publications. For more on memoristas, see Rappaport (1994).

5. Pre-Columbian burials have been discovered throughout Pasto territory. Nevertheless, it is only when memory is jogged by something as legitimate as a museum poster that obvious historical referents are incorporated into public displays. In the same way, it was only after the appearance of "Glory", a film about an all-black Civil War regiment, that the Massachusetts 54th Volunteer Infantry Regiment began to be incorporated into re-enactments of the Civil War (*Washington Post*, 20 May, 1990).

6. The traditions of Andean Christs described for the Peruvian and Bolivian Andes (see Allen 1988, Gow 1980, Nash 1979, Sallnow 1987) or of the Virgin Mary and various saints among the Colombian Páez (see Bernal 1953, Rappaport 1980–81) are not to be found in southern Nariño, whose indigenous population is considerably more culturally integrated into the dominant mestizo society. I heard re-workings of biblical stories situating Christ in Andean landscapes: being forced to drink bitter quinua water instead of vinegar, hiding from the Romans in a field of the typically Andean *chocho* or *tarhui* (lupins), which made noise when he moved and betrayed his presence. But an Andeanisation of Christ comparable to that of other areas, where he essentially takes on Andean traits, is absent from Nariño.

7. Similarly, voices of the indigenous movement have rewritten native history so that it corresponds to, legitimises, and is legitimised by the Christian past. Manuel Quintín Lame (1971), a turn-of-the-century Páez militant whose published works have influenced the native people of Nariño, included indigenous figures in his reworking of the Nativity, much as did native chroniclers of the colonial period.

8. See Harvey (in this volume) for a critique of the memory-history distinction.

9. Even before its publication, *Los pensamientos* was a source of inspiration for the native people of Ortega, Tolima; it was only after repeatedly hearing unusual metaphoric language uttered by the people of Ortega that editor Gonzalo Castillo-Cardenas (1987: 1–3) began to suspect that there existed some kind of template for their clichés, resulting finally in his discovery of Lame's manuscript.

II

MULTIPLE MEDIA:
RITUAL, WEAVING, AND
THE MAKING OF MEANINGS

CATHERINE J. ALLEN

When Pebbles Move Mountains

Iconicity and Symbolism in Quechua Ritual

Say it! No ideas but in things.

William Carlos Williams

Before sunrise, on the Monday before Corpus Christi, many small groups of pilgrims climb toward the glacial sanctuary of Qoyllur Rit'i in the highlands of southern Peru. Delegations from many communities bring small icons of crucified Christ to "visit" Christ of Star Snow in his chapel among the powerful and sacred mountain lords. They time themselves to end this first leg of their arduous journey before sunrise; that way they can enter the sanctuary as the first rays of the sun strike the snowy peaks. There are many aspects to this complex and beautiful pilgrimage, which epitomises in many ways the contradictory social and cultural experiences of southern Peruvian peasants.[1] Here, I will focus on one small but significant ritual practice—the "pebble game", the practice of playing with miniatures.

During their climb to the sanctuary, pilgrims stop beside the steep path at a level place called Pukllay Pampa (the playing ground), where they rest their icons in a stone windbreak. Michael Sallnow's rich account of the Qoyllur Rit'i pilgrimage includes this description:

> Here there was a strange interlude. . . . Groups of people . . . began to leave the
> circle to engage in various kinds of foolery. All around, members of other
> *naciones* were doing the same. Some indulged in general horseplay, leaping and
> jumping around amid much shouting and laughter. Others played at games of
> make-believe. One of our number bought a cow from a companion, in reality a
> lump of quartz, for which he gave a handful of scraps of paper representing

73

money and which he tethered with a strand of wool from his cap. He then took his cow over to a group from another *nación* and proceeded to sell it to them in turn. The original vendor's scraps of paper, meanwhile, had become seeds, which he went off to plant. Others, meanwhile, occupied themselves privately in the construction of elaborate miniature houses and corrals out of rocks, with stones representing llamas, alpacas, and sheep, to indicate to the spirits of the shrine the devotee's desires. Everyone from our party without exception joined in some of these antics, though not all with equal enthusiasm. Participation seemed to be mandatory. (Sallnow, 1987: 190)

I witnessed a similar scene when I accompanied pilgrims from the community of Sonqo (Paucartambo Province) in 1975, although my companions were somewhat less spirited than Sallnow's. I was struck by the intensity of the young couples as they searched for stones shaped like alpacas, llamas, sheep, and cows and then carefully placed them in their little stone corrals.[2]

The next day, at the sanctuary itself, this make-believe continued. Scree-covered slopes around the small shrine devoted to the Virgin of Fatima were bustling with miniature house-building activity. There, most of the participants were young men in a more urban style of dress, speaking Spanish as well as Quechua. Indeed, their little houses reflected a more urbanised style of life and a commercial orientation. There were fewer domestic animals and many *artefactos*—pebble sewing machines, refrigerators, televisions, and Volvo trucks. Small groups of these pilgrims carried on games of buying and selling articles of pebble property for bits of paper representing money. Sallnow observed that some of these compounds "had written labels identifying them as the desired property of this or that family", adding that "the combination of this surreal spectacle and the rarefied mountain air was dizzying" (Sallnow 1987: 193).[3]

When I returned to the Qoyllur Rit'i pilgrimage in 1980 I found that some of the pilgrims from Sonqo had shifted their house-building activity from Pukllay Pampa to this area around Fatima's shrine and that their little houses included the artefactos increasingly present in Sonqo: record players and loudspeakers, sewing machines and Coleman lanterns.

The Virgin of Fatima, or "Mama Sinakara" as she is called by some pilgrims, is thought to be an *awaq mamacha* (little weaver mother, the patroness of weaving). Women sit next to her shrine, weaving small, doll-sized samples of their handiwork to leave as offerings. They say that as they weave, their hands "learn" from the mamacha, and they depart more accomplished in their craft. I should add that one sees folded pieces of paper inserted in the nooks and crannies of Fatima's shrine as well: these are letters left by literate pilgrims, who sidestep the process of house building by writing their desires down on paper. Meanwhile, the *taytachas* (little fathers, or icons representing crucified Christ) "visit" their prototype Christ in the chapel in order to return revitalised to their home communities.

This "play" in the heart of an exhausting and difficult pilgrimage does indeed have a surreal quality for an outside observer. The house building looks like a child's game; the women look as though they are making doll's clothes; and the playful buying and selling with fake money rather resembles the game of Monopoly. It is hard to write a description of the scene without smiling—and, indeed, the pilgrims themselves enjoy these activities and refer to them light-heartedly as *pukllay* 'playing'. Nevertheless, it is obvious that there is more to these activities; they are neither child's play nor party games. They give that impression because, out of all the pilgrimage's complex ritual activity, they are probably the most difficult for a cultural outsider to fathom.

The activities at Qoyllur Rit'i present two different kinds of textuality side by side: there are miniature iconic texts built of pebbles, and there are abstract symbolic texts, letters to the saints, in alphabetic writing. Both make requests of powerful beings (whom I will call "deities" for lack of a better word), but the ways that they communicate these requests operate on different assumptions about the relationship of form, substance, and human action. In the following pages I will explore this miniaturised "play" activity as a mode of communication between human beings and deities. Approached as texts, the pebble households are iconic messages presented to the mountain lords and saints to request specific material favours. I will not explore the pilgrim's use of writing in any depth (but see Lienhard and Lund, in this volume). Nor will I analyse a specific pebble text or corpus of such texts. Rather, I will explore the general process of communication involved in the production of these texts. In the process I hope to indicate some angles of approach to these textual strategies.

Much Andean textuality has proved notoriously resistent to interpretation. Attempts to "decode" pre-Columbian communication devices, such as the *kipu* (complex knotted strings used for record keeping) and the *toqapu* (abstract geometric designs), have met so far with limited success. It is not simply the extreme abstraction of these texts that baffles us; it is their semiotics. Pre-Columbian expression operated on premises about form, matter, action, and meaning quite distinct from those that produced western alphabetic writing.[4] At Qoyllur Rit'i, these two types of textuality operate side by side, often employed by the same individuals. I hope to show that the making of miniatures in pilgrimages illuminates some fundamental aspects of a peculiarly Andean type of textuality through which ideas and values are communicated in presentational forms. I hope that eventually this exploration may contribute to our understanding of pre-Columbian communication systems like the Inka kipu; on the other hand, it should provide some insight into the kinds of adjustments and difficulties Andean peasants encounter as they incorporate literacy into their lives.

I will argue that these textual strategies must be understood as active, interactional techniques for changing the lived-in world; they include synecdoche (or envelopment of the whole as part of a larger whole) and play with dimensionality. They are premised on a principle of consubstantiality, the assumption that all beings are intrinsically interconnected through their sharing a matrix of animated substance. In other words, these strategies make sense within a worldview that assumes the inseparability of mind and matter and attributes animacy of some kind to all material objects.[5]

Play, skill, and reciprocity

The pebble play at Qoyllur Rit'i is one special example of the pervasive and important role of miniatures in Andean ritual. These miniatures are viewed as tiny storehouses of prosperity and well-being. They are carefully tended—"fed" and even on occasion clothed—and ritually manipulated to bring their keepers the well-being they represent.

Usually these miniatures are bestowed by super-human agencies—a mountain lord, the earth, or the lightning.[6] During pilgrimages such as Qoyllur Rit'i, human beings are temporarily empowered to create the miniature texts themselves as they "play" at the sanctuary.

Why does this childlike play—lighthearted yet intent—figure as an important, even mandatory part of a long and difficult complex of ritual actions? For childlike it is: the miniaturised activity at Qoyllur Rit'i does resemble the play of children back in the pilgrims' home communities. During my fieldwork in Sonqo, for example, I often saw small children playing with pebble "herds"; little girls' first attempts at weaving were carried out on miniature looms, "as if for a doll".

Bruce Mannheim provides a clue to this problem in an article entitled "The Language of Reciprocity in Southern Peruvian Quechua" where he reports that children at play "are said to *ayni* with God" (1986b: 267). *Ayni*, a basic form of reciprocity, has also been called the "ethos" of indigenous Andean culture (D. Núñez del Prado 1972). Oscar Núñez del Prado comments that "life is an *ayni*, and must be returned at death" (1973: 30–31). At the most abstract level, ayni is the basic give-and-take that governs the universal circulation of vitality.[7] It can be positive, as when brothers-in-law labour in each others' fields; or it can be negative, as when the two men quarrel and exchange insults. This circulation—be it of water or human energy—is driven by a system of continuous reciprocal interchanges, a kind of dialectical pumping mechanism (Allen 1988: 93). Every category of being, at every level, participates in this cosmic circulation. Humans maintain interactive reciprocity relationships, not only with each other but also with their animals, their houses, their potato fields, the earth, and the sacred places in their landscape.

Participation begins during childhood play when an individual begins to acquire the skills necessary for adult life. This learning comes not through didactic instruction but through progressively successful efforts to master a skill (Franquemont et al.: n.d.; Allen 1988: 50). In Sonqo, for example, every adult skill is said to have been invented by a specific saint; a person who masters a skill—spinning, for example—is said to be *santuyuq* (endowed with the attributes of the saint) for that activity. The same idea can be phrased in terms of stars rather than saints: every skill has its *istrilla* (star); a person who is good at a skill is *istrillayuq* (endowed with the star).[8]

The statement that children at play "do *ayni* with God" tells us that a child's first entry into this universal world of reciprocity occurs outside the context of society as, through play, she or he interacts directly with sacred power sources (God, saints, stars). Gradually the person is drawn from this decontextualised play into a network of adult interactive relationships. An adult person's basic responsibility in life is to use acquired skills in order to participate in the web of reciprocal exchange. Throughout adult life, the internalised saint is paid out through skilled work—producing spun thread, woven cloth, ploughed fields, cooked food, dances, chewed coca, and so forth.

Adults consume the products of each others' skilled work; I consume my fellows' work (through its products), while my own work is consumed by my fellows.[9] Failure to participate in this circulatory ayni leaves one unable to die properly; one becomes a *kukuchi*, or *condenado* (condemned soul)—trapped in a rotting body and consumed by the desire to eat one's closest relatives. The kukuchi's insatiable, cannibalistic appetite exposes it as a kind of microcosm gone wrong and collapsed in upon itself.[10]

This vision of the cosmic circulation as a complex, organised, and highly controlled system of mutual consumption is important for understanding the pilgrims' activity at Qoyllur Rit'i. It reveals the significance of play as it recurs ritually in adulthood. In pilgrimage, one comes into direct contact with the most powerful saints and with the snow and ice of mountain lords who are normally viewed from a great distance. It is, to the pilgrims, like walking into the face of god—a liminal state that returns them to the decontextualised, open, and direct condition of childhood play. It is not surprising that this ritual play occurs on a place called Pukllay Pampa. Billie Jean Isbell has shown that the word *pampa* (a flat stretch of ground devoid of landmarks) connotes openness and potentiality, a condition of being undefined, as yet unmarked by distinguishing features.[11]

On Pukllay Pampa, the 'playing ground', adult pilgrims play freely in the realm of possibility, on a space of transformation, in immediate contact with the greatest mountain lords and the powerful shrines of saints. Their play has the effect of reinvigorating skill and creativity. Thus women sit at the side of the awaq mamacha and "weave with her hands". Young married couples build their households, and young entrepreneurs play at commerce.

Pebbles and power objects

Beyond the "pebble game", miniatures abound in the highly charged ritual atmosphere of Qoyllur Rit'i. We have already encountered one example: the little taytachas (Christs, literally 'little fathers') brought to "visit" the great image of miraculous Christ at the sanctuary. At the pilgrimage's end, these taytachas return home revitalised, a process Sallnow (1974: 127) likens to "recharging their batteries". Taytachas and other images of Catholic saints are thought to store their community's well-being and prosperity. If denied their feast days, they feel too sad and tired to support the community.[12]

Among the pilgrimage dancers are formidable *ukuku* (bears), many of whom carry little replicas of themselves. A widespread folktale about the bear tells how a doll helps the ukuku to fight and subdue a ferocious damned soul (kukuchi). Ukuku dancers on the pilgrimage face a similar trial, for they spend the night up on the glacier, amid the hordes of cannibalistic souls thought to inhabit these frozen wastes. Reminiscent of the folktale, the dolls seem to function as power objects.[13]

Outside the context of pilgrimage, miniatures and other small objects are also ritually important. In peasant communities, persons favoured by the *apukuna* (mountain lords) may acquire power objects of various kinds. For example, at the age of nine years, an acquaintance of mine in Sonqo found an antique religious medallion while playing on a hill named Picchu. She recognised it as her istrilla, the source and storehouse of her well-being (*allin kawsay*). At the age of fifty, she still treasured it as a gift from her guardian, Apu Picchu. On the eve of 1st August, she brings it out of its hiding place and lovingly "feeds" it with coca leaves, red wine, and cane alcohol.

Another type of power object, similar to the istrilla, is the *misal*, which is guarded by ritual specialists (*paqo*) as the source of their power and special insight. I am told that these misales are usually quartz crystals, considered to be the residue of lightning bolts. In fact, any place or thing struck by lightning is considered to be possessed of special and immediate potency, called *qhaqha*. People or animals killed by lightning are buried on the spot, and thereafter are revered with offerings of coca and alcohol. A person who survives being struck by lightning is himself called qhaqha, and becomes a paqo (ritual specialist). The condition of being qhaqha, and/or the possession of a misal is what enables the paqo to perform divination—that is, to communicate with sacred places.[14]

Certain sacred places are intimately connected with the welfare of domestic animals. These *apu* may favour fortunate and deserving individuals with *inqa* or *inqaychu*, small stones shaped like domestic animals. A few places in Sonqo—for example, a confluence (*tinku*) of three streams, and some marshy hillsides—are described as 'possessing inqaychus' (*inqaychuyuq*). There, the little inqaychus come out to graze on 1st August, and if you listen carefully you can hear them bleating 'prettily' (*munaychata*). They allow people with insight to recognise them and take them home, while the foolish or unlucky see only common stones and pass them by.[15] Jorge Flores Ochoa reports that in Paratia, the animal itself enters a fog and disappears into the ground, leaving the stone behind. He quotes a herder as explaining: "You must look carefully and quickly throw over them either an *inkuña* [woven napkin for keeping coca leaves] or a *ch'uspa* [woven coca bag]. If you succeed, then the animals disappear and in their place remain white or black stones, still warm and palpitating" (Flores Ochoa, 1977b: 221; author's translation).

During the miraculous events of 1780, which are said to have given rise to the Qoyllur Rit'i pilgrimage (Ramírez 1969, Gow 1974, Sallnow 1987), the Christ child behaved remarkably like one of these inqaychus. One day he appeared as a mestizo child to a shepherd boy pasturing alpacas alone in the high *puna* (mountain tundra). The two children played nicely together; the herds multiplied marvelously, and the shepherd boy was given food and beautiful clothes. When an official delegation from Ocongate came to investigate, they were blinded by rays of light shining from his white clothes, like light reflected from a mirror. When they approached, the Christ child threw off his clothes and disappeared into a rock, which afterward bore his imprint: "So in this way, in this rock, our father Jesus Christ entered naked, and from that time our miraculous father was formed there" (Sallnow 1987: 210). Like the pretty little inqas, Christ allowed himself to be recognised by the favoured but fled from the foolish, appearing to them as a rock. According to Flores Ochoa: "*Inqa* is the generative and vital principle. It is the source and origin of happiness, well-being and abundance. Herders say that the *illa* and *inqaychu* both 'are' and 'have' *inqa*" (1977b: 218; author's translation).

Arguedas relates inqa to the word *inka*:

INQA: (*incca*, according to the traditional spelling) and not "INKA" is how this word is pronounced by the Canas Indians; and "INQA" not only signifies emperor, "INQA" is the name for the original model of every being, according to Quechua mythology. This concept is more commonly known by the term "inkachu". Then "*Tukuy kausaq uywakunaq INKAKUNA*" should be translated as the model or original archetype of every being (Arguedas, 1955: 74, quoted in Gow, 1976: 199; also see Gow, 1974: 69).

The inqa does not simply provide a model, in miniature, for the living creatures it represents; as a prototype it gives rise to the animal itself in its vitality as well as its physical form.[16] A household's prosperity is intimately connected with its inqaychus, which store the fertility and vitality of the herds. They are described as 'caring protectors' (*khuyaqkuna*) and are passed from generation to generation, divided among a couple's children, just as the animals also are divided for inheritance purposes. There are inqas for other aspects of the household economy as well: one collection, for example, included smooth pebbles representing potatoes and a triangular stone described as a *michiq warmi* (herder woman). The collection also included carved stone tablets representing the house compound and its fields. Sonqueños say that these carved inqas, too, have been passed down for generations, and claim not to know their origin.

On the eves of 1st August, Carnival, and St John's Day (24th June), a family brings out its inqas to "graze" on offerings of coca leaf and to "drink" libations of alcohol. While adults comment on the beauty of their little stone herd, their children fondle the inqaychus and play with them delightedly. Chewed coca wads are called the inqas' excrement, and are buried in the family's corral.

The inclusion of artefactos—loudspeakers, sewing machines, televisions—in some pilgrims' pebble households at Qoyllur Rit'i can be understood simply as an elaboration of these indigenous Andean rituals, practised to secure the well-being of the peasant herds and crops. In rural high-altitude communities, much of a household's wealth and local prestige is invested in its herds; peasants who migrate to towns and cities like Cusco, on the other hand, invest much of their wealth in artefactos. They find that saving money is pointless in conditions of staggering inflation, while manufactured articles can be used to augment the family income and often can be resold. Like the animal wealth of the countryside, they also provide a source of prestige and personal satisfaction. Seen in this light, the trucks, televisions, and refrigerators fit less jarringly into the little archetype households left on the mountainside.[17]

The activity of commerce, so central to many pilgrims' lives, has also been integrated into this context. Like weavers, who leave Fatima's shrine with their hands newly instructed, young entrepreneurs ply their commercial craft in miniature—in miniature, not only because the material goods are represented by pebbles and the money by bits of paper, but because the participants do it as a game.

Moments of ritual potency

In order to encapsulate personal and community well-being, power objects like inqas, misales, and istrillas have a connection with mountains on the one hand and with celestial light on the other. In fact, inqas may be called *illa*, a word referring to a ray of light. During their ritual "meal", the inqas should be positioned facing the door "because that is *inti haykuna*" (sun's entrance; commonly refers to the east) where the first rays of light will enter the house in the morning. Interestingly, the house is treated as a microcosm with its own orientation to the sun; the door need not be facing east.

At ritually powerful times of the year, most importantly on 1st August (near the sun's anti-zenith passage), many Andean peasants compose a burnt offering (*despacho*) to "feed" the earth and sacred places.[18] The offering is folded in an envelope of paper that has a "head" and "feet", like a miniature human being. When the despacho is burned, its head must point toward the place on the horizon where the sun is expected to rise, again called "inti haykuna". If not properly oriented, the offering will pass upside-down or sideways to the sacred places.

Like other ritual practices that are intended to promote prosperity, pebble games require a proper orientation toward sources of light. The directness of contact with sacred power sources is facilitated by both the site of the sanctuary, and the time of year—shortly before the winter solstice when the sun is on the verge of renewal. The rays of the sun are especially potent during this period. On the Qoyllur Rit'i pilgrimage, too, sunrise is a moment of great potency and ritual importance. Many pilgrims time their trek to arrive at the sanctuary at the moment of sunrise; later, at the end of an all-night walk, the pilgrims dance on a pampa beneath Apu Ausangate at the moment of sunrise.

In general, the shining of reflected light is felt to be creative, amplifying the realms of possibility.[19] On 24th June, the Feast of St John (formerly the Inka's Inti Raymi, or Sun Festival), the sun is said to "dance"; stream water is thought to have powerful medicinal qualities at the moment the sun's light first strikes them, and many people try to draw water at this very instant. The combination of solstitial sun and glacial ice is especially powerful. After their all-night vigil on the glacier, the ukukus chip off chunks of ice at dawn; these are melted down as "holy water" and kept for medicinal and ritual purposes.

Elsewhere I have written that "(the) power of the inner world is the inverse, a kind of crystallization of power emanating from the upper world. We human beings live at the interface, in this world, where exchange and transformation take place" (Allen, 1988: 66).[20] Small power objects are particularly potent results of that transformation, produced at times and places in which both terrestrial and celestial forces are most powerful. They are created at moments when the configuration of *pacha* (the world) is sundered: on 1st August, when the earth opens; when lightning strikes; when the solstitial sun turns in its course.

Garcilaso de la Vega (1963 [1609], part I, bk. 2, ch. 4) seems to be employing the same idea when he explains that the word *huaca* (sacred earth shrine) refers not just to mummies and earth shrines but to anything whose appearance causes surprise or fright.[21] I was reminded of his statement when, before I left Sonqo, I asked a paqo how I might continue to grow in insight back in my own country. He answered that I must dream "after being frightened by the *relámpago*" (lightning bolt). To be startled is to experience a momentary sundering of one's internal microcosm, a moment which is potent as well as dangerous.

The pebbles at Qoyllur Rit'i, like the inqaychus on 1st August, come into human hands at a time of opening, a kind of crack in the world's fabric. Thus, the miniature houses with their corrals of animals and artefactos are like inqaychus—but in a curiously reversed way. Pilgrims wilfully enter a powerful place at a moment of opening and transformation; in their play, it is they who define the identity of the stones by arranging them into iconic statements of their needs and desires. Then, rather than keeping them, they leave them behind to be absorbed back into the mountainside.

Conclusion: miniatures and iconicity

We are now in a better position to understand the processes of miniaturisation and iconic representation that take place in this potently charged playground. Let us turn back to our opening question: what kind of communication is this, and what kind of textuality does it involve? That the communication is iconic in nature, is clear enough: the pebble households are little models of the things they stand for. However, there is a deeper purpose to this iconicity beyond simple representation.

In his famous discussion of miniatures, Claude Lévi-Strauss asks a similar question: "What is the virtue of reduction either of scale or in number of properties"? (1966: 23). He concludes that miniaturisation facilitates instant apprehension of the whole and that this produces a "very profound aesthetic emotion". Miniatures make us "reverse the normal process of understanding", for knowledge of the whole precedes knowledge of the parts: "More exactly, this quantitative transposition extends and diversifies our power over a homologue of the thing, and by means of it the latter can be grasped, assessed and apprehended at a glance" (ibid.). This analysis illuminates the Andean miniatures and yet falls short of explaining them in some interesting ways. Andean miniatures do more than simply delight their owners; they change the lived-in world. The pebble texts of Qoyllur Rit'i, inscribed on a ground of potentiality and transformation, serve a communicative and even coercive purpose.

Throughout Andean culture one encounters a pervasive tendency toward envelopment, or synecdoche. The Oxford English Dictionary (1971: s.v.) defines *synecdoche* as "A figure by which a more comprehensive term is used for a less comprehensive one or *vice versa*; as whole for part or part for whole, genus for species, species for genus, etc". I am using the term to refer not so much to a figure of speech as to a figure of thought. Synecdochal thinking[22] comprehends the world in terms of mutually enveloping homologous structures that act upon each other: ayllus are contained in ayllus; places are contained within places; every potato field contains its own vertical ecology. Textile patterns contain other patterns in amazing arrays of symmetries and inversions.[23] The word *tirakuna* (from Spanish *tierra* plus the pluralising suffix *-kuna*) refers to the whole collection of individual named places contained within the world. The many-armed ridge called Sonqo is one of the tirakuna; but Sonqo itself contains hundreds of named places who are themselves tirakuna. The scale of one's purview can expand or contract endlessly.[24] Every microcosm is a macrocosm, and vice versa.

In Andean ritual, synecdochal thought works on a world premised on consubstantiality: all beings are intrinsically interconnected through their sharing a matrix of animated substance. Thus, small and large imply each other concretely; a powerful miniature informs the cosmos with its own form.

Pilgrims at play in the charged atmosphere of Qoyllur Rit'i are empowered with the potential of actually shaping and directing a piece of the world according to their own wishes and needs. Thus a pebble text actualises the prosperity—the herds, trucks, sewing machines—it represents. When a pilgrim picks up a pebble at Qoyllur Rit'i, he is in a kind of world-defining situation. The fact that pieces *of* the mountain are presented *to* the mountain to communicate *with* the mountain is an extreme condensation of the normal cycle of reciprocity in which deities provide human well-being and are in turn sustained by that well-being.[25] To pick up a piece of the mountain in this time and place of potency and transformation is to pick up the world itself and form it in one's own terms, according to one's own desires and needs. Animals, buildings, and artefactos are ultimately a transformation, or crystallisation, of well-being that flows from the mountain; in that sense, what the pilgrim does is to shape a bit of the mountain's potential energy. I believe that this is the crux of iconicity in the ritual activity.

Epilogue: "No ideas but in things"

"The Spanish brought writing", my friend don Luis told me, just after we had finished preparing a burnt offering for Mother Earth and the Sacred Places. "The Inkas did not know writing; they knew stonework". He was praising the Inkas when he said this, trying to convey to me their power and wisdom. As with many of his deceptively simple statements, the significance of these words does not easily reveal itself. What does it mean to "know stonework"? Why should stonework stand in opposition to writing? And why do many Qoyllur Rit'i pilgrims—especially those who most look to the Inkas as ancestors—communicate requests to the deities by practising stone-work in miniature?

The contrast between the two types of textuality—symbolic versus iconic, abstract versus concrete—brings to the surface deep prejudices in a literate society: we think of iconic representation as crude and pictographic, a barbaric precursor of civilised literacy. The Inkas have long stood as a puzzling challenge to this assumption. Such a complex and sophisticated society can hardly be called "uncivilised"—but why did they never develop anything we can recognise as writing? To explore the textuality of stonework—in whatever dimension—is to explore the relationship between the material world and human agency, between thought and matter—as apparently both the Inkas and don Luis understood it. I hope that this preliminary exploration of miniature stonework may indicate some angles of approach to the textual strategies involved. These textual strategies are active, interactional techniques for changing the lived-in world; they include synecdoche (or envelopment of the whole as part of a larger whole), and play with dimensionality, and they are premised on the assumption that all beings are intrinsically interconnected through their sharing a matrix of animated substance.

It follows that all action is interactive because all beings are animate; activity is dialogic and governed by reciprocity. It also follows that the world is subject to transformation; specific life forms are transitory expressions of a single underlying substance.[26] Specific creatures exist only as long as their interactive relations with the world maintain and support their given forms. Finally, all representations (verbal, plastic, and graphic) are themselves active agents in this world of becoming. They do not just encode—they embody and enact—human thought, memory, and desire.

ACKNOWLEDGMENTS   Field research on which this paper is based was funded over a ten-year period by the Doherty Foundation, the Wenner-Gren Foundation for Anthropological Research, and George Washington University. A fellowship in the Dumbarton Oaks Center for Pre-Co-lumbian Studies provided time in which to rethink my ideas and rewrite the paper during the

1993–94 academic year. Many colleagues have helped me through conversations or comments on the paper, especially Rosaleen Howard-Malverde, Tom Cummins, and Bruce Mannheim. Responsibility for any errors contained here is of course my own. Finally, I extend many thanks to the individuals in Sonqo who have been thoughtful consultants and gracious friends.

Notes

1. For further sources on the pilgrimage to Qoyllur Rit'i, see, among others, Ramírez 1969; J. Núñez del Prado Béjar 1970; Gow 1974, 1976; Sallnow 1974, 1987; Randall 1982; Poole 1982, 1984; Getzels and Gordon 1985; Allen 1988.

2. I am using Qoyllur Rit'i as a representative example of a widespread activity common to pilgrimages throughout the Andean region. According to Rosaleen Howard-Malverde:

> The trade in home-made miniatures is a prominent feature of the pilgrimage to the shrine of the Virgin of Copacabana, Bolivia (6th August); people buy these from traders, who set up their stalls on the slope leading up to the calvary; then [they] have the little lorries, houses, even degree certificates and passports blessed both by the *yatiri* [ritual specialist] and by the priest. The manufacture of mini-artifacts is virtually a cottage industry in Bolivia. (personal communication, 23rd August 1994)

3. See also David Gow 1974: 71. According to Howard-Malverde, "the practice of making *artefactos* from stone and trading in them also occurs in the context of funeral rites in Northern Potosí, Bolivia" (personal communication, 23rd August 1994).

4. I am much indebted to Tom Cummins's thinking on this point. See his paper presented at the Dumbarton Oaks conference on "Native Traditions in the Post-Conquest World" in October 1992 (Cummins, in press).

5. I developed this argument concerning Andean animatism in my book, *The Hold Life Has: Coca and Cultural Identity in an Andean Community*, Washington, D.C.: Smithsonian Institution Press, 1988.

6. Also see Lapidus de Sager 1968; Flores Ochoa 1977a, 1977b, 1988; Aranguren 1975; Tomoeda 1988; Allen 1988.

7. For other work on Andean reciprocity, see, among others, Alberti and Mayer 1974; Isbell 1978; H. Skar 1982. The circulation of energy through *ayni* has been discussed by several other observers in addition to myself (Allen 1988). For example, see, among others, Earls and Silverblatt 1976; Urton 1981; Valderrama and Escalante 1988.

8. By analogy with the English term 'office holder', we might translate *istrillayuq* as 'star holder' and *santuyuq* as 'saint holder'.

9. Lawrence Sullivan, in his perceptive analysis of South American Indian religion, refers to this as "an endless cycle of consumption" (1988: 69). The theme of mutual consumption is powerfully expressed in Andean ritual through the practice of forced feeding (see Allen 1988: 169–175).

10. In the district of Paruro, *kukuchi* are described in terrifying terms as all-devouring black holes (Deborah Poole, personal communication, July 1980).

11. See Isbell and Roncalla (1977). In Ayacucho, riddles begin with the phrase, "In that *pampa* ... " (*Waq law pampapi* ... ; Isbell and Roncalla 1977: 25). See also Arnold, in this volume, for a discussion of the term *pampa* in textile language.

12. As ayllu members participate in treks and dances, they pour out their energy in a sacrifice that vitalises their patron deities. See Allen 1988, especially chapters 6–7.

13. For other sources on the *ukuku* as a figure in folklore and ritual dance, see, among others, Morote Best 1957; Barstow 1981; Allen 1983; Poole 1982, 1984.

14. Concerning Inka religion, Sabine MacCormack comments: "Lightning and the dead epitomize a cosmic imbalance tending either to generation or destruction" (1991: 286).

15. Also see Randall 1990: 27.

16. Claudette Kemper Columbus's article, "Immortal Eggs: A Peruvian Geocracy; Pariaqaqa of Huarochirí" (1990) is also relevant here.

17. Manufactured goods are thought to have a self-hood imparted by their makers (Allen 1982). Although machines—unlike hand-made ponchos, houses, and cooking pots—have no identifiable maker, they do have a certain kind of animation when connected with their power sources. The conceptual parallel with domestic animals was expressed, for example, by an acquaintance from Sonqo who purchased a radio in Cusco and immediately carried it back to my hotel room to perform its *tinka*, a form of ritual homage paid to domestic animals.

18. On the relation of Inka ritual activities to Inka astronomy, see the works of R. T. Zuidema (for example, 1980, 1988).

19. See, for example, Tristan Platt, in this volume. Also see MacCormack 1991, and Arguedas 1978, in which reflected light is a recurring motif.

20. See, among others, Earls and Silverblatt 1976; Zuidema 1980; Urton 1981; Isbell 1982; Allen 1988; Valderrama and Escalante 1988; Salomon 1991.

21. Harrison (1989: 45–48) gives an interesting discussion of Garcilaso's definition of huaca. Salomon (1991: 16–17) provides a good general discussion of huaca as a concept, as does MacCormack (1991). Zuidema's work explores Inka huacas in great depth (see, for example, Zuidema 1986).

22. The Oxford English Dictionary goes on to define synecdochism: "b. *Ethnol.* Belief or practice in which a part of an object or person is taken as equivalent to the whole, so that anything done to, or by means of, the part is said to take effect upon, or have the effect of, the whole". I want to extend this definition beyond metonymic part-to-whole relationships and emphasise situations in which part and whole are structurally homologous, causing metonymy and metaphor to collapse into each other.

23. For example, see Ascher and Ascher (1981: 54–55); Cereceda 1986, 1987; Franquem-ont et al., (n.d.); also see the suggestive articles by Harris (1986), Platt (1986), and Kemper Columbus (1990).

24. See Salomon and Urioste (1991: 14–15).

25. At Qoyllur Rit'i, the mountain is offered a part of itself, perhaps an ultimate case of Andean ritual forced feeding (Allen 1984, 1988).

26. See, for example, Ossio 1973; Sharon 1980: 170–174; Bastien 1987: 69–74; Allen 1988: 37–66; Salomon 1991: 14–19. On transformation in the cosmologies of South American Indians in general, see Sullivan 1988.

PENNY DRANSART

Cultural Transpositions

Writing about Rites in the Llama Corral

An elaborate ritual event observed by individual families in Isluga, an Aymara community in the highlands of northern Chile, has its focus of action in a certain type of corral. It is said by the human actors to be aimed at ensuring the reproductivity and fecundity of their animals. This ritual has an almost liturgical character since each family performs the events in a very similar manner, although no sacred text exists. Incorporated in the ritual are songs, gestures, actions, and material objects (some of which are used in everyday contexts, but which now take on highly charged roles). The contextual meaning of these events is not easily translated into words; instead, the significance for the participants should perhaps be seen in the insertion of the ritual into a fuller temporal and spatial setting—that is, in its position in the annual ritual cycle and in its topographical siting within an animated landscape.

If we accept that texts may occur in verbal form and also as the products of other generative channels, then the events that take place in certain types of llama corral may be considered to constitute texts. In the Andes, the *kancha*, or corral, is a site or space where humans and animals produce words, noises, gestures, and actions. Colour and shape in the form of material objects (some of which are used in everyday contexts) now take on highly charged roles and are incorporated into the activities. The emphasis here is on the unfolding of action or, in other words, the production of a meaningful ceremony, meaningful at least to the human participants.

Roland Barthes uses textual analysis as a way of understanding a text as the means for producing what he calls *signifiance* (moving play of signifiers), and the text in question is not treated as "philological object, custodian of the Letter" (Barthes 1977:

85

26). Although Barthes is careful not to regard texts as objectified words, the curious capital L of the phrase "custodian of the Letter" should be noted. It is as though a residual notion concerning the dominance of verbal over non-verbal performance is being dragged along with the volatile but generative play in which meaning is produced.

Catherine Allen (in this volume) argues that pre-Hispanic non-verbal communication operated on a different set of premises concerning "form, matter, action, and meaning", which may be contrasted with that which underlies Western alphabetic writing. She demonstrates how "playing" with pebbles as part of the rituals performed on a pilgrimage undertaken by the Quechua of Sonqo also shares this different "relationship of form, substance, and human action". It is my purpose here to contextualise in particular the visual and tactile aspects of Aymara ritual observance. I wish to emphasise that it is the very manipulation of colour, texture, and sound that enables the participants of the ritual to articulate various parts of the ceremony in a meaningful manner.

The Aymara of Isluga have developed an ability to compartmentalise Western alphabetic writing from other areas of experience. To Western educationists, most Isluga people would be regarded as functional illiterates. Writing is part of school learning, and school is an institution from city life imposed and controlled from beyond the boundaries of Isluga territory. As an institution, the school and its teachers are perceived as promoting Chilean city values which, all too often, are seen as being in opposition to Isluga Aymara values, but to which parents must send their children. This intrusion from city life is grudgingly accepted in Isluga. All too often, people gradually lose their reading and writing skills after leaving school.

In contrast, the events in the kancha corral take place in an arena that is inserted into an Aymara temporal and spatial setting. In other words, they have a temporal location in the annual ritual cycle of Isluga, and a topographical siting within a landscape with which Isluga people are intensely involved through their herding activities. Moreover, they consider the landscape to possess animated qualities. The events considered here are not underwritten by an inscribed discourse.

The ceremonies observed in corrals are ritual acts of remembrance undertaken by different individual families. During these celebrations, the greater part of one or two days is spent within the llama corrals. As the event unfolds, there is disorder, chaos, and drunkenness. Confusion reigns. Panic-stricken llamas and alpacas jump over and dislodge precarious dry stone walls of the corrals. All the same, the ceremonies to which I was invited in January, February, and March 1987, displayed a liturgical character, for although no sacred inscribed text existed, each family conducted its individual ceremony in a very similar manner. When the ritual is not being performed, all that remains is the potential and the willingness in people to perform it, along with a carefully wrapped bundle of items that is stored away in a dark corner of a house.

It is worth mentioning that Leach maintains we engage in rituals in order to transmit messages to ourselves (1976: 45), but I would add that the verbal content is not necessarily apparent or dominant. Aijmer says that "language and culture are quite different sorts of codes and there is no easy and immediate way of translating from one into the other" (1987: 4). We should, he says, understand non-verbal codes in their own right, because ritual is the expression of linguistically irretrievable information (ibid., 12). Therefore, the written text that offered here constitutes a transposition of activities in the llama corrals into words.[1] To advocates of textual theory, all meaning is contextual. The context of these events is the landscape itself, and in Isluga, people understand their landscape through their own close association with their llamas, alpacas, and sheep, which frequent the pasture grounds and water sources.

An Aymara landscape contextualised

The Isluga livestock ceremony reveals two sets of relationships: first, the relationship between humans and their herded animals on the one hand and the landscape and its pasture on the other; second, that between human and animal lineages. The former consists of a married couple and their children, and the latter of herded animals and their progeny. To a certain extent, human and animal lineages are seen as being parallel. Both herded animals and humans are associated with mythical points of origin in the landscape. The former are associated with *juturi*, hollows considered to lead from the Inner World, from which camelids or sheep emerge. Each village recognises several juturi, and there are different ones for camelids and sheep. These juturi are *uywiri*[2] (herders or providers) which are spatially located in the landscape as springs or dry places. However, they are inconspicuous and do not constitute imposing geographical features such as the hills and the awesome volcano that dominates much of the landscape in Isluga.

In contrast, the generation of humans who lived in the previous world age are associated with *t"aqsu*, which are located on ground with sparse vegetation at the juncture between the gently sloping arid pampa and the rocky, steep lava flows at the foot of the volcano in the village where I did my fieldwork. T"aqsu are said to be like small corrals, but people say, emphatically, that they were never used to shelter animals.

The land—that is, the body of the "Wirjin Tayka", as the Pachamama, or earth divinity, is referred to in Isluga—is the site from which herded animal and human lineages spring. Moreover, soil and water produce pasture, which is eaten by llamas and alpacas who produce fleece. The livestock ceremony symbolises the metaphorical transformation of pasture into fleece, which is an important component of the material conditions of Isluga social life. The *wayñu*,[3] as it is known in Isluga, or the *uywa k'illpaña* (the marking ceremony of the herded animals) presents itself as the culmination of the herding cycle. It takes place in Isluga during the rainy season, and it is a celebration of the herded animals held by a nuclear family (mother, father, and children) in honour of the Wirjin Tayka and the uywiris. The ceremonies are addressed to the Wirjin and the uywiris by the human supplicants, and husband and wife respectfully kneel down to ask for permission to proceed at various stages of the long event.

Because of the complexity and richness of the event, I will not consider all aspects of the ceremony in detail. Therefore, my text is incomplete. However, I wish to point out that the combination of components is meaningful to the people who conduct the events. Seen in another perspective, it is the use of matter derived from the land itself—products such as fleece, feathers, grass, fragrant firewood, maize, and stone—

that contributes to the liturgical character of the ceremony. The articulation of colour, texture, and aural effects are the means through which the people of Isluga produce this particular text.

As an example of how substance is manipulated in Isluga, the mother of the family offers smoke from fragrant embers to the Virgin (the Christian Virgin is implied), while both mother and father offer coca leaves to the Wirjin Tayka. The father grinds black and white maize kernels, and the flour is mixed in separate cups with water. These mixtures of maize flour suspended in liquid are known as *ch'uwa*; the black mixture is offered to the T'alla (the female uywiris) and the white to the Mallku (the male uywiris). Thus the human participants ask the powerful Wirjin Tayka and the uywiris to grant them an audience with them and their animals.

Such is the awe and respect with which these beings are held in Isluga that participants, especially the mother and father of the family observing the wayñu, are expected to achieve a state of ritual drunkenness. Thus the long all-night vigil is an important part of the ceremony which precedes the colourful events that take place in the corral. The mournful sounds produced during the vigil and in the corral form an essential complement to the strong colours (red, pink, and orange and tonal gradations of green, red, and orange).[4] Traditionally, Isluga people avoid the excessive use of colour in daily life, employing it only in certain contexts (Dransart 1988: 44–48). Also, alcohol is not normally consumed on non-festive occasions. Hence the abundance of strong colour and the need for humans directly to address the uywiris, with their higher status, means that a state of drunkenness is enjoined upon the participants.

The wayñu ceremony in Isluga

Isluga families usually celebrate two wayñu ceremonies, one for their camelids, which takes place between New Year's Day and Carnival, whenever that may fall, and another for their sheep, if they possess any, which usually takes place immediately after Carnival. Here I will concentrate on the former, the wayñu of the llamas and alpacas. The ceremony takes the form of a symbolic investiture of the animals, and the ritual "dressing" of the animals is accompanied by songs and mandolin music, which are designed to ensure the fertility of the herds. Without this music, it is said, the ceremonies would have little effect. Each family has its own date, which must fall on a Thursday or Saturday. These days of the week are known as Día Compadre (godfather's day) and Día Comadre (godmother's day) respectively; the former refers to the day of the Mallku and the latter to the day of the T'alla.

The wayñu ceremony requires a considerable investment of labour in preparing for the event, and some families may celebrate it every other year. Alternatively, they may conduct an abbreviated version known as *ch'allta* one year, and the wayñu proper the following year. Individual families have some flexibility in deciding how often and when to observe the ceremonies. The health and well-being of the animals is a decisive factor, for if they suffer ill health or meet with misfortune, a family may well decide to change its customary date.

Preparations begin in advance with the making of *chicha*, a maize beer, and of the *sarsillu*, *chimpu*, and *wistalla* with which the animals will be "dressed". Sarsillu are ear ornaments, in the form of tassels of coloured yarn, in which red predominates. Four different types are made for different categories of llamas and alpacas: *tilantir sarsillu* for the guide animals, often older females with no offspring to accompany them; *tama* for the female animals of the herd; *wantilurita* or "flags" for the male animals; and *sombreros*, pompons that sit on top of the ear, also for the males. Chimpu is unspun llama or alpaca fleece, dyed red, pink, or orange; yellow is sometimes used as well. It is tied to the backs of the llamas and alpacas. In the case of female animals, chimpu will be tied in a cluster over the withers, but in male animals it is tied lineally along the length of the spine. The third item, wistalla, is a neck piece which consists of a series of coloured yarns in tones of pink, green, and orange, which hang from a thick cord that will be tied round the neck of the camelids (the word "wistalla" is also used for a small bag used by women and men for holding coca leaves). It is important that all these colours be strong and clear; any faded colours are rejected as being useless for this ceremony. The responsibility for the making of the maize beer and the tassels, neckpieces, and chimpu lies with the women of the household, but the men often make some of the items, especially the sarsillu called "wantilurita" and "sombreros" (which will be worn by the male animals), and the wistalla. Neighbours may lend a hand with these preparations.

The ceremony begins with an all-night vigil during which the father and mother of the household may go to visit the juturi and pasture grounds that their herds are accustomed to frequent. The juturi, which are said to be the owners of the animals of both husband and wife, must be properly acknowledged. Offerings to the juturi may include flamingo feathers which are burnt in the hope that the camelids will behave like flamingos, which habitually cluster together in cohesive flocks. The feathers are burned so that the llamas will not wander, but will stay close together. In the meantime, the rest of the family and other relatives and friends sing mournful songs inside a house, where they make libations of chicha and alcohol, and drink. As dawn begins, the people are still inside and maintain the vigil. It seems like a wake.

Early in the morning, the llamas and alpacas are released from a large corral where they have spent the night. As they leave, their owners sprinkle the ground with liquid libations. A young woman and a young man herd them out onto the wet *bofedal* pastures and beyond to the dry scrub pasture grounds. Later, about midday, they will bring them back to the village, this time to a kancha corral, to where the focus of attention turns.

First of all, the wife enters the kancha, moving in an anti-clockwise direction round the central stone and wafting the smoke of fragrant-smelling embers to each of the four corners. The kancha is an enclosed space in which ceremonies designed to encourage the reproductive vitality of male and female animals will take place, and from which the animals with their ritually enhanced reproductive powers will emerge in due course.

The llamas and alpacas enter the corral. An animal is selected for slaughter, but first its back is sprinkled with chicha, maize flour, and alcohol. Brightly coloured chimpu fleece is tied to its back. Then a neighbour or a relative cuts the jugular of the sacrificial llama, and spoonfuls of the blood of the dying animal are scattered over the ground of the kancha by the husband, who directs the rest of the blood into a hollow dug into the ground, known as a *wiña*. All persons present lie down, head to the ground, in an act of obeisance to the uywiri. This silent act of remembrance is usually performed along the rear wall of the corral.

Later on, the animals are marked. The marking takes two forms. First, llamas and alpacas are "dressed" with chimpu (the dyed fleece; this word really means 'mark'), ear adornments, and neck pieces of coloured yarns. Second, animals that are approaching sexual maturity—that is, animals born in the previous birth season—have an owner's mark cut into one or both ears. The ear tassels which are pierced through the ears of the animals cause the ear to bleed slightly, but the ears of the one-year-old animals are made to bleed profusely. The ceremony is therefore a rite of passage for the animals at the time of their initiation into sexual maturity. It parallels the ear piercing ceremonies and the ritual investiture of the breechcloth which are recorded for Inka noble boys (held, admittedly, at another time of the year, as part of the Qapaq Raymi celebrations at the time of the winter solstice). The initiation of the llamas and alpacas thus becomes a celebration of the social identity of the herded animals, and the recognition of one of the stages in the process of achieving "animalhood" experienced by all herded animals in Isluga.

This part of the ceremony, the marking, will probably not finish until the following day. After the female animals are marked, they are allowed to go free. The next morning, the ritual *misa* table is transferred inside the corral. Then the male animals are marked and finally allowed to join the females. In the intervening evening, a group of men go off to make a symbolic journey to the valley. They return, playing the role of a herder and a caravan of llamas. As they enter the village, the herder attempts to keep his "llamas" under control, but they escape to chase young women as they endeavour to indulge in sexual buffoonery by mimicking the copulation of llamas. The mood and pace of events changes, and the apparently dirge-like and repetitive music that took place inside the corral yields to dancing and cheerful music. A communal meal to which all are invited is served. This is called a *comilona* (feast) or *boda* (wedding).

The llama corral as site and source of regenerative vitality

Having presented an account of the wayñu ceremonies, let us focus our attention on the kancha, with its creative inner space. This, after all, acts as the nexus for the ceremonies, within the wider context of the landscape. At first sight, the kancha seems like a simple rectangle of casually built dry stone walling, which is often in a state of disrepair. However, it is designed to suit the needs of the wayñu ceremony, and it is furnished with some significant features (figure 6-1). The majority of the kancha in Isluga are constructed so that the entrance faces east, toward the rising sun like most of the houses. Some, however, have an entrance facing north, looking toward the mighty, multiple summits of Mallku Kawaraya. Most are furnished with a small, more or less square stone, which is placed in the interior space of the kancha. They all have a large, flat stone placed outside, to the left of the entrance as one looks in, but on the right of the entrance from the point of view of someone sitting behind the stone, with

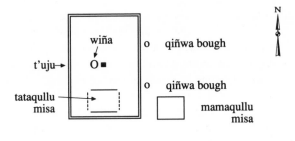

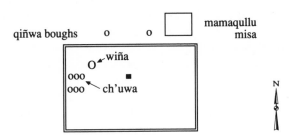

Key

Wiña   Hollow for containing the sacrificial blood of a llama
Qiñwa   A tree which grows at high altitudes in the Andes
T'uju   A niche in the corral wall at ground level
Mamaqullu misa   The ritual table which is laid out on a large flat stone for the part of
   the ceremony during which the female animals are symbolically dressed
Tataqullu misa   The ritual table which is laid out on the ground inside the corral for
   the part of the ceremony during which the male animals are ritually dressed
Ch'uwa   A series of dishes filled with the so-called *ch'uwa* libations

Figure 6.1   The design of the *kancha* (llama corral) in Isluga.

one's back to the kancha wall. This large stone serves as the *mamaqullu misa*, the ritual table for the female animals.

Some kancha are provided with a niche (*t'uju*) in the middle of the rear wall, low down on the ground, directly opposite the entrance. This is the place where the *ch'uwa* libations are placed in a double row on the ground. Before the llama or alpaca is sacrificed, a hollow is dug in the ground between the central stone, on which embers are placed. The ch'uwa dishes are arranged in front of the t'uju. It is between this blood-filled hollow and the rear wall where material objects are placed that the people lie on the ground in silence, withholding speech and song. In this instance, the material objects consist of clay dishes and enamel cups containing ground substances mixed with water. These dishes hold the substances that will be libated to the earth and hills;

they are evidently positioned to play a mediating role between humans and supernatural beings. Once again, the human supplicants hesitate to address the powerful Wirjin and the uywiris; instead, they prepare to proffer material substances that will be ritually sprinkled on the ground. For the purposes of the ceremony, branches of *qiñwa* trees are placed on both sides of the entrance to the corral, which is closed when the animals are inside by means of a rope held taut across the walling, over which a blanket is draped. Qiñwa is a high-altitude tree which grows in sheltered places; locally it can be obtained from a great valley on the volcano above the village.

As an outsider who has read the work of Santacruz Pachacuti Yamqui Salcamaygua, an early seventeenth-century author of native Andean descent from the Lake Titicaca area, a striking visual analogy came to my mind. This is, of course, not a connection which the people of Isluga would make, although they do recognise certain archaeological sites as being the work of the Inkas. The view of the entrance to the Isluga kancha, flanked by boughs of trees, with the interior t'uju niche behind, resembles the central part of the early seventeenth century drawing by Santacruz Pachacuti of the three exits from the inner world through the Paqaritampu (the house, or inn, of origin) from which the first Inkas crawled into this world (figure 6-2). The central part of the drawing depicts a rectangular geometric design flanked either side by a tree, representing Apo Tambo and Pachamamaachi, according to the written account. The ancestors were perceived as the progeny of the earth itself, that is, of the Pachamama, and the lineages were expressed visually as rooted and branching trees. On the lower left and right are two more rectangles of simpler design. The three openings or "windows" are named by Santacruz Pachacuti as Tampottoco, Marasttoco, and Sutittoco, belonging respectively to the uncles, maternal grandparents, and paternal grandparents of the first Inka ruler, Manku Qhapaq, who was said to have emerged from the cave with his three brothers and four sisters.

It would seem that the three exits were the points of origin for the royal *panaka* lineages of the Inka rulers.[5] The drawing by Santacruz Pachacuti refers to human lineages. Yet the word *ttoco* as written by this author is the same as the modern "t'uju". The focus of the elaborate wayñu ceremony in Isluga turns on the generative interior space of the kancha, where songs are sung, bright colours are used, libations are offered, and the symbolic dressing of the animals takes place to ensure that lineages of camelids multiply. The qiñwa tree, besides providing a genealogical metaphor, is also a symbol of the source of life and of longevity, and, according to Sherbondy (1988: 112), as a strong tree which is resistant to the cold, it was probably the symbol of Imperial Cusco.

With this emphasis on the importance of lineage, the root of the word "wiña", the hollow in the corral which is filled with red blood and green coca leaves, should be explained more fully. *Wiñaya* is the Aymara and *wiñay* the Quechua word listed in early-seventeenth-century dictionaries as 'always, eternal, forever'. The Quechua dictionary of Gonçález Holguín (1952 [1608]: 352) adds 'the generations and descent', while Bertonio translates *viñayana viñayapa* into the Latin *saecula saeculorum* 'generations of generations' (Bertonio 1984 [1612] bk II: 388). Since *saecula* implies 'successive generations [of people or animals]' (Simpson 1973: 529), my understanding of the wiña hollow is that of a source of vitality which is regenerated in the llamas and alpacas through the ritual performance of the wayñu ceremony.

The very design of the kancha reinforces the idea that the creative interior is the space from which ever-multiplying lineages of camelids will emerge. The fact that the ceremonies are undertaken by a husband and wife in partnership suggests that the animal lineages are considered to be parallel to human ones. Llamas and alpacas require constant attention, as do human children, and herders worry constantly about their herds lest they go hungry, fall into a river and drown, or fall prey to predators. However, imagery manipulated by the people of Isluga is multi-faceted, since the ritual term by which llamas and alpacas are designated during the wayñu is *p"aqalli* 'flower'. A herder may say, "these are my flowers".

The simple idea of a bud forming and blossoming forth appears to be replete with meaning that has lasted over the centuries through changing social contexts in the Andes. A pair of Inka ceramic vessels with a long flaring, flower-like neck are painted with a row of stylised women holding birds, above which are flowers (Purin 1990, 2:193). We should recall that some of the Inka empresses depicted in the early seventeenth century by Martín de Murúa (Ossio 1985) and Guaman Poma (1980) show

Figure 6-2 The Paqaritampu (the house of origin) of the Inkas, drawn by Santacruz Pachacuti Yamqui Salcamaygua, 1615. Reproduced by permission, Biblioteca Nacional, Madrid, ms. 3169.

a woman standing holding a flower. It is clear from the text that Guaman Poma is interested in the importance of lineages. However, his drawings are more suggestive than the text, for in some cases—for example Mama Huaco and Mama Anahuarque— the empress is shown inside a room with two windows, one at each side of the monarch (figures 6-3 and 6-4). My interpretation of the scene is that Guaman Poma is presenting in visual form the theme of the procreation of lineages, which originally in Inka myth emerged from the body of the Pachamama through the cave of Paqaritampu. The room stands for the cave, and the windows are the two lateral entrances, while the body of the empress contains the vital inner space from where the lineage or panaka emerged into this world.

It is worth recalling that Gabriel Martínez (1976: 271) pointed out that the Aymara verb *amtaña* and the Spanish *recordar* are both used as ritual terms in what he calls a liturgical act which is full of meaning. He cites the work of Rodolfo Kusch, who draws a parallel between the root *amu*, which appears in Bertonio's dictionary as *amu*, meaning 'boton dela flor' (flower bud) and *amutaatha* 'acordar' (to remember, to recollect) (Bertonio 1984, bk II: 17). This clearly indicates that the acts of remembrance honouring the Wirjin Tayka, uywiris, Mallku, and T'alla that I have analysed are not just an acknowledgment of their existence. When a supplicant lists a litany of names of the places frequented by his or her llamas, and then adds "Uywir mallku amtata jan amtata, Uywir t'alla amtata jan amtata" (Male uywiris remembered and not

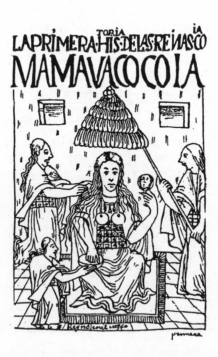

Figure 6-3 The first Queen Quya of the Inkas, Mama Huaco, drawn by Guaman Poma de Ayala.

Figure 6-4 The ninth Queen Quya of the Inkas, Mama Anahuarque, drawn by Guaman
Poma de Ayala.

remembered, female uywiris remembered and not remembered), it indicates that the
person who has uttered these words is actively involved in feeding and nourishing
these beings, just as the Wirjin Tayka and the uywiris are held to nourish fortunate
supplicants. Equally, the fact that families invited me to accompany them in their
wayñu involved active participation. One cannot be an observing bystander in Isluga
without being made to feel intensely uncomfortable.

Acts of remembrance, acts of negation

The events in the llama corral are not, as I said, underwritten by an inscribed text, and
yet I appealed to some visual parallels from early seventeenth-century records. This
would seem to imply that certain formal, visual aspects have persisted over some time.
However, the seventeenth-century Quechua context and the Aymara context of the
late 1980s are discontinuous in time and space. One of the reasons for proposing this
analogy is that visual manifestations may be endowed with a disquieting character
which admits of multiple meanings. If they are considered to constitute cultural texts,
then they do not serve to fix essentialistic meaning. Yet, in Isluga, the use of the
material objects serves to underpin the articulation of sensuous phenomena as the
ceremonies proceed. This would explain the apparent longevity of the imagery and
also account for my observation that the different families who invited me to their
wayñu all performed the ceremonies in a very similar manner.

Since I was first introduced to Isluga in 1986, I have no long-term perspective on how the ceremonies might change through time. On a return visit to the village in 1989, I found that some of the families of the village where I did my fieldwork no longer have the willingness to perform these ceremonies. They have become evangelical Protestants, a cult that shuns the taking of alcohol and dancing, and which tells its membership to forget the Wirjin Tayka and the uywiris. I am using the verb 'to forget' in the sense of positive rejection, in contrast to the Aymara *amtaña*, to remember.

The events I observed in 1987 in the llama corral took place against a Catholic background which, through its inability to intervene in village life, was tolerant of non-Christian Andean beliefs and practices. Throughout my main period of fieldwork from 1986 to 1988, the village maintained a staunch anti-Protestant stand of which it was proud. Indeed, the mother of one of the families which later converted to Protestantism was most insistent that outsiders from the city (for example, the district nurse and government agency officials) should attend her wayñu; she seemed so proud of being able to show to them that this was her Aymara-ness and that she was in her domain. And it was clear that the outsiders were reluctant to accept the proffered *copita* of alcohol; they only stayed to take one gulp, barely hiding the grimace, before they left to return to their domain.

The full implication of the co-existence of those who remember the Wirjin Tayka and those who do not remains to be explored in Isluga.

Conclusion

To return to my opening remarks regarding textual theory, I wish to offer some comments. Proponents of textual theory such as Julia Kristeva concentrate on the speaking subject as producer of verbal utterances, where language is considered to be a complex signifying process rather than a monolithic system. Similarly, for Barthes, *signifiance* is a process in which the text is read as "a moving play of signifiers". Thus, oral practice results in new combinations and transformations of what went before. Yet the wayñu ceremony, with its remembrances and songs, seems to revolve round non-verbal imagery, for some of which parallels can be found in seventeenth-century sources.

There is an apparent contradiction here where the potentiality for verbal performance to change is matched by invariance in certain aspects of non-verbal performance. In examining the relationship between words and images, let us consider the well-known essay entitled "Rhetoric of the Image" by Roland Barthes. Barthes is moved, when confronted by a visual image, to suggest that "the image is felt to be weak in respect of meaning" (1977: 32) while dismissing the question whether "signification cannot exhaust the image's ineffable richness". The image he is considering is extremely banal: it is, in fact, an advertisement for Italian pasta. Yet, in a footnote, he reveals that he is worried about the banalisation of the verbal content, not that of the visual content (p. 40). Barthes wonders if there is always textual matter under or around the image, and he recommends "go[ing] *back* to partially illiterate societies, to a sort of pictographic state of the image" (p. 37, emphasis added). To talk in such terms is to prioritise the written word, for Barthes claims that the linguistic message is present in every image, and that writing and speech constitute the full terms of informational structure (p. 38). I seriously doubt that the verbal context is as dominant as Barthes suggests (how else would I be moved by paintings by Mark Rothko—which I am—without feeling the need to read the title underneath?). My experience of Isluga life is that people have very acute and developed visual awareness, and they are producers of visual phenomena that cannot easily be translated into words. The wayñu ceremony is a vehicle of symbolic thought which brings together images and sounds that are constellations of significant signs displaying varying degrees of abstraction. This thought pervades all other areas of life and all aspects of herding technology, linked, as it is, to the use and knowledge of the animated landscape. Until recent developments in visual anthropology, the discipline of social anthropology has been hampered by its reliance on mere words. I wish to stress the power of imagery. And on this imperfect text which I have written, I rest my case.

ACKNOWLEDGMENTS   I gratefully acknowledge the receipt of scholarships from the Pirie-Reid Fund, and from the Emslie Horniman Fund, which enabled me to undertake fieldwork in 1986–88, and for travel expenses from the British Council in Santiago in 1989. I would also like to thank most warmly the people of Isluga who made me feel at home with them during my fieldwork. This account is based on ceremonies observed in a village belonging to Araxsaya, which is the Upper Moiety of Isluga in the highlands east of Iquique, Chile.

Notes

1. In this article I am concentrating on the whole ceremony, especially on the ritual action and the space where it takes place. Songs with a verbal content are, of course, an important component (see note 3). At the time of the marking of the animals, different songs to the guide animals are sung by the people in a constantly repeated refrain. However, on this occasion I wish to emphasise the over-arching non-verbal content of the livestock-marking ceremony.

It is also worth pointing out that the non-human participants of the ceremony contribute their utterances, in the form of a whinny or, in quieter moments, a mournful "y-y-y" (as written in Spanish; the English equivalent would be an 'e-e-e') sound. While I was herding, an Isluga woman said her llamas were crying when making this noise. This would be in keeping with the dirge-like songs sung by the humans in the llama corrals during the ceremony. It is all very reminiscent of Guaman Poma's drawing of the Inka emperor and empress singing in a similar fashion to their red llama (Guaman Poma 1980: 320).

2. In Spanish they are also known as *aviador*, which has been translated as 'él o ella que provee' (he or she who provides) (Martínez 1976: 281).

3. Strictly speaking, *wayñu* is the term for 'song'. However, it is also the word adopted by Isluga people for referring to the livestock-marking ritual discussed in this article. Sound and colour are the two important motivating elements, without which the events would have no effect. My concern here is to examine the visual and tactile aspects of the ceremony. For a corresponding consideration of the role of music in the equivalent ritual observed by the northern neighbours of the Isluga people, see Manuel Mamani Mamani (1990).

4. See the next section for a description of the colourful ear tassels, neckpieces, and dyed fleece with which the animals will be "dressed". The use of colour during the wayñu and its relationship to woven textiles is discussed more fully in Dransart (1991).

5. *Panaka* were royal lineages that have been interpreted by R. T. Zuidema as exogamous, matrilineal groups, in which a man belongs to his sister's group, hence his children cannot classify themselves with him; this is discussed further by Rostworowski (1986: 138–141).

7

DENISE ARNOLD

Making Men in Her Own Image

Gender, Text, and Textile in Qaqachaka

A number of recent ethnographies, though distinct in time and space, have compared and contrasted the weaving of cloth, as women's work, with men's writing of texts, as two hierarchically related orders of gendered activity.[1] Moreover, this gendered distinction is often implicit in the wider debate about orality and literacy, in the supposed superiority of "literate" societies as opposed to those with more "oral" cultures. This chapter will challenge such a hierarchical viewing of these gendered activities in the Andean case, where even a distinction between weaving and the writing of texts is problematic. In Andean studies, the existence and status of "written texts", both before the Spanish conquest and immediately afterward, is a subject of continuing debate (Murra 1975a and b, 1989; Adorno 1986; Platt 1992 and this volume; Arnold 1993; Ferrell, 1994). Moreover, the increasing interest in the pre-Columbian mnemonic technique of recording information as diverse as bureaucratic records, genealogies of the noble Inkas, and tales of their exploits on the knotted threads called *kipu* in Quechua, or *chinu* in Aymara, has shown that this characteristically Andean art of memory bridges any supposed divide between weaving and the writing of texts (Cereceda 1987; Zuidema 1989; Arnold and Yapita 1992; Pärssinen 1992).

When we examine the same proposition in relation to the contemporary men and women of Qaqachaka, an *ayllu* commmunity in highland Bolivia (department of Oruro), the case is just as problematic. In Qaqachaka, both men and women weave cloth, although the cloth that women weave technically is the most complex, and with the introduction of compulsory education in 1952, both girls and boys have had the opportunity to learn to read and write. But even though historical evidence suggests that women's weaving and men's writing of texts have been different orders of gendered activity in the past, there is no evidence that the two activities were related hierarchically; rather, they were viewed as parallel domains of gendered activity.

I shall suggest that these different orders of gendered activity may derive instead from some perceived metaphysical differences in memory and intelligence, whereby men are believed to think "with their heads" and women "with their hearts" (Arnold and Yapita 1994: 53ff). It is a common expression in Qaqachaka, for instance, that men wrote their historical texts with plumed pens and blood ink, using the force of spirit in their heads, whereas women "wrote" their textiles with their weaving picks, using the memories and inspiration held in their hearts.

I shall examine how these particular gendered differences in intelligence are evident not only in such tasks as weaving and writing, but even, for example, in certain garments which men and women still make for themselves. However, the main argument here challenges the idea of any hierarchy between women's weaving and men's writing of texts by showing how contemporary women weavers in Qaqachaka mediate any such hierarchy simply by using their weavings as a form of text. In weaving certain gendered garments for themselves and for their menfolk, in creatively manipulating their woven texts and the symbolic language embedded within them, women are able to order and define, within the symbolic domain, the relative powers of production and the relative generative powers of reproduction of each gender, and to decide on their relative hierarchical value. A woman weaver is thus able to define in practice the limits and obligations of both genders as social constructions in Qaqachaka society.

In the first section, I examine the activity of weaving in its broader social and cultural context. Here I shall show how common ideologies of gender, and ideas about creation, transformation, production, and reproduction, are not only embedded in the finished cloth as a kind of "text", as Cereceda (1978) and others have shown, but in turn form the basis of the spoken texts: descriptions, narratives, myths, songlines, sayings, and so on, which accompany such practical tasks and relate them to other associated tasks. In the second and third sections, I focus on some specific representations of gender in two distinct woven garments: the woman's over-mantle, called *awayu* in Aymara, and the man's poncho, a term borrowed into Aymara as *punchu*. Aspects of gender will be compared in the two garments as items of dress. In particular, two characteristic patterns of weaving from these finished textile garments will be examined as mediators of a symbolic language about gender, production, and reproduction. In these final sections, I shall pay particular attention to the women weavers' own discourse about the use and significance of these gendered garments.

The social and cultural context of weaving

The arts of the hand and the arts of the voice

Weaving as an activity is related to other practical tasks, and these interrelated activities give rise in turn to the interrelated "texts" that accompany them: whether in the more formal performance of songs or tales, or simply in the multilevelled analogies expressed in the more everyday comments and sayings that interweave the different tasks in a complex "intertextuality", which others have described (see, for example, Tedlock and Tedlock 1985; Howard-Malverde 1989; Hanks 1993 after Kristeva 1980).

The Tedlocks, most particularly, have noted how the practical arts of the hand are necessarily interrelated to the arts of the voice. They criticise a Saussurian semiotics as describing a closed code that exists prior to any of its particular manifestations in the material world, disengaging language and the verbal arts from hand and tool and, ultimately, from face and voice. Semioticians, they argue, merely follow codes across the boundaries of various genres, and human action from this point of view is merely reducible to the terms of the code. They prefer instead the work of Bakhtin who examines "interrelationships" rather than "codes", or the work of Julia Kristeva on "intertextuality". The Tedlocks use the notion of intertextuality to explore the relationships between, and among, various arts of the Quiché Maya of Guatemala, pointing out that rarely is an adult specialised exclusively in just one activity. Rather, they practice and collaborate on several of them, interrelating the various levels of their performance.

LEARNING TO WEAVE, LEARNING TO WRITE

In Qaqachaka, too, this crossover between different activities occurs. I have mentioned elsewhere how the building of a house is compared to the setting up of a loom, and how, in a much broader sense, certain weaving designs and their modes of repetition—in reflections, serial repeats, staggerings, and bilateral symmetries—are repeated throughout distinct media. Thus, homologous configurations can be found in the different garments of rustic woven and knitted cloth and in sophisticated modern factory-made jumpers, in braided slings and ropes, in dance choreography and the patterns of song verses, or in the decoration of simple pots and the decorative elements of urban architecture (Arnold 1992a and b, 1994).

It is not surprising, then, that such analogies are made between women's activity of weaving and men's activity of writing. Moreover, a parallel manner of learning these two different activities is acknowledged. Before 1952, there was a distinct gendered division of labour, whereby boys, but not girls, tended to be sent to school to learn to read and write. It was thought that boys had greater need of these skills than girls in their journeys to the cities and, even more importantly, in order to read and defend their title documents to the land. Moreover, a girl's labour in herding was considered to be too important for her to have time to go to school. Her knowledge was focussed instead in her weaving and her recognised ability to "read" the ayllu textiles. In a parallel manner, too, boys were believed to learn to read in school by exercising the power of spirit (*ispiritu*) in their heads, like hens—all birds are associated with spirit—pecking seeds of knowledge from the ground, whereas girls were believed to learn to weave by exercising the inspiration and memory (*amta*) held in their hearts. And in the parallel processes of learning, boys learnt to read and write, first of all, letters, then syllables and words, and finally sentences and whole pages of script, enabling them to understand and interact with the world outside the immediate ayllu, above all with the urban domain and the offices of city bureaucrats. A girl, on the other hand, learnt first of all to weave small garments, such as skirt and belt fasteners, manipulating just a limited number of two to five warp-threads (*chinu*) to make easy designs on her first simple loom. Then, as she grew older, she learnt to weave more complex cloth, moving from one garment to another until she reached the highest degree of complexity in her mantle, with designs of up to one hundred warp threads. At the same time, the range of meanings of her designs, and her own discourse about them developed to increasing degrees of complexity (see also Rodríguez 1994).

In Qaqachaka, girls initially learn their weaving designs from the women who surround them—from their mothers, aunts, and grandmothers. Girls often form a special apprenticeship to an older weaver, who shares her weaving skills in return for help in pasturing her animals, and she often recalls this relationship between weaving and pasturing in her first song performances in public, later in her adolescence. They also learn from contemporary apprentices, girls of the same age, whom they respect as weavers, as they are pasturing their animals in the hills. Young girls begin to spin wool from the time they are large enough to hold and spin a spindle. The first weaving venture is usually undertaken when a girl is about eight or nine, when she weaves her first skirt-fastener or hat-band. Both of these weavings, small as they are, introduce the basic understanding of many more complex weaving techniques that they will require later on. Afterward, a girl rapidly moves on to a belt, a small food bag, and then to her first mantle (awayu). However, she weaves her first poncho only when she is married or has acquired a permanent male partner. The weaving techniques and designs that a girl has learnt in each of these early textile ventures are still evident in her awayu when she is a mature woman, married and having set up her own household. The design section of the awayu continues to incorporate the small design bands, reminiscent of her early skirt-fasteners and first belt designs. And she often carries some of her own mother's designs into her mature mantles.

This is not to say that a boy does not develop skills comparable to a girl's weaving. His musical ability develops, in the playing of various flutes and pan-pipes, incorporating musical elements that are often compared to weaving designs (see Stobart 1987). And young boys quickly learn to imitate their father's technical ability to knit the fine and brilliant knitted hats known throughout the region, and to braid ropes and slings. They, too, begin with simple designs of just four or eight threads, developing their technical abilities until, in the most complex braided ropes and slings, grown men are able to manipulate complicated designs of bilateral symmetry based on a minimal scheme of sixteen component threads, working up to seventy-two-thread designs.

THE GENDERED DIVISION OF LABOUR IN WEAVING

In this way, the cultural rules that differentiate activities by gender give rise to different gendered domains, social realms with their own distinct lexicons, utilised more by men working with other men or by women working with other women. No doubt, too, this contemporary gendered division of work in weaving has been influenced historically by Inka and later colonial demands on household labour. For example, the lexical difference between the term for a mature woman, *warmi*, a woman who can weave as opposed to a woman who cannot weave, called *yajiru*, may be the result of centuries of household obligations toward the state during the Inka and colonial periods, whereby a married woman was required to weave a prescribed number of garments for state use each year (see Murra 1975a and b, 1989). Similarly, married men as the named heads of the household, registered in the state census rolls, were required to weave a certain yardage of coarse homespun cloth in both historical periods.

Nowadays in Qaqachaka, men weave on the upright loom introduced by the Spanish. They weave homespun cloth made from sheep's wool, in two thicknesses; this cloth is called *wayita*, a term Aymarised from the Spanish *bayeta*. From a thick yarn, they weave various clothes: men's trousers, men's shirts, also women's dresses (*allmilla*), blouses, and skirts. From a finer yarn, they weave men's jackets and women's mantillas. Fathers still make their children's trousers, skirts, and blouses from wayita. In the gendered division of labour related to weaving activities, men spin sheep's wool for the coarse homespun cloth, but they also spin the llama wool necessary for the food sacks (*kustäla*), although the sacks are woven by women. Men spin the strong warp threads for most weavings. They weave belts (*wak'a*), and in the recent past they wove the large blankets called *apichusi*. In addition to weaving, they twist thick hanks of wool, plaiting it into ropes (*wiska*) and slings (*q'urawi*). Men also knit the characteristic finely detailed woollen caps of the region (*ch'ulu*), on five wire knitting needles, using modern acrylic wools. It is in their knitted woollen caps, rather than in their coarse homespun garments, that men practise the most technically complex of their weaving art, including the technique of 'taking out designs' (*apsu salta*).

Until a couple of generations ago, the women of Qaqachaka wove larger garments, such as the mantle and poncho, on a backstrap loom which they called a 'loom on poles' (*lawat sawuña*), usually set up in a sheltered spot in the courtyard of the house. Nowadays, however, they weave them on a horizontal loom (*ch'akur sawuña*) formed from four stakes set into the earth, and fastened back to other wooden ties with ropes, reserving a miniature backstrap loom for small items such as belts and fasteners. Older women comment that the weaving of these larger garments was much finer in the past, 'right bald' (*suma q'ara*), since the tension was much easier to adjust by a slight body movement, rocking backward on your waist. But although there are disadvantages with the modern horizontal loom, it has more flexibility. For instance, you can roll up the working weaving and take it with you to weave up in the hills while you are pasturing the animals. Weaving is usually done in a sheltered spot, often in a walled corral near to where the animals are grazing.

In the gendered division of labour in weaving, women weave the smaller modern blankets (*p"irsära*) from sheep's wool, women's mantles (awayu) and overskirts (*urk"u*), and men's ponchos, in a mixture of alpaca and sheep's wool (see figure 7-1). They also weave belts (wak'a), skirt-fasteners (*t'isnu*), babies swathing-bands (also called wak'a), as well as the food sacks woven from llama wool. Women and young girls weave the decorative hat-bands (*irsipilla*) for fiestas. And women plait various forms of ties and fasteners, as well as the edge decorations of their finished weavings. In a typical year, a woman might weave two blankets, two mantles, and a variety of other smaller weavings.

Figure 7-1 María Ayka Colque weaves an *awayu* on a horizontal loom as she sits in her own field.

GENDERED ASPECTS OF TEXTILE LANGUAGE

Gendered distinctions are also evident in textile language. Recent studies of the relationship between textile language and speech are beginning to suggest ways of understanding the linguistic parallels between the formal structure of textile designs and the syntax and discourse organisation of spoken Andean languages (Arnold and Yapita 1992; Pärssinen 1992). For example, particular spatial configurations of textile layout may refer us analogically to the different levels of ayllu organisation, as they are perceived according to gender relations.

In this way, women's mantles may be worn as items of dress, hanging down their backs, although the precise configuration depends on a woman's age and standing in any one community. A young woman usually wears the patterned area of her mantle hung horizontally in the style called *k'illp"a*, the top two corners fastened at her chest with a large sewing needle or, alternatively, with a large safety pin. Curiously enough, this horizontal configuration is explicitly compared to the horizontal web of female blood ties, both human and animal, which interconnect the more localised patrilines across space, since women usually move after marriage with their inheritance of animals to the household of their new husband. This same idea is enacted ritually through the spilling of blood in the maternal line during the important annual animal earmarking ceremony called by the same name: "k'illp"a" (see Arnold, 1988: 229ff.).

Or, more commonly for married and older women, the mantle is folded in half, doubled up, like the married couple, and then draped over their shoulders and fastened at their chests. If a married woman wears her mantle single, people might ask her: "Do you want to become a widow"?

One cannot overemphasise the importance of weavings in the Andes as containers. Mantles are used as carrying cloths, containing anything from raw food products collected from the fields to cooked lunch snacks, from skeins or balls of wool to rolled-up weavings in progress, and not least of all small babies. The mantle as a container is worn horizontally across the back of the shoulders, and the two outer corners are pinned together at the chest.

Young men sometimes use a small awayu as a carrying cloth, although they wear them differently from women. The load is worn behind, bundled up behind their waists, and the two outer corners of the mantle are tied at the front, rather than fastened with a pin. Young men often wear colourful and decorative mantles this way in fiestas, to show off their girlfriends' or young wives' weaving skills. If older men should use a mantle for carrying, once again it is worn in a distinctive fashion, slung diagonally behind one shoulder and then down around the waist, where the two outer corners are tied.

Men use their ponchos as women use their mantles, as warm overgarments. They are worn draped over their shoulders with their head through the opening in the central seam, called its 'mouth' (*laka*), but with the patterned areas hung vertically. Or they use them as carrying cloths, to carry anything from extra clothing to heavy burdens of firewood, over their shoulders with the two outer ends of the poncho tied together at the chest or waist.[2]

INTERTEXTS BETWEEN AGRICULTURE AND WEAVING

Weaving as a gendered activity has analogies with other such transformatory activities, and the play of analogies between them, as "intertexts", continually negotiates gender status in the different domains. This can be amply illustrated in the multiple analogies between men's ploughing of the land and women's weaving of textiles, viewed as gendered forms of work, or in those between women's songs as they weave and display their textiles, and men's music making as they admire the young women and their skill as weavers. The Andean equivalence between weaving and food production is evident historically in pre-Inka and Inka obligations between the peasantry and the state (Murra 1989: 285–286), and modern analogies between these tasks still lie at the heart of traditional systems of exchange of gendered gifts between men and women and in the songlines that accompany them.

In contemporary vernacular discourse, the female activity of weaving as a task still has many direct analogies with men's work in ploughing and planting the earth. The motion of weaving the weft threads into and out of the warp threads on her horizontal loom is considered to be like a man's action with the tip of his ploughshare, ploughing furrows into the earth. A man's action ploughing the land opens the ground preparing it for the placing of the food seeds into the earth, while a woman's action in weaving a mantle opens and closes the working mouth of her loom by the heddle movements, leaving behind woven seeds embedded in the textile designs. Incidentally, both activities are, in turn, related to writing. The written lines on the white pages of my field notebooks, for example, were frequently compared by visiting women to furrows in the earth, and the movement of my pen on the page to that of a ploughshare or to a weaving shuttle.

Although these analogies between agriculture and weaving—and writing—are also present in relation to men's weaving activities, they are much more muted. Men's weaving of coarse homespun cloth and the simpler motion of the Spanish upright loom is much simpler technically than the women's weaving of fine cloth, and does not seem to merit the same layering of analogies and metaphors related to the complex picking and heddle movements of the horizontal loom. Only in relation to men's knitting of their woollen caps may we find a weaving discourse that is at all comparable with the women's weaving discourse described here.

Qaqa women, then, overtly counterpose the language of agriculture with their own weaving discourse. In the formal layout of the mantle design, they acknowledge that the *pampa*, the wide expanses of a single colour, are those that are newly under cultivation. The patterned areas of the mantle are called in Aymara *salta* 'to stand up', a term with double significance: referring to the complexity and movement of the weaving technique in this zone of the fabric whereby the salta designs "stand up", and marking the stage of growth of the food crops as they sprout up from the newly worked earth. The salta—or its Quechua equivalent *pallay* (gather up)—can thus be compared to the collection of food products from the harvest piled up at the sides of the zone under cultivation, the agricultural field called "pampa". These intertexts between weaving and agricultural activities and the discourse that surrounds them are also evident in other regions of the altiplano. In the region of Pacajes, for example, the cultivated fields are described in drinking language as *Qipa Mama* 'Weft Mother', the people of the region are compared to the loom, and everything they produce with the weft (Arnold and Yapita with Apaza, in press).

The Origins of, and Inspiration for, Weaving

It should not surprise us either that both weaving and writing share the same spoken origin myth, which alludes to the transitional interface between the prehistoric dark ages of Qaqachaka and its more Christian present. The Qaqas themselves generally agree that the ancient *chullpa*, the ancestral occupants of the chullpa houses whose bone remains from mummy bundles can be found throughout the ayllu, did not know how to weave. The origins and inspiration for weaving does not come, then, from the ancestral chullpa in their age of darkness. They come, rather, from the dawning of another age of light, and the oral histories concerning these origins narrate the common myth about the destruction of the chullpa with the birth of a new sun and the burning of its resplendent light. Some authors have argued that this is a myth concerning the Spanish conquest. However, the same myth also appears to be related to an Inka presence in the area, for the Qaqas acknowledge that weaving—and writing—came into existence with the birth of the Inka sun god, *Inti Tala*, and that with these two skills the Inkas were able to dominate the chullpa peoples.

Nevertheless, the same chullpa mummy bundles, but recast as the god-saints of the new Christian age, are acknowledged as the source of inspiration for weaving. The various *mamitas* such as Mama Tulurisa, Mama Pitunisa, Mama Kantilayra, Mama

Waralupi, and Mama Qupakawana are called 'the weavers', *sawuri*, and women chew coca and pray to them when they weave "for a good hand, a good pulse, and a good eye":

Mamita Waralupi	Little mother Guadelupe,
amparam churitanta.	you will give me your hand.
Sawu Tawaqu umt'añani	Let's drink to the Young Girl of the Loom,
Waralup tayksataki	for Guadalupe, our mother,
amparamataki, wich'uñataki, mä wulsutaki.	for your hand, for a weaving-pick, for a pulse.

Depending on the day on which you weave, you may pray to a dead ancestress who was a good weaver on a Monday, the day when the dead are remembered; you may not weave on a Tuesday, which is a devilish day. You may pray to one of the mamitas as you weave on a Wednesday or a Saturday, or pray to a male god-saint, Killak Tatala or Panakach Tatala, as you weave on a Thursday, but you may not weave on a Friday, another devilish day. Sunday is a day of rest. Catherine Allen (1988 and this volume) also mentions the importance of female saints to women weavers in Sonqo, Peru.

Manifestations of the Inka ancestral spirits make a seasonal appearance when they become an important inspiration for weaving. During the entire period of the rainy season, from the Feast of the Dead in November until the following Carnival, the *jira mayku* and *jira t'alla* 'the spiralling lords and ladies', often compared to Inkas, are present in the ayllu. They are a part of the realm of the mountain spirits and are believed to come from the distant ocean, the rain clouds, and the inner world. They are the spirits of the dead, ambiguously a dangerous and deathly force, but one that may also generate fertility (see also Harris 1982; Arnold 1992b). Women are inspired by them to weave from the time of their arrival in the ayllu from the western ocean at the beginning of the rainy season at the Feast of the Dead to their departure back to the ocean at Carnival with the end of the rains. A weaving that a woman is working on before each of these feasts, the Immaculate Conception of the Virgin and Carnival, must definitely be completed by the date of the feast; otherwise they believe that it will never be finished, the woman will become lethargic, and the strong earth will grasp her. At these times of the year, there is the most frantic desire to weave.

Apart from these wet and diabolic sources of inspiration or their more Christian counterparts, women also acknowledge a metaphysical source for their individual inspiration, which they say comes from their hearts, *chuyma*. The term "chuyma" describes literally the chest organs, including the physical heart (*lluqu*), lungs (*sama sama*), and liver (*k'iwch"a*), and the mass of blood and breath located there. But in its more metaphorical sense, it translates more as "conscience", or perhaps even better as the old Nordic "pluck". The woman agree among themselves that certain women have special gifts for weaving, and these gifted women weavers they call 'lifted hearts' *alax chuyma*, intelligent women who just observe a design once and are able to copy it down from memory. Most women chew coca as they contemplate their weaving forms, colours, and designs. At the precise moment that their heart opens like a bud, then spirit flows and they are inspired to weave, grasping the designs from the blood mass in their hearts.

Inspiration for weaving also comes from the world that women observe around them as they weave. Above all, it comes from the natural world of the hills and the wild animals, birds, and plants that dwell there. Women are inspired most in their creative tasks of weaving during the most fertile times of the year, especially the rainy season when the earth is green and flowering. The Aymara verb *p"anchayaña* describes both the opening of a bud and the opening of the heart, at the moment when it is lifted and inspired to weave. As Dransart observes (in this volume), this powerful notion of "flowering" at once interrelates the activity of remembering in the heart as the female locus of memory and inspiration with the female capacity for the perpetual generation of lineage, both human and animal. "Heart, make me flower", *chuyma p"aqartatistanta*, they say. Then their animals are happy and they are happy. Women do not like to weave in the dry season, when it is cold. There is no vegetation or food. The animals walk about disconsolately, and so do the women. The dry dust blows about, making the new weaving on the loom dirty, whereas with the rains the air is clean and fresh, and so are the weavings.

Steps in the process of weaving

I shall now consider in stages the different processes of transformation involved in the conversion of the woollen fleeces of the animal herds, through specific tasks of work, into woven cloth. At each stage, the precise relations of a gendered division of labour, not only in the human but also in the animal domain, give rise to a series of gendered analogies between people and their animals, expressed in the vernacular texts that accompany their work tasks.

Wool from male and female animals are used for different weaving tasks, associated with the different genders. Wool from female animals is said to be softer. It is used for making skeins, and women weave with it for their mantles. Wool from male animals is said to be coarser, and men use it to weave the coarse homespun cloth. Wool from both male and female llamas is used for making food sacks and the smaller food bags. Woven textiles that use dyed wool are generally woven from female animals, as the wool is softer and easier to manage. The main gendered division of labour, then, is between women using wool from female animals to weave fine cloth of dyed colours and men using wool from male animals to weave coarse homespun cloth.

In Qaqachaka, as they shear their animals, weavers and herders also mutter this direct comparison between the woollen fleece of a given animal and the weavings they will make from it after the wool has passed through various stages of transformation. The men murmur:

Punchusim, närak puncht'asï.   Take off your poncho, I shall put on a poncho, too.

while the women murmur:

Awayusim, närak awayt'asï.   Take off your mantle, I shall put on a mantle, too.

The animals, too, are addressed in humanised and gendered terms as they are sheared. Alpacas are left with special clumps of wool dangling from their coats, which are called their "coca-cloths" (*inkuña*) if they are females or "coca-bags" (*wallqipu*) if they are males:

T'arwa inkuñyañaw jisk'ita, warmipiniw, taqpach warminak inkuñani.	The wool is for making a coca-cloth, a little one, she's really a woman, and all women have coca-cloths.

NATURAL HUES AND COLOURED DYES

The wools used for weaving come in the raw natural hues of tan (*paqu*), grey (*uqi*), black (*ch'iyära*), white (*janq'u*), coffee, and chestnut (*ch'umpi*), and a variety of combination in tones between them. The llamas traditionally reared in Qaqachaka, called *ch"uwa*, have fleeces of one single colour, and these are the most favoured animals for the yarns of natural colours used in weaving. It is these natural colours, particularly black and chestnut, that are used for the broad plain-coloured areas of everyday garments, the pampa of women's mantles, and the *saya* of men's ponchos. The prized 'painted llamas' (*pinta qarwa*) introduced into the ayllu more recently, with their broad patches of mixed colours, tend to be used only for the coarse ropes and slings where mixed coloured yarns may be used.

Or the wools may be dyed. Each colour set has its distinct set of uses. However, the weavings that are considered to be the most pretty (*k'achitu*) are those that have dyed colours, above all the colour scarlet, or blood-red *wila*,[3] used with other colours that "grasp" each other well in combination. It is a predominantly red colour, for example, which is used for the salta figurative area of the woman's mantle, contrasting with the plain and naturally coloured pampa. Ideally, the variety of colours used will be somewhat like the rainbow, but not too like the rainbow which is dangerous. As opposed to the contrast between the reddish salta and the plain-coloured pampa in normal everyday attire, however, festive garments are infused with the colour red all over. Even the pampa becomes infused with red.

DYEING THE WOOL

Dyeing the wool entails making it cook (*q"atiyaña*). The plied wool, wound into skeins, is immersed in boiling water containing the dyes. In the past, these were made from special herbs, roots, and stones, which are still recorded and remembered in the words of the women's songs. Specialist dyers provided the dyes and dyed the wool. Nowadays brighter aniline dyes are preferred as they are more colourfast, and the Aymara term for the modern dyeing technique, *tiñiña*, is a direct borrowing from the Spanish *teñir*. There is even a move toward factory-made acrylic wool, whose bright and clear colours, with their characteristic of longevity, have brought them to the height of fashion among the younger women of the ayllu.

Qaqa women explain that making the skeins of wool cook over fire "introduces light" into the wool, making it brighter in colour, thus reminding us of yet other associated narratives about the civilising function of cooking-fire as well as of the resplendent sunrise at the very origin of weaving as an activity. However, while blood red may be the bright and cooked colour par excellence, the Qaqas' definition of tone and intensity in the dyed colours of woven cloth depends on the amount of white or black added to the primary colour. Lighter colours, with white added, are regarded as drier colours, whereas darker colours, with black added, are regarded as more moist.

WEAVING A MANTLE

Now we focus on the weaving and design of the woman's mantle, called awayu, examined here as a kind of text. I concentrate on the ethnocategories used by the weavers themselves (see Gavilán and Ulloa 1992), but in a wider sense. In order to weave her awayu, a woman first sets up her loom in a sheltered and quiet spot in the hills, beating the four corner stakes into the earth and speaking her request to the earth virgin to receive her offering as she does so. She ties the stakes back to other smaller stakes in the earth with ropes and then begins the process of setting out the warp threads. With a partner, she throws the warp threads (chinu) to and fro, looping them over the timber poles of the loom, the double threads of one complete loop forming one chinu of the cloth.[4] She already has in mind the entire layout of her finished cloth, the threads of which she will select in a process called *apsu*. She sets out the first half of her mantle, with its broad divisions into areas of plain or "ordinary" weave (*inaki*) in plain dark-coloured natural hues in the centre, the pampa, with the narrow decorated outside edge, to be used for fastening the mantle at her chest, to one side. The wider decorated area of cloth, called 'large salta' (*jach'a salta*), is set out to the other side, with its mixture of dyed-coloured stripes in plain weave, its checker patterns (*k'utu*), also in plain weave, with the most detailed patterned areas, called 'small salta' (*jisk'a salta),* formed in a complementary warp-faced weave using three warp threads and two wefts. The three warps form the three layers of cloth in this complex figurative zone (see figure 7-2).

The small salta may be set out in boxed units, called *tika* (as in figure 7-2), or in a continuous design, depending on the time the weaver has at hand. The boxed pattern is repetitive and easiest to weave, and is used mainly at the higher levels of the ayllu where women have larger flocks of animals and less time to concentrate on their weaving. The continuous patterns that require constant attention are found at the lower levels of the ayllu where the flocks are smaller, and even there only among the best weavers. The salta designs are selected and organised by the process of counting the warp threads, called chinu, and each woman knows a certain range of figures that she may weave in any precise number of chinu (see figure 7-3).

The finished mantle as a text: the pampa and salta

Various authors have commented how Andean cloth, as a kind of text, is a woven expression of ayllu territory (for example, Platt 1978; Cereceda 1978; Gisbert et al. 1987; Torrico 1989). Many of these studies have been inspired by taxonomic or semiotic readings of the cloth, rather than by a study of the weaving techniques involved or of the language that the weavers themselves use about the component

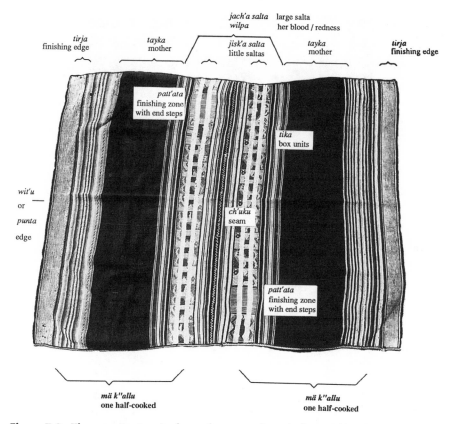

jach'a salta   large salta
wilpa   her blood / redness

tirja
finishing edge

tayka
mother

jisk'a salta
little saltas

tayka
mother

tirja
finishing edge

patt'ata
finishing zone
with end steps

tika
box units

wit'u
or
punta
edge

ch'uku
seam

patt'ata
finishing zone
with end steps

mä k"allu
one half-cooked

mä k"allu
one half-cooked

Figure 7-2 The weaving terminology of a woman's typical everyday *awayu*.

elements of their work. The weaving terms for the distinct zones of the cloth have been analysed semiotically, sometimes in a structuralist pairing of binary opposites, particularly with reference to the supposed distinction between categories associated with "culture" and those associated with "nature".

A definition of the broad areas of one single colour, called "pampa" in the woman's mantle and "saya" in the man's poncho, has been particularly problematic in weaving studies to date. It is often concluded that the pampa area is related to the large expanses of flat uncultivated land, outside the main cultivated zone (see, for example, Cereceda 1978; Bouysse Cassagne 1987: 190–91). It has been observed that the thin coloured stripes (of just one or two chinus) that border the pampa areas and make up the salta figurative areas have names related to the boundary zones between cultivated fields, the stone walls (*jalja*) that divide communities and agricultural fields, the walls that surround small cultivated plots of land (*uyu* and *tini*), and the streams (*jalaqa*) that flow down the mountains, some of which also form boundary zones (Arnold 1988; Torrico 1989). Usually these distinctions between the two principal zones of the cloth

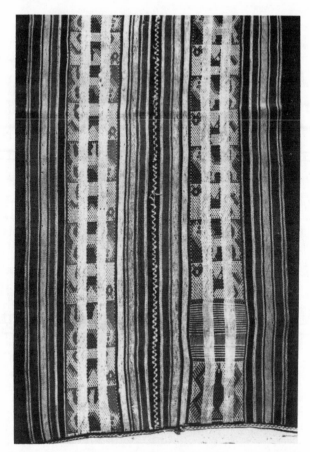

Figure 7-3 Typical everyday *awayu* with the *salta* enlarged. Note the box-like *tika* figures of horses and tigers alternating. Note also the striped end detail called *patt'ata* and the final figure of a bird.

have been drawn in terms of nature and culture. The pampa is inevitably associated with the category of nature, the wilder zone outside inhabited and cultivated space, while the figurative design, the salta, is associated with the cultivated and domesticated space around the immediate hamlet.

In Qaqachaka, these structuralist distinctions do *not* seem to be appropriate. Although there is a coding of elements in its designs, the mantle is still essentially figurative. The wide expanse of a single colour in the mantle, called pampa, is directly associated by the Qaqas themselves with an area of flat land periodically brought under cultivation, land where the animals may also graze, on occasion. Pampa as a textile zone is related then to an agricultural field which may be cultivated. As doña Lucía Quispe Choque, one elderly Qaqa weaver, explained:

Yapuchañ pamp sataw purapa.	Both are called agricultural fields.
Manq'an pampat jaqi manq'i,	It's a field where people eat from,
manq'an pampapinij sha,	it's really a field for food-crops,
ukat ukan sawupt"a.	and it's where we weave.
Sawuñ ch'utun sawupt"a, jisk'a pampanaka.	We weave in the weaving places, which are little fields.

The raw and the cooked: the mother and her offspring

A further clue to the nature of the textile term pampa is given in its alternative name, *tayka*, meaning 'mother'. The entire zone of cloth called pampa may also be contrasted with the central and decorated part of the cloth, called salta. Salta is the weaving term for the whole expanse of the patterned and coloured area, as well as for its distinct "figures". The weaving term salta is probably derived from the Aymara verb *saltaña*, in turn a borrowing from the Spanish *saltar*, meaning 'to stand, or jump up'. These two principal textile zones with their different weaving techniques and uses of colour, the pampa and the salta, are contrasted by the Qaqa women themselves as 'raw' (*ch'uqi*) and 'cooked' (*q"ati*) zones. Their own categories echo the technical processes they have carried out in the stages of weaving. The unpatterned and monochrome pampa of an everyday mantle, as we have seen, is more usually woven from undyed wool in natural hues, usually of black or chestnut-brown, while the patterned and coloured salta is literally "cooked", being woven from the cooked and dyed yarns of various bright colours.

But the relationship between pampa and salta designs are also phrased by the Qaqa women weavers themselves in other ways. The salta designs are described as the 'offspring' (*qallu*) of the pampa, or using the pampa's alternative name of "mother", as "the young one of the mother". Sometimes the pampa is related to the salta as the 'large mother' (*jach'a tayka*) to the 'little mother' (*jisk'a tayka*). Then the salta patterned area is further subdivided, so that the "little mother" salta has her many "offspring", which are the smaller figurative designs within the overall patterned area of cloth. Weavers, like doña Lucía, say that the "large mother" is broad, whereas the "little mother" designs, her offspring, are "sprinkled about" inside her.

This formal organisation and taxonomy of textile zones into "mother" and "off-spring" units has been observed in other textile genres: in Cereceda's study of the small food bag called "wayaqa" (Cereceda 1978), in Torrico's study of the large food sack called "kustäla" (Torrico 1989), and in Zorn's study of the coca-cloth called "unkhuña" (cf. "inkuña" earlier in this chapter; Zorn 1986). As to the woman's mantle, called "awayu", however, its very technical complexity appears to give rise to even more layers of meaning concerning this relationship between mother and offspring. There are, for example, some further clues to their possible formulations in the differential emphasis given to these two textile zones by older and younger women. Young women, showing off their skill as weavers, and thus their marriageability, make a point of weaving the largest saltas that current fashions will allow. They have introduced more and more complex weaving techniques into the salta designs, using up to five large sets of heddles in the most complex saltas of all, the *t'isnu salta*. Their pampas, on the other hand, are in relation shrunken in size. The scale of the pampa space withdraws in relation to the salta space. The Aymara verb used for this process, *irkataña*, emphasises this notion of contest between the red and the black parts of the textile; they say that the red part, *wilani*, "rises against the black". Thus, the saltas of the young women, as a textile zone, become shamelessly large, so much so that the sheer scale of the young women's saltas shocks the older women of the ayllu, those who were brought up on modestly scaled saltas which were not even to be seen until they were completed.

Older women sometimes suggest that this generational gap in the scale of the salta designs is due to the modern influence of schooling. They say that now is the 'time of reading' (*liyi timpu*) and that younger women, with their reading and writing abilities, are able to just 'pick out' (*p'itaña*) designs without the necessity of using the design models that the older women were accustomed to copy from in their youth. Interestingly, the Aymara verb they use here for weaving, "p'itaña", has the more specific meaning of 'picking out' the design with a pointed object, like a weaving pick, or a plumed pen, or a modern pencil. It is also the same verb used when men knit their woollen hats with pointed knitting needles, or when hens pick out seeds from the ground with their pointed beaks. Are the literate young women "writing" their designs into their woven texts? (See figure 7-4).

There are other functional reasons for this difference in scale between pampa and salta. Older women, in contrast to the younger women, have less time for weaving. With their failing eyesight, they weave much less elaborate saltas and much broader pampas. The "large mother" weaves less salta design-space than her "little mother" daughter. The only exception to this general rule is doña María Ayka Llanque, an older woman in her seventies, whom we affectionately call "Punk" on account of her youth-

Figure 7-4 Doña Juana picking out her *salta* designs.

fulness and her propensity to wear numerous safety pins here and there on her mantle. Doña María is generally acknowledged in Qaqachaka to be one of the best and most prolific weavers, in spite of her age. She regards herself as an "eternal maiden", saying that she weaves "just how she likes"! She is an exception that proves the rule.

Learning the salta designs

Are there other reasons for this difference in age and modesty in relation to the salta designs of most other women of the ayllu? Further clues to this difference in approach between generations emerge when we study how women learn the salta designs.

Qaqachaka as a whole has its own characteristic style in the organisation of its textile zones and use of colour, above all in the proportion between its pampa and salta and the number of patterned bands, the 'little saltas', which the large salta incorporates. These factors make Qaqa cloth recognisable to insiders and outsiders alike in the region, marking Qaqachaka ethnic identity and history, recording and reproducing it in cloth. Nevertheless, each individual weaver has her own distinct style in weaving, her own idiosyncratic discourse about it, and she is considered to be the personal owner of her textile designs. In relation to the complex and patterned salta designs, a woman says that her inspiration for them comes from her 'design heart' salta chuyma), but more generally her love for the saltas. Women explain that their designs are already "just inside their hearts", allowing them to select whichever salta they wish:

Chuyma manq"sanki,	They are just inside our hearts,
saltas kuna palltañasa.	letting us select whatever salta design.

They say that they just contemplate the designs and then "draw them out".

In the process of weaving a mantle, the finished cloth is usually formed from two identical but separate halves. Each of these sections is called *mäk"allu*, *mä* meaning 'one', and *k"allu* meaning 'half-cooked'. In Qaqachaka, there is a clearly aspirated /kʰ/ in the naming of this component of the finished textile, and it cannot be confused with the term *qallu* 'offspring' for the same component that Zorn (1986) suggests is used in the region of Macusani in Peru. The weaving term *qallu* is reserved for other component parts of the mantle in Qaqachaka, as we have already seen. Furthermore, the term *k"allu* 'half-cooked' evokes another stage in the transformatory process of converting raw wool to a cooked and finished cloth. Finally, the two component halves of the cloth are sewn together. The generative central seam is called *chuyma ch'uku* 'heart-seam', since this central seam is regarded as the "heart" of the animate mantle.

The pathways of the salta designs

Then, once the salta design of a weaving is in progress, a woman must follow its unique pathway (*t"ak"i*). She tries not to get lost or to move from the salta pathway, for then she will make a mistake. In following the pathways of her designs, she is also analogously following the pathways of her territory, for the textile paths are compared to "the veins of the earth". Thus, she follows the pathways of her animals, and in this way she incorporates the pathways she treads with her animal flocks in her daily task pasturing the animals, moving from the main *pueblo* or her hamlet to the hillside houses and their surrounding pastures, from corral to corral, into the textile designs. The seeds that fall accidentally with the animal droppings onto the daily pathways form another design feature, which a weaver integrates into her cloth. Other pathways of growth woven into the cloth are those of the wild plants and shrubs that she is familiar with as she pastures her animals in the hills, the patterns of which she has copied in her designs.

The most common salta designs are inspired by the wild beasts of the hillsides, the condors and falcons, partridges and quails, vizcachas and foxes, lizards, toads, and snakes, as well as the water birds that frequent the lakes and watering places in the upper levels of the ayllu. These wild beasts and plants are described by the women as the beasts, the shrubs, and plants of the virgin earth. Each salta is regarded as animate. It has a beginning, an end, and a centre, its "navel".

A woman's capacity to weave thus expresses her transformative skills; weaving activity is regarded as vital and magical. In weaving the pathways of her salta designs, of her animal herds and her cultivated fields, a woman not only copies them from the memories held in her heart but also manipulates them, working on these miniature elements in microcosm to transform them and bring their larger counterparts into being in the ayllu macrocosm. Through weaving, she maps and records ayllu history in a more figurative way, and by embedding the seeds of future production in her designs she provides the reproductive matrix that guarantees this future production (Arnold 1988; Arnold et al. 1991; Allen, this volume).

Analogies between pampa, salta, and the earth

The relationship between the two principal zones of the mantle, between the plain pampa and the patterned salta, also follows the yearly sequence of the agricultural cycle. The women weavers say that the pampa is the earth resting. They call her the 'black mother' *ch'iyar tayka*. "She has not been worked", they say, meaning she has not been ploughed. The pampa, like the earth, is black and unturned, she is still lazy and unwilling to procreate. She is strong, and her blackness indicates that she will bring forth, but not yet. Qaqa women, like doña Asunta Arias, another weaver, emphasise yet again the relationship between cloth and production when they observe how older women wore black dresses and overskirts, when the earth produced well, "Whereas nowadays", she says, "women wear just any colour and production in the ayllu is declining".

The salta, by contrast, has been churned up well: *ch'ata*. They say that it is as if she has been amply ploughed and then planted. "Ploughing thus, like the fields that we plough, thus it is then, thus it could be, the salta designs", explains doña Asunta. *Ch'ata*, the churned-up area, is another term for the plough handle that does the turning.

The salta, with its bright dyed colours, also has to do with the coming of the rains, and the greening of the vegetation. The rains, like the devil spirits which bring them, are believed to come from the western ocean. When they are late, people complain, using the verb *saltaña*:

Salt'amay carajo,	Get up then, damn you,
purxatpanay carajo.	oh, that it would rain over the earth, damn it.[5]

Weaving terms for the narrow stripes that border the little saltas echo this preoccupation with water. They may be called *taniqa* 'to flow down'. Or they may be called 'irrigation canals' (*larqa*), and the little salta designs that they supply "are like the fields". Sometimes the entire mother salta is called 'large river' (*jach'a jawira*) and the small saltas are called 'little rivers' (*jisk'a jawira*). It should not surprise us, then, that the wild birds and beasts which animate the salta domain are most specifically those "that announce the rains": the toad or birds flying in groups, the animals of the virgin earth.

However, the precise nature of the difference between the plain pampa and the coloured and figurative salta zones of the woven cloth becomes most explicit in relation to an alternative term for the salta. This key term emerged one day in a casual conversation about weaving with doña Juana Ayka Colque. She called it *wilpa*, incorporating the root-term *wila* 'blood' and the third-person possessive suffix -*pa*-, a term we might gloss as 'her redness', or 'her blood'. This "redness" is most evident in the edge zone of the salta, where it borders the pampa, although, as we have seen, it may flood the entire salta and even overflow into the pampa zone in a festive mantle. Women say that the salta is predominantly red in colour "because the earth has her blood and is fertile". The rains have run into the earth and made the soil turn red. Doña Asunta explained:

Wilaw sas	It is blood, saying,
jumintukichix uraqix, ch'ata laq'a,	the earth is damp, the trampled earth,
uka wilpaw sapx nanakax . . .	this is her blood we say . . .

"Thus she produces her fruits, her babies, the *wawas*, the food products", she added, "the blood of the earth is her fruit".

Is it for this reason, then, that young women exaggerate the scale of their salta into outrageous sizes, and shrink back their pampas? In doing so, are the young women exaggerating their fertility, their blood flow, their womanliness, and their marriageability? Are the older women content to shrink back their saltas to a more modest scale, to acknowledge the passing of their blood flow and fertility, and their return toward an ample pampa and a time of rest?

Other textual connections can be made here. It could be said, for example, that it is precisely a woman's blood flow at her first menstruation that gives her the inspiration for developing the most complex techniques of her weaving career in the beautiful large salta designs, those that will become a visual expression of her new fertility and her potential reproductive powers. This blood flow is the first signal of her potential capacity to form a new human lineage with her future husband, as well as relating her to the equivalent stage in an animal's reproductive life marked analogically by blood at the important ear-cutting ceremony called "k'illp"a", and to the local birth of the Inka sun in the region. Then, in the following reproductive years of her life, the rhythm of her cyclical blood flow and her increasing powers as a weaver are continually nourished by the mass of blood in her heart, providing a continued source of inspiration for her textiles throughout the middle years of her life with their large and impressive designs. Only in her final years, when her blood flow has ceased, is she more modest again in her weaving designs.

In a similar vein, this key symbol of blood flow is also evident in relation to men's creative powers, but in a quite different manner. While a young man uses the powers of spirit that reside in his head, in the past, at least, certain "literate" men used the matrix of sacrificial blood from the animal herds to provide the blood ink that expressed their developing powers of writing on the page. And it is this same sacrificial blood that a man still offers in a ritual context to the Inka sun god in a more exclusively male domain.

The pampa and the salta can be compared in other ways. The pampa in everyday garments, whether in a woman's mantle or a man's poncho, is usually of a dark hue and natural colour. It is without fire and raw (ch'uqi). It is unproductive like the dry season. The salta, by contrast, is cooked (q"ati), with firelight glowing from within, making its colours clear and bright. It is fertile, irrigated, and damp, like the earth in the rainy season. The two zones of cloth could even perhaps be opposed as shadow to light, as night and day, or as dark moon to full moon; the opposing poles of light pulsate the cyclical rhythm that brings into being female blood flow. But it is important to point out that Andean weavers do not, like structuralists, experience a binary reality of either/or. Even within the most complex of the salta designs themselves, the t'isnu salta, the purposeful juxtaposition of dark and light colours in the three layers of cloth is manipulated in order to contrast the two sides of the cloth in a complementary weave, like night and day. Both co-exist, as a weaver looking at the upper face of the cloth understands the other below.

The poncho as a text

We continue here to examine the differences in meaning represented by the unpatterned pampa and the patterned salta areas of cloth, but in a comparative study of the formal organisation of these textile zones in two gendered garments, in the man's poncho, on the one hand, and the woman's awayu, on the other. In this way, I shall attempt to offer some final observations about gender and its ideological manipulation through weaving in Qaqachaka. First, though, I shall outline the formal design of the man's poncho.

Like women's mantles, men's ponchos are woven in two identical halves, joined at the centre by a sewn seam. However, there is a difference between the poncho and the mantle in the zones of cloth that are joined by this central seam. In the poncho, it is the central unpatterned zone of the textile that incorporates this central seam, whereas in the mantle the central seam joins the two halves of the patterned salta. The broad design of each half of a typical everyday poncho in Qaqachaka is generally of two wide bands of patterned areas made up from coloured stripes of varying widths, called *lista*, located between three wide bands of unpatterned textile, called *saya*, woven in the same natural colour (see Figure 7-5).

The naming of parts of the poncho

The weaving term "lista" recurs at several different levels in the formal organisation of the patterned areas of cloth of the man's poncho. One entire striped band of the poncho, comparable to the salta of the woman's mantle, is called "lista". This wide coloured band, which we might call the "maximal" lista of the poncho, is then further subdivided into a series of smaller vertical stripes, also called "lista". These smaller stripes are organised into identical formal groupings, once again called "lista", the "minimal" lista groupings of the poncho. A typically everyday poncho usually has up to five minimal lista groupings in each maximal lista band, whereas a festive poncho may have up to ten. (see Figures 7-5 and 7-6).

Each minimal lista group is usually composed of four coloured stripes, also called lista, commonly of darker and lighter hues of the same tone, or, alternatively, of two complementary colours. In the poncho, the four coloured stripes of the two outermost minimal lista bands, those that border the unpatterned saya on each side of each maximal lista, are usually red in colour. This is like the same reddened zone of the salta in the mantle as it borders the pampa. Each of the four coloured stripes of the minimal lista, usually of between three to four warp threads, has other alternative terms. They may be called 'group' (*qutu*) or pampa. In the minimal lista group, the four wider stripes of colour are sub-divided into two pairs by even narrower stripes of just one warp thread, the narrowest lista of the entire poncho (see Figures 7-7 and 7-8).

The weaving terminology of these narrowest stripes depends on their precise position in relation to the minimal lista grouping as a whole. Each minimal lista group is symmetrical around a central narrow stripe, flanked on each side by a pair of wider stripes, which are then, in turn, bordered by two outer narrow stripes. These inner and outer narrow stripes have distinct names. The outermost narrow stripes are called *taniqa*, meaning 'to run down', the directional suffix -*qa*- denoting the direction

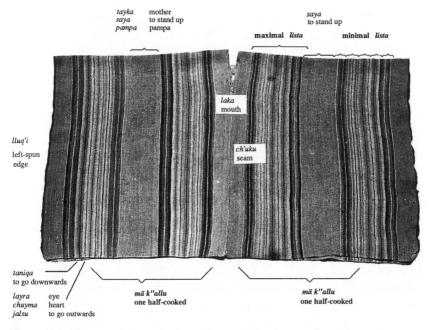

Figure 7-5   The weaving terminology of a man's festive poncho with a red *saya*.

Figure 7-6 A man's poncho in use.

downward. An alternative name for them is *larqa*, a term that was also used for the narrow stripes bordering the smallest salta design of the woman's mantle and having the meaning in both garments of 'irrigation canal'.

The narrow stripes that form the central 'heart' (*chuyma*) of the minimal lista grouping, on the other hand, are most commonly called *jalsu*, a weaving term derived from the Aymara verb *jalsuña* meaning 'to go or to run outward', the directional suffix *-su-* marking its direction of flow outward. Weavers compare the jalsu to a spring of water bubbling up from the earth. An alternative term for the inner stripes is *tansu* 'to run outward' using the same directional suffix. And sometimes these inner stripes may be called 'eyes' (*layra*).

Besides these differences in weaving terminology, there is also a difference in the use of colour between these inner and outer sets of narrow stripes. The taniqa outermost stripes may be black, but they are more usually white. They are not dyed, but natural hues of wool, whereas the jalsu inner stripes should ideally be dyed red in

Figure 7-7 A maximal *lista* group in the poncho.

colour. As a rule, even if not all the jalsu stripes in a maximal lista band are red, at least some should be red. Table 7-1 summarises these differences.

Differences between the woman's mantle and the man's poncho

There are many pertinent differences in the weaving techniques and weaving terminology of the woman's mantle and the man's poncho. I shall examine some further differences between them, and then attempt to relate these differences to aspects of social and gender organisation in Qaqachaka as a whole. Finally, I shall suggest how the differential gender relations of Qaqachaka society are manipulated by women through a means of cultural or ideological production of cloth.

Table 7-1 Differences in terminology of the narrowest *listas*.

Outer narrow stripe	Inner narrow stripe
taniqa	*jalsu*
-*qa*- 'to go downward'	-*su*- 'to go outward'
'irrigation canals'	'eyes' or 'heart'
black or white	red
natural hues	dyed colour

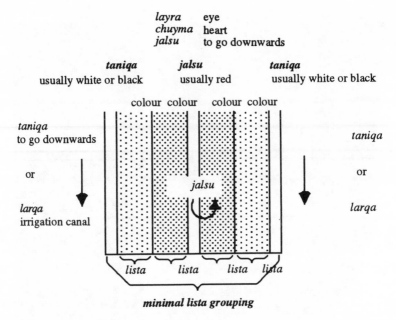

Figure 7-8 A minimal *lista* group in the poncho.

A primary difference between the patterned zone, or salta, of the woman's mantle and the saya of the man's poncho is that the mantle's salta is essentially figurative, whereas the man's poncho comprises a much simpler pattern of stripes, the lista. A further gendered difference that is immediately noticeable to any observer is in the way in which the respective patterned section is worn by each sex. Young women wear their mantles with the patterned salta hung horizontally, in the style called "k'illp"a", whether the garment is worn hung down the back or doubled up and hung over the shoulders, whereas men usually wear their ponchos with its lista stripes hung vertically.[6]

There is also an immediate difference in the weaving techniques of the patterned and unpatterned zones in the woman's mantle and the man's poncho. In the woman's mantle, the unpatterned pampa is woven in a plain weave of a single natural colour, which contrasts with the more elaborate complementary warp-faced weave of its patterned salta, with its variety of figures in natural and dyed colours, whether in the most complex multi-layered warps of the t'isnu salta or, alternatively, the simpler apsu salta. In the woman's mantle, then, the flat pampa and the "standing up" salta are differentiated with regard to both weaving technique, non-figurative and figurative designs, and the use of colour. In the man's poncho, by contrast, both zones are woven in a flat plain weave (*llanu*). The difference between the patterned and unpatterned zones in the man's poncho is not marked, as in the woman's mantle, by a difference in weaving technique, but by the use of colour and pattern. The unpatterned saya of an everyday poncho is woven in natural hues of a single colour, whereas the patterned lista is woven mainly with dyed colours in a striped pattern.

Further differences become apparent in the weaving terminology of each garment. Although there are some common weaving terms for the parts of each garment, particularly in relation to the two main textile zones, there are also distinct differences. As in the woman's mantle, the unpatterned zones of cloth in the man's poncho can be called pampa, meaning 'flat place', whereas the patterned and coloured areas of cloth can be called salta, meaning 'standing up'. The pampas of the man's poncho can even be called 'mothers' (*tayka*), as in the women's mantles. However, there is more usually a distinct gendered difference in the weaving terminology of the two primary zones of cloth in each garment. The unpatterned zones of the man's poncho are most commonly called by their weavers "sayas", another weaving term with the inter-changeable meaning of 'standing up'.[7] And instead of using the term salta, reserved more for the woman's mantle, the patterned zones of cloth of the man's poncho are more usually called lista, the weaving term meaning 'stripe'. (I shall return to other important dimensions of the significance of the weaving term "lista" later on). The terms pampa and salta, then, are reserved more for use in relation to the woman's mantle, whereas the terms saya and lista are used in relation to the man's poncho. Like the differences in orientation of the patterned area of each gendered garment as they are generally worn, mentioned earlier, these differences in weaving terminology similarly define a dominant orientation of the unpatterned areas of cloth according to gender. The female pampa is a "flat" and horizontal place, whereas the male saya is "standing up" vertically. These weaving terms and gendered modes of dress thus reinforce the common notions that women as a gender are associated with the flat places, the pampa or *t'alla*, and men with their respective higher mountain peaks. Table 7-2 summarises these differences.

Mantle pampa and salta, poncho saya and lista compared

With these similarities and differences in weaving terminology, technique, design, and styles of dress of the two gendered garments in mind, we might venture a comparative study of their respective parts. Despite their superficial dissimilarity, it seems that certain elements of the woman's mantle and the man's poncho deal with similar semantic domains, and a comparison between them helps to clarify the function of the puzzling range of stripes, called lista, in the poncho. For example, the variety of figures in the coloured and patterned salta of the woman's mantle appears to be in many ways a female equivalent of the repetitive sequence of minimal lista stripes in the man's

Table 7-2 Different terminology and use of the mantle and poncho.

	patterned zone	patterned zone
WOMAN'S MANTLE	*pampa* 'flat place'	*salta* worn horizontally
MAN'S PONCHO	*saya* 'standing up'	*lista* worn vertically

poncho. Similarly, the monochrome pampa of the woman's mantle appears to be a female equivalent of the unpatterned zones of the man's poncho, whether they are called in weaving terminology pampa, tayka, or saya. Thus, the mantle's salta and the poncho's lista, on the one hand, and the mantle's pampa and the poncho's saya, on the other, appear to treat essentially the same semantic domains. Perhaps we can be more precise, then, about a comparable meaning of the lista stripes in the man's poncho?

If the maximal lista group of the poncho is like the patterned salta of the mantle, then does the minimal lista grouping of the man's poncho express the same kind of significance as the minimal small salta of the woman's mantle? There is distinct evidence for this. For example, we can note the same preoccupation in the weaving terminology of the minimal lista grouping with the idea of flowing liquids, in its use of such terms as *jalsuña* 'to flow out' and *taniqaña* 'to flow down', as there was in the figurative salta of the woman's mantle, with its "irrigation canals" and "streams that flow down" the hillside. An alternative term for the minimal lista grouping is, once again, *taniqa* 'to flow downward', and weavers say that these minimal striped bands "flow down from the plain saya" of the poncho, like the salta in the woman's mantle "comes down from its mother field". Even the basic weaving term salta, in the woman's mantle, as we have seen, referred in the wedding songs to a moist and female-gendered parcel of land, a *salta q"uchi*. Within the microcosm of the minimal lista grouping of the man's poncho there is also the same organisational logic as there is in the salta of the mantle. There are the similarly wider stripes of colour, which may be called pampa, divided at the centre by the narrow, usually red, stripe called "jalsu", just as the broad plain-weave pampa of the woman's mantle is divided at the centre by the predominantly red salta (see again Table 7-2).

The relationship between pampa and salta in the woman's mantle, and their respective gendered equivalents, the saya and lista in the man's poncho, also have to do more explicitly with the gendered social formations in Qaqachaka. The various hamlets, formed around patri-, viri-local households are conjoined across space by a network of female ties. Male ties of semen are passed down vertically through the seed or semen lines of the male lineages called *chacha kasta*, most often localised in space through generations, whereas the female ties of blood are passed down through the bloodlines called *wila kasta*, connecting the patrilocal groups horizontally across space "like a web" in each generation.

In each gendered garment, too, it is as if the patterned and coloured salta of the mantle or the striped lista of the poncho has to do predominantly with the respective generative powers of women and men. Thus, the difference in orientation of the salta or lista in each respective garment as it is worn is analogous to these primary gendered social formations in the ayllu. The man's poncho hangs with its coloured lista stripes vertically, like the vertically organised male kindreds, whereas the young woman's mantle hangs with its figurative and predominantly red salta horizontally, in the k'illp"a style, like the female (both human and animal) web of blood ties connecting the patrilineal groups horizontally across space.[8] The weaving terminology of pampa 'flat-place' for the unpatterned monochrome zone of the woman's mantle and saya 'standing up' for the equivalent zone of the man's poncho further reinforces these proposed analogies. The only exceptions to this general rule are those that seem at the same time to prove it—namely, older women who may wear their mantles with the salta hung vertically (in the style called *pulu*) like the man's poncho stripes. They themselves say that this style of dress "keeps them warm", but they also insist that it confirms their status as older women "who have lived in the same place for many years". "Like men", they say, they are "standing vertically in one place".

We must remember, however, that it is a woman weaver in Qaqachaka who weaves both of these garments, her mantle for herself (or her daughter) and a poncho for her husband (or her son). In doing so, it is as if she skews both of these gendered social formations of female bloodline and male semen line toward the female side. It is as if, in her mantle, a woman weaver displays two different but associated aspects of autogenesis. On the one hand, she displays the power of her human bloodline of female ties as revealed in her predominantly blood-red "large salta", and, on the other, the generative capacity of her household and ayllu, the wild birds and beasts of the hills, the domesticated animals reared there, and the food products that the ayllu may grow within its boundaries, as revealed in the "little salta" designs. In the festive mantles, these female blood ties have even greater predominance. In this case, even the monochrome pampa of the woman's mantle is flooded with a dyed-colour red, as if to display during the fiesta the moments of greatest creativity of a woman, her household and ayllu, mediated through redness. It is as if the passage of the fiesta condenses the most fertile moments of the year into this single hue.

Even in a man's poncho, a woman weaver displays the same preoccupation with marking a reddened bloodline in the central space of the minimal lista grouping, the heart-place where it springs forth like water. It is as if she wishes to emphasise that a man's own blood relationship to his mother and maternal kin is the primary one. Then, in the narrow outer stripes of the minimal lista grouping, those which are most often white, and "semen-like", according to doña Asunta, a woman weaver marks what appear to be the connections of male ties of semen, the semen lines or chacha kasta, between social groups. But then, in the festive ponchos, with their dyed-red saya, these male ties of semen are once more mediated through female ties, ties of blood. What a woman has done in both examples, then, is to place female ties of blood at the centre of the weaving design and to relegate male ties of semen to the periphery. And in doing so, she has re-organised and re-defined the gender relations and social formations of Qaqachaka for both women and men.

The meaning of the stripes called lista

I shall conclude with a final hypothesis about a difference in signification between the man's poncho and the woman's mantle as gendered garments. The hypothesis has to do with further observations on gender relations in Qaqachaka and the way that they are represented in the textile zones, form, and colour of these two woven items. A vital clue to this difference lies in the use of the weaving term "lista", a term that we have noted is used most often in relation to the coloured striping pattern of men's ponchos. I argue here that although the term "lista" has a range of meanings associated with agricultural and herding activities, these meanings in a woman weaver's hands are deliberately muted in the man's poncho, as compared to their raised significance in their own mantles. Women are thus able to emphasise through the manipulation of their weavings, as texts, the relation of men with more productive tasks and themselves with more reproductive and regenerative powers.

The use of the weaving term "lista" in the poncho of Qaqachaka is puzzling. "Lista" as a term can also be used in the women's mantles, but its use is restricted to the narrow bands of colour in plain weave that decorate the outer fastening edge of the cloth, as well as the narrow bands of colour that decorate the large salta area of the cloth, those which generally border the small saltas. As a weaving term, "lista" is rather underplayed in the terminology of the mantle. It is in the man's poncho that lista are predominant. Why should this be?

"Lista" appears to be derived from the Spanish term for a stripe, fringe, or narrow band. When we study its etymology, the introduction of the Spanish term "lista" into Aymara weaving terminology is first noted in Bertonio's Spanish-Aymara vocabulary of 1612, collected in the region of Juli on the southern edge of Lake Titicaca. Bertonio mentions several kinds of stripe called "lista", and he notes what appear to be a number of contemporary Aymara terms for these stripes still in use in the region in the seventeenth century, such as *hattu*, *koli*, and *caruma* (Bertonio 1984 [1612], I:293; II:37, 56). These archaic Aymara weaving terms are not known in Qaqachaka and do not seem to be used in Bertonio's region today, either. Bertonio does, however, mention an equivalence between the Spanish verb *listar* and an Aymara verb still used by weavers around the southern edge of Titicaca, *sukochatha*, and he implies that the adjective 'striped' may be translated into Aymara as *suko suko*. *Suk'u suk'u*, but with a glottalised /k'/, is still a weaving term in the lakeside region to the present day for a narrow stripe in a man's poncho. Our puzzle is why, in Qaqachaka, the Aymara term for a poncho stripe of colour has disappeared and the Spanish term, "lista", has been introduced to the exclusion of any other?

Bertonio also relates as synonymous the Spanish verbs *listar* and *baretear* 'to open trenches with a bar or pick' with the Aymara verb *sukochatha*, whose modern meaning is 'to open furrows with a plough', thus drawing the meaning of the weaving term "listar" into the realm of agricultural production (Bertonio 1984 [1612], I:293). The concept of a ploughed furrow may have been foreign at first to an Andean population used to using the hand plough and only turning over clods of earth in order to place the food-seeds inside, and the Spanish term for furrow, *surco*, is borrowed directly into Aymara as *suku*. The close equivalence between the terms for furrows, stripes, and the action of breaking open trenches does nevertheless imply an analogy between the narrow lista stripes in a woven poncho and each furrow in the turned field of the modern salta design. As long as anyone can remember, the Spanish foot plough has been used in Qaqachaka to plough the land into furrows. Only the ayllu elders remark how the sharp point of the Spanish ploughshare injures the virgin earth more than the older indigenous foot plough, and they request her forgiveness before the ploughing begins.

There are associations of the term "lista" with herding activities as well as with agricultural ones. According to Cassandra Torrico, the term "lista" among the Macha of northern Potosí, neighbours of the Qaqas, is used for the coloured woollen earrings placed in the notched ears of the animals during the marking ceremony or on their saint's day (Torrico 1989). "Lista", in this context in Macha, is thus comparable with the Quechua terms *t'ika* or *chimpu* elsewhere, or *p"aqara* 'flower' in the Aymara terminology of Qaqachaka. When the animals are marked in Qaqachaka, they are regarded as being "flowered". In this notion of "flowering", there are further sugges-tions of maternal ties. In the marking ceremony of the animals, the woollen earring is placed in the notched ear of an animal, and the marking by notching, as we have shown, draws forth a flow of blood marking a continuous bloodline of animals, since the marking passes from mother animal to offspring (Arnold 1988: 229ff.). Torrico also notes the association of certain colours of wool for the lista earrings in Macha with distinct family lines of animals.

The more common definition of "lista", however, that which survives into modern Spanish, is as a 'list', a roll call or register, such as a bill of fare, a college roll call, and so on. It is this modern definition that I shall pursue here. The poncho designs of Qaqachaka have changed significantly in the past fifty years, and it is possible that these modern changes might have been decisive in the implementation of the use of the weaving term "lista" for the poncho stripes, to the exclusion of other garments. There have been particularly dramatic changes in poncho design since the Bolivian Revolution and the Agrarian Reform of 1952–53, design changes that have been accompanied by major social and cultural changes, such as the introduction of mechanised transport, public education, and greater access to the external market system. Could it be that the stripes of the poncho may have taken over a vestigial function, one that was no longer necessary after this period of major change? Could this function have been in a listing of items which are no longer displayed or counted in this manner?

The poncho stripes as a mnemonic device

Silverman-Proust, in her study of the striped wayaqa food bag in Q'ero in Peru (1988), suggests that the lista stripes of the food bag, with their various different widths and colours, were homologous in many ways with the older kipu system of counting. She gives evidence that the broader stripes of the food bag signified larger quantities, previously marked by the wide knots of the kipu cords, while the narrower stripes of the food bag, like the smaller knots of the kipu, marked smaller quantities. She also elaborates a possible coded system of colours for the products represented in the stripes, as the various varieties of maize and potatoes produced in the ayllu of Q'ero, as well as the different colours of llama fleece reared there. She even notes the use of certain colours in the coded system of the food bag as associated with family lines. She confirms, too, that the information recorded nowadays on the food bags was previously recorded on the kipu cords within the living memory of the older residents of Q'ero. This information, concerning ayllu production, was presented by the cord-keepers of Q'ero to the outside authorities who visited them on occasion.

Might I tentatively suggest that the poncho stripes, called "lista" in Qaqachaka, may also have expressed similar domains of knowledge to those annotated on the historical kipu or chinu cords? This would presumably have occurred during the period of cultural change, from an older mnemonic system to the introduction of modern writing in the programmes of enforced literacy in the newly built schools of Qaqachaka. There are clues in Qaqachaka, as there are in Macha, that family lines are marked by certain colours in the stripes, as they were once in the various kipu cords. There are also clues that certain products of the ayllu may have been colour-coded into the stripes of the poncho, in the same way that they are always recited in a certain sequence in the food libations, as modern intertexts of the older kipu. Doña Lucía confirmed to us how:

List ukat, aka maq'añaspa,	This stripe could be the food products,
aka ch'uqïspa,	this one could be potatoes,
ukat akaru tunqüsp, tirijüsp,	then this one could be maize, wheat, beans, then
jawasäsp, ukat yaranüsp,	barley,
uk"amasjipï,	thus it is, then,
surtiñans uk"ampinï.	even in the libations it is so.

As yet, however, we have not found such a clearcut relationship between the lista stripes of the man's poncho in Qaqachaka and the older system of counting by kipu that Silverman-Proust has encountered in Q'ero in Peru.[9] It is not common practice in Qaqachaka, either, to extend the chinu threads of a poncho into a fringed border, like those of neighbouring regions, to suggest even more pertinently, visually at least, the appearance of the coloured pendulant cords of a kipu device. Such fringes do still figure, however, on the special ponchos used by the ayllu authorities of Qaqachaka when they take office, those who might have once presented such coded information to the external authorities.

The poncho and mantle compared as gendered garments

At a more general level, however, it seems likely that the preponderance of lista stripes in the man's poncho and their underplaying in the woman's mantle is related to important gendered differences to do with their respective functions: on the one hand, of representing a coded system of information on ayllu production for outer consumption, and, on the other, of representing the inner resources of the ayllu as a more figurative form of beauty and aesthetics. Might we tease out this distinction even further, to suggest that an essential gendered difference between the two garments might lie in a differential emphasis in the man's poncho on "production" and in the woman's mantle on "reproduction"? Qaqas themselves do suggest such a distinction when they differentiate between men who, like silver, enter into circulation and participate in the productive cycles of external exchange, whereas, women, like gold, embody the wealth that grows within, in the bowels of the earth of their ayllu. Doña Lucía also points out that since the poncho is "flat" it can only represent food as the result of men's agricultural work. Whereas, she says, the woman's mantle with its "standing up" salta design represents in more general terms "all of the blessings that the earth provides, in animals and food products, and even in birds".

The men's ponchos with their lista stripes do seem to mediate a more abstract and codified system of representing the elements of ayllu production than the women's mantles, in both agricultural and herding domains. This information is in turn displayed by men, who since colonial times have been the named heads of households, the named mediators between the inner ayllu and the outer world of the external market system. Historical evidence suggests that male kipu-keepers, the *kipukamayuq* of the region, once presented their knotted cords, with their detailed inventory of ayllu production, to an external system of authority. Perhaps, in a similar way, modern Qaqa men might still be displaying in their poncho garments "lists" of items for both internal and external consumption. That being so, a man also readily acknowledges that his productive work in farming agricultural produce and earning money from the market-place is, finally and inevitably, given up to his wife, to deposit in the household stores, where she will control it.

Besides their powers of production, men's powers of reproduction and auto-genesis are also represented in the ponchos that they wear. It seems possible, for example, that more personalised patrilineal family lines, the chacha kasta, are revealed by their colour-coding as owning certain sets of ayllu produce. In the colour-coding of the stripes, too, there seems to be embedded information about the seminal nature of male reproductive and generative powers. But I would argue that representations of these overtly male powers are underplayed in the poncho as compared to the colourful display of women's reproductive and generative powers in the excessively red and blood-like salta designs of the mantle. The modern association of the stripes in a man's poncho with the historical kipu cords does remind us of the historical association of men with the writing of such texts, but it is a woman weaver who is defining this association, and she does not give it a high status. Overall, I would argue that, in her woven poncho, a woman weaver is defining men in her own image.

There are other important reasons why a woman weaver may underplay male reproductive powers in the poncho as a garment. According to a gendered system of metaphysics, women are believed to think "with their hearts". As the female locus of thought, intelligence, and memory, the heart is believed to be the source of their songs and their weaving designs. The heart is viewed as a mass of concentrated blood and breath and is a locus of transformation. It is the essence of their femaleness. And it is the mantle as a garment of dress that wraps that part of their bodies which encloses their hearts. By contrast, a man is believed to think "with his head". As each individual woman's first blood flow initiated her greater creative powers of weaving, so her continuing blood flow, like her later salta designs, marks the memory of the birth of the new Inka sun god in the region, the memories of which are held in her heart. Similarly, a man's equivalent powers are believed to reside in the spirit in his head, only mediated through the sacrifical blood ink with which he once wrote, in memory of the same Inka sun god. His poncho as a garment of dress wraps only his body. It is, in fact, only when men knit headgear for themselves that we find any similar degree of expression of their respective powers of virility, but this will be the subject of another essay.

Conclusion

Weaving in Qaqachaka is a necessary form of productive activity for both men and women. It is functional in the productive domain of household tasks, as well as in the social and cultural obligations of a married couple toward each other and toward their kin and affines for the rest of their married lives. However, I have argued here that the wider interpretation of the significance of weaving within Andean cultures must take into account not only the various aspects of weaving as a gendered activity but also weaving as a part of a multi-layered and intertextual discourse which is also gendered. I have therefore argued against the interpretation of the proprietorship of land and its products or of the animal herds, the means and relations of production that make weaving possible, according to an exclusively male discourse or one that is external to the culture. In listening instead to the alternative layers of gendered discourse in Qaqachaka, most especially to what women say about their work as weavers and its significance, we become aware of other levels of action and meaning: weaving as work or as exchange, weaving as production or as a part of reproductive and transformatory processes, weaving as an art of the hand with its own aesthetic and information system embedded in it—each forming a separate but interrelated part of a gendered vernacular discourse.

When we return to the main issue here, the gendering of such activities as weaving and the writing of texts according to a supposed hierarchy, then we cannot ignore the evidence from Andean history, nor can we ignore the Andean present. However, the most challenging evidence that confronts us emerges from women's own discourse about their weavings. In weaving garments such as the mantle for herself and the poncho for her menfolk, it is a woman weaver who defines through her work the limits and obligations of each gender as a social construction. She does so through a symbolic language, a means of cultural and ideological production continually re-invented from generation to generation, which defines her own place of power in the inner and domestic domain of the ayllu, and her husband's place of power on the periphery and outside of it. In her weavings, a woman not only invents the symbolic language to express the metaphysical postulates of Qaqa society, but, by manipulating the woven texts of such gendered garments, she is able to counter-pose the two different orders of gendered activity and their relative powers of production, reproduction, and creative intelligence. If any hierarchy exists at all within this symbolic domain controlled by women, then surely it is one in which women define for themselves the central place of power, and only then do they make men in their own image.

ACKNOWLEDGMENTS   This essay emerged from a paper given originally to the anthropology workshop on "Gender relations, work and proprietorship among the indigenous peoples of South America" held on 7th–8th December 1990, at the Institute of Latin American Studies, University of London, and from a departmental seminar given to the Department of Anthropology at the University of St Andrews, Scotland, in February 1991. Thanks to Nicole Bourque, Tristan Platt, Penny Dransart, Peter Gow, Joanna Overing, and Rosaleen Howard-Malverde for their comments. Of all the weavers of Qaqachaka whose words I remember here, special thanks to doña Guadalupe Colque Quispe, doña Bernaldita Quispe Colque, doña Juana Ayka Colque, doña Nicolasa Ayka, doña Mauricia Mamani Choque, and most especially doña Lucía Quispe Choque, doña Asunta Arias Tarki, and doña María Ayka Llanque. Thanks also to Juan de Dios Yapita, for the fieldwork we did together and the discussions we had afterward about it. The paper would not have been written at all without him.

Notes

1. See, for example, Watson Franke 1974 on this distinction in the Guajiro culture of Colombia; March 1983 on the Buddhist Tamang of Tibet; Niessen 1985 on the Toba Batak of Indonesia; Messick 1987 on the Islamic Berbers of Azrou, Morocco; and Bergren 1983 on ancient Greece.

2. Historically, the poncho as an item of dress was in use by the Spanish in the seventeenth century, although the older Andean tunic (*urk"u*), or short poncho (*q"awa*), continued to be worn underneath (Money 1966, cited in Barriga Barahona 1981). The poncho's origin is usually attributed to the Araucanians, or Mapuche, who are said to have invented it after the introduction of the horse. I should like to thank Penny Dransart for drawing my attention to this reference.

3. I have used the translation 'blood red' for the Aymara *wila*, a term that denotes both blood and its scarlet colour. There are, however, several other colour terms that refer to the distinct colours of different types of blood: the blood at birth, menstrual blood, and so on. There are also taboos on using these colour terms in certain contexts.

4. For a more technical definition of *chinu*, see Gavilán and Ulloa 1992: 123ff.

5. Literally: 'Get up then, damn you, it should arrive over (the earth) then, damn it'.

6. Sophie Desrosiers (1988) discusses the horizontality of women's garments and the vertically of men's garments.

7. *Saya* in everyday parlance may also refer to the two moiety-like configurations of Qaqachaka, *patxasaya*, meaning 'upper' moiety and *manq"asaya*, meaning 'lower' moiety. The term "saya" is also used in relation to the ritual battles once held in the main plaza, when the dancing groups of warriors entering the four corners of the plaza were referred to as four "saya" of warriors.

8. For a historical perspective on the gendered use of horizontal and vertical bands of colour in styles of dress, see the description of the *succullu* ritual in Bouysse-Cassagne 1987: 233ff.

9. However, in a comparative study, in the lakeside community of Chukiñapi in the department of La Paz, we have found similar analogies between the food products and the coding of colours in the textile stripes (see Arnold et al., in press).

INSIDE THE TEXT: PROCESSES OF TEXTUALISATION IN WRITTEN QUECHUA DISCOURSE

Willem F. H. Adelaar

Spatial Reference and Speaker Orientation in Early Colonial Quechua

The introduction of writing constitutes a major landmark in the history of a language. When language is transmitted through writing, the mechanisms governing the production and the interpretation of speech are different from those that obtain in an oral communication process. If the introduction of writing is successful, two separate traditions may arise, one of which is the direct continuation of the existing practice of oral transmission. For the second tradition, that of written speech transmission, to develop, a series of adjustments is required in the language system. These adjustments occur both at the morphological and at the lexical levels. Subsequently, the interaction of the two traditions may result in a number of new varieties combining elements of both. Such complex configurations of several co-existing and interrelated traditions are found in the national languages of today's modern nations.

In written communication, knowledge of the situation surrounding the speech event can be absent. The identity of the participants, in particular of the addressee but also of the speaker-writer, is not self-evident, as it usually is in oral speech events. In spoken language, the categories space and time are identified in relation to the place of speaking and the moment of speaking. When language is written, information about space and time has to be presented in a different, more precise way. A producer of written speech not only must refer to time or location in the situation described, he

135

may also feel compelled to refer to locations in the text. The latter tendency is less prominent in oral speech.

The revolutionary character of the introduction of writing must be mitigated somewhat. Traditional societies usually entertain a practice of oral transmission of narrative discourse. Narratives are often presented in a standardised way and must be understood in a context unrelated to the place and the time of speaking. As in the case of written text, some adjustments with respect to plain oral communication are in order, and do, in fact, occur. It is not unusual for an incipient writing tradition to inherit some of the mechanisms that separate narrative discourse from plain oral communication.[1]

Incipient literary tradition and the Huarochirí document

In the specific cases of Quechua and other languages of the Andean region, writing was introduced abruptly with the arrival of the Spanish conquerors. A tradition of oral transmission of texts was in existence. Discursive features of this oral tradition may have set the path for changes in the language that later accompanied the shaping of a written linguistic practice. A strong literary tradition never developed in any of the Andean languages, most written texts being more or less direct reflections of oral speech.[2] Nevertheless, a written tradition in its incipient stage can be observed in one of the longest and oldest running texts available in Quechua, a document originating from the province of Huarochirí, not far from Lima. It was written on behalf of one of the most zealous of Peru's idolatry crusaders, Francisco de Avila.[3] The Huarochirí document has been dated 1608 (Acosta 1987).

The authorship of the Huarochirí document remains in doubt. Apparently, the author or authors deliberately chose to remain anonymous. Except for a marginal note on one of the pages of the manuscript, any reference to a possible authorship is avoided. Whoever wrote the text frequently uses the inclusive plural "we" form, dealing with his audience of readers, one might say, as if they were his co-authors.[4]

In chapters 20 and 21 of the Huarochirí document, a principal role is played by one of Avila's most efficient assistants, don Cristóbal Choquecaxa. The vivid description of his adventures is full of detail from personal experience and would make him a good candidate for the authorship of the document.[5] If he were indeed the author, Choquecaxa would have made efforts deliberately to hide his identity. The stories concerning him were all written in the third person and in the hearsay form.[6] In normal speech, use of the hearsay form indicates that the speaker disclaims having witnessed the events he narrates.

The role of the speaker in Quechua discourse

In a Quechua discourse, speakers are compelled to express certain aspects of their relationship to the events they describe. The grammatical markers used to such effects cannot be suppressed from the utterance without bringing about substantial modifications in meaning, if the utterance remains acceptable at all. It follows from the above that Quechua grammar requires a specification of the speaker-event relation, even when the speaker's involvement in the event or his identity become less important or even irrelevant. For a language with an oral tradition this is not surprising. Since there is always a speaker who pronounces the discourse or a narrator who tells the story, there is no reason not to take note of the speaker's or narrator's attitude toward the event described, his involvement in the action referred to, and so on. But as soon as the oral tradition is replaced by written text, the need may be felt to eliminate all reference to the speaker's identity. One may wish to leave unspecified the speaker's feelings or his participation in the activity described in order to give the text a general truth value. The compulsory use of grammatical markers referring to such categories may then be experienced as superfluous or even bothersome.

When a written tradition is about to develop, grammatical markers referring to the speaker's involvement in the event are either likely to disappear, or to become merely decorative and fixed. Alternatively, their functions may change. There are at the least two aspects in which the identity of the speaker and his experience play an essential role in the make-up of a Quechua sentence. One of them has to do with the source of the information supplied, which can be from personal experience or observation, from hearsay or inference, or simply be a matter of conjecture. Since the grammatical markers used to these effects are found in virtually every single sentence, the speaker is constantly compelled to specify the degree of certainty and the source of his contentions.[7] A second speaker-related element that must be explicitly indicated in the discourse is his location in space with regard to the events described. In Quechua, events have to be specified for certain spatial features for which the position of the speaker at the moment of utterance serves as a point of orientation. In what follows I will briefly discuss the different ways in which this phenomenon is dealt with in the Huarochirí document. Two categories, one syntactic and one morphological, will receive particular attention.

The role of the proximal demonstrative pronoun

Two demonstrative pronouns, *cay* and *chay*, occur in the language of the Huarochirí document. They correspond roughly to English 'this' or 'this place' and 'that' or 'that place', respectively.[8] There are no separate roots for spatial adverbs such as 'here', 'there', and 'over there'. Instead, the demonstratives are used in combination with the locative (*caypi* 'here', *chaypi* 'there') or directional case markers (*cayman* 'hither', *chayman* 'thither'; *caymanta* 'hence', *chaymanta* 'thence').

As a first approximation, *cay* can be characterised as "proximal" ("place of the speaker", "object near the speaker"), whereas *chay* is "non-proximal" ("any place but that of the speaker", "object not near the speaker"). The proximal demonstrative *cay* does not constitute an obligatory element in the sense that a grammatical marker would be. It can be replaced by the more neutral *chay*, or be omitted altogether. As a deictic element, however, it is essential for reference to the location of the speaker.

The Huarochirí document contains many passages that are direct quotations from a grammatical point of view. In Andean languages, such as Quechua, the use of quotations is not a stylistic option but a grammatical necessity. Verbs are sub-categorised for the type of complement they require.[9] In the language of the Huarochirí document, as in most conservative dialects of Quechua, the verb *ñi-* 'to say; to consider; to intend' requires a direct quotation as its complement. Semantically, *ñi-* refers not just to verbal communication but to mental activities as well. The content of such a mental activity is presented as a quotation that has the same shape as would have a stretch of speech actually pronounced by the subject of *ñi-*. The following example illustrates this:

(1)   chaysi quiquillantac huc huata chica ñoñonhuan causachircan "pip churinh
      *cay*ca" ñispa. (chap. 2, sec. 12)[10]

   [For about a year she kept him alive with her own breast, while saying: "Whose
   son could *this* be"? *Or:* For about a year she kept him alive with her own breast,
   wondering whose son he could be.]

In quotations of thoughts, as illustrated in (1), the place-of-speaker function of the proximal pronoun *cay* is preserved in the sense that the narrator chooses as a point of reference the location of the speaker he quotes. Embedded quotations are treated as independant utterances in their own right, reflecting the structure of such full sentences in which the narrator would describe his own experiences. No relevance is accorded to the fact that the quoted speaker does not actually speak.

The following example refers to actual speech uttered by two distinct personages. As is often the case in Quechua, one direct quotation is embedded within the other:

(2)   chaysi yayantaca "yaya, *cay*pim huc huaccha 'yayaiquicta alliyachisac' ñimuan"
      ñispa villarcan. (chap. 5, sec. 48)

   [She told her father: "Father, there is a poor man *here* who says to me: 'I shall
   cure your father' ".]

In portions of the text that are not quotations, the speaker orientation of *cay* is preserved when there is a reference to the geographical point at which the writing of the text occurs. In some cases, the place of writing is explicitly mentioned; in others, it is not. See, for instance, example (3):

(3)   chaysi chay quintecunaca anchatac *cay* checacunacta chicnircan. (chap. 11, sec.
      153)

   [Those Quintis held *these* Checas in extreme contempt. *Or:* The Quintis there
   held the Checas *here* in extreme contempt.]

We know from other sources that the text was probably written in the *reducción* village of San Damián de Checas, where the survivors of the Checa nation had been brought together. At the moment of writing, the author was presumably surrounded by Checas. Whence his use of the expression "these Checas". The Quintis, on their side, lived near the town of Huarochirí, a considerable distance away. A rather remarkable example in which knowledge of the place of writing is a prerequisite is (4):

(4) *cay*cunaca riman ñispa "hunanchanchic 'ychach ari chay' ". (chap. 4, sec. 35)

> [*These* ones speak of it saying: 'We believe that such may actually be the case'.
> *Or*: The local people *here* comment on it, saying that they believe that such may
> actually be the case.]

In examples such as the above, it is not always evident which area functions as the domain of speaker orientation. It requires imagination to determine the location of the narrator and find out which people surrounded him at the moment of writing, a difficulty that will not normally arise in a situation of oral communication.

Proximal *cay* is frequently found in expressions referring to extensive areas that include the place of writing. This fact is illustrated in (5) and (6):

(5) chaysi *cay* quitipi ancha hunay puricorcan ancha ahca llactacunacta runactapas llollachispa. (chap. 2, sec. 28)

> [For a long time he wandered about in *this* province deceiving many gods and people.]

(6) *cay* llactacunaman ñatac miticamurcan. (chap. 2, sec. 28)

> [He fled towards *these* communities.]

In these cases, the area is not specified. The writer is confident that his readers will understand which area is meant. *Cay quiti* 'this region' and *cay llactacuna* 'these communities', 'this region', refer to highland provinces, or simply to the high Andean region in general, as opposed to the lowlands near the ocean. Even when the narrator maintains a certain distance from what he is writing, he is constantly aware of the place where he finds himself at the moment of his writing.

Beside this geographically motivated use of the proximal pronoun, we can also observe a text-adapted version of it. The demonstrative *cay* may, in fact, mean 'this place in the text', as in (7) and (8):

(7) *cay*pim churani cay huc yayayuc guarocheri ñiscap machoncunap causascanta. (preface, sec. 2)

> [*Here* (in the text) I put (write down) the traditions of the forefathers of the people of Huarochirí, who descend from a common ancestor.]

(8) *cay*mantam ñatac pariacacap pacarimuscan callarinca. (chap. 5, title)

> [From *here* (in the text) will start (the story of) Pariacaca's beginnings.]

The demonstrative *cay* frequently refers to what follows in the text. Illustrative examples are (9) and (10). Example (9) is a recurrent expression in the document of Huarochirí:

(9) chay simiri *cay*mi. (chap. 3, sec. 29)

> [That story is *this*. *Or:* That story is as follows. *Or: This* is how the story goes.]

(10) *cay*tam *cay*saua quillcasson. (chap. 20, sec. 259)

> [*This* we shall write down *here*after.]

The demonstrative *cay* may also refer to the preceding section of the text, 'what we have just been talking about', 'what we have just explained', as in (11):

(11) *cay* isconnin capitulopi . . . (chap. 10, sec. 141)

[In *this* ninth chapter (just finished) . . .]

(12) *cay cay*cunacta villanacuptinsi chay huatyacuri ñisca huyarcan. (chap. 5, sec. 46)

[While they told each other all *these* things, Huatyacuri was listening.]

In cases of recurrent reference to several persons or entities of more or less equal importance, *cay* can be used in order to keep the attention fixed on the principal topic of the account. Digressions or asides are characterised by the presence of *chay*, the main thread of the account by *cay*:

(13) chaymantas pariacacaca *cay* huallallo caruinchocta atipac rispas . . . (chap. 8, sec. 98)

[Then, when Pariacaca set out in order to defeat *this* Huallallo Caruincho . . .]

The use of *cay* is rather consistent. Apart from the original deictic place-of-speaker reference, we find several uses that fit well in a narrative tradition, either oral or written. In some cases, *cay* refers explicitly to a place in the text. This fact may be interpreted as a first adjustment to the needs of written language. The demonstrative *cay* is more marked semantically than *chay* and less frequent. The function of *chay* varies from a clearly deictic one to something near to a definite article in English.

The role of the verbal derivational marker -*mu*-

The one grammatical marker that implies reference to the location of the speaker is the verbal suffix -*mu*-. Like the other verbal affixes traditionally described as derivational,[11] it is inserted between the verbal root and the endings referring to tense, mood, and person. The suffix -*mu*- is extremely frequent. Although Quechua dialects may differ substantially in their morphology, the suffix -*mu*- is not known to be absent from any of them. Also, its use is quite constant throughout the dialects.

Verbs that imply motion in a particular direction are obligatorily marked with -*mu*- if the motion to which they refer is directed toward the speaker. Alternatively, a narrator may choose a point of reference different from his own location to which motion denoted by a verb with -*mu*- is directed. In an unmarked situation, the location of the speaker will be automatically interpreted as the point of reference for -*mu*-.[12]

The absence of -*mu*- from a verb referring to a change of location implies a movement away from the speaker or a movement that is neutral with respect to the location of the speaker. The following elementary examples illustrate the way movement toward the speaker and its opposite are indicated in present-day Quechua dialects:

(14) apa*mu*y   apay

   '*Bring* it (to me)!'   'Take it away (from me)!'

(15) apa*muy kay*man   *apay kayman

   '*Bring* it *here* (to me)!'   (ungrammatical expression)

The presence of a noun phrase specifying direction toward the speaker (e.g., *kayman* 'hither', *kay llaqtaman* 'to this village or town') may accompany a verb with -*mu*-, but can never replace it. This is shown in (15), where the expression *kayman* 'hither' can be combined with *apamuy* but not with *apay*.

The semantic contrast emerging from the absence or presence of -*mu*- is comparable to the difference in meaning that separates the members of the lexical pair *ri-/hamu-*. The verbs *ri-* and *hamu-* are used in the southern Quechua dialects and in Huarochirí Quechua with the meanings 'to go' and 'to come', respectively.[13] The verb pairs *ri-/hamu-* and *apa-/apamu-* are reminiscent of the Spanish lexical pairs *ir/venir* and *llevar/traer*. Both in Quechua and in Spanish, the semantic contrast is mainly based on the criterion of whether or not there is a motion toward the speaker.

In Quechua, the use of -*mu*- in its function of indicating direction towards the speaker is not restricted to events referring to real movements. It can also manifest itself in events that imply some sort of a psychological approach to the speaker. As a result of such an event, the subject of the verb that contains -*mu*- becomes more visible or otherwise perceptible to the speaker than it was before the event took place. Verb stems that are frequently used in this way in the Huarochirí document are listed under (16):

(16) non-existing   to existing   pacari*mu*- 'come into existence' (chap. 3, sec. 36)

   not living   to living   causari*mu*- 'revive' (chap. 1, sec. 4)
                                         yuri*mu*- 'be born' (chap. 5, sec. 51)
   not active   to active   pucori*mu*- 'start to blow (of wind)' (chap. 18, sec. 225)
   invisible   to visible   llocsichi*mu*- 'cause to come to light'; 'cause to come out' (chap. 6, sec. 83)
                                         ricuri*mu*- 'appear' (chap. 13, sec. 175)
   silent   to speaking   rimari*mu*- 'speak up (in a meeting or after silence)' (chap. 3, sec. 30)
   rolled-up   to spread out   pahya*mu*- 'explode', 'break out' (chap. 31, sec. 435)
   few   to numerous   mirari*mu*- 'increase in number' (chap. 3, sec. 34)

A second, but optional use of -*mu*- is found with verbs that do not primarily refer to motion in a particular direction. With such verbs, -*mu*- refers to a definite place at a substantial distance from the speaker, usually involving a previous movement from the speaker's location to that place. At the same time, there is the suggestion of a circular movement, as the effects of the action referred to are expected somehow to revert to the speaker. The suffix *-mu-* in these cases can be translated as 'there', 'over there', or 'where I am telling you'.

This second function of *-mu-* is less frequent and not obligatory. If a noun phrase referring to a place indicated by *-mu-* is added to the verb, the presence of the suffix is no longer required. It is a different situation from that which obtains when *-mu-* occurs in its 'direction toward the speaker' function. As we have seen, agreement with a possible directional noun phrase is obligatory in the latter.[14]

In what follows, several characteristic instances of *-mu-* as it occurs in the Huarochirí document will be discussed. In them, the use of the marker *-mu-* is quite similar to that in present-day dialects of Quechua. It is best preserved in direct quotations. Examples (17) and (18) illustrate the function of speaker-directed motion of *-mu-*; (17) also contains the lexical counterpart of *-mu-*, the verb *hamu-*:

(17) huc atoc añas huarminhuan *hamu*nca, chaymi huc huchoylla porongollapi ashuanta apa*mu*nca. (chap. 5, sec. 58-59)

   [A fox and his wife, a skunk, will *come* this way. They will *bring* 'chicha' in a small jar.]

(18) pana cauellaca, *cay*man cahuaycu*mu*ay. (chap. 2, sec. 17)

   [Sister Cauillaca, please look at me *here*!]

In (18), *cahuaycu-* 'to look into a particular direction' is treated as a verb of motion as a result of the presence of the suffix *-ycu-*. It should be observed that there is no strict sub-categorisation of the verb class based on the motion vs. non-motion distinction. Some verbs, such as *chaya-* 'to reach, to arrive, to hit' can be used both as motion and as non-motion verbs. *Cahua-* 'to look' becomes a motion verb through the extension of the stem by means of the suffix *-ycu-*.

The use of *-mu-* in the verbs listed in (16), which refer to an increase in perceptibility, are frequently found in the Huarochirí document. As we have seen, such verbs can denote change, appearance or sudden diffusion. They occur in direct quotations, as well as in the embedding narrative:

(19) cayaminchallam yuri*mu*nca. (chap. 5, sec. 51)

   [One of these days his birth will take place.]

(20) chay llamaca runa yna rimari*mu*spa ñispa ñircan . . . (chap. 3, sec. 30)

   [The llama suddenly began to speak like a human being and said . . .]

Example sentences (21) to (23) from the Huarochirí document illustrate the use of *-mu-* referring to an action that occurs at an indicated place at a distance from the speaker ("action over there"). It occurs both in quotations and in the main narrative:

(21) cayallatacmi chaypi chasquechi*mu*son. (chap. 9, sec. 128)

   [*There* tomorrow we shall make him receive them.]

(22) huatyacori sutioc pariacacap churin ñiscatac ñaupaclla ricu*mu*orca[15] yacha*mu*rca. (chap. 5, sec. 38)

   [Huatyacuri, Pariacaca's son was the first to (go and) see him *there* and learn about him *there*.]

(23) ña cay rarcacta pichayta puchoca*mu*spari runacunacta anchapunis combidac carcan saracta purotucta. (chap. 7, sec. 94)

[After having finished this canal-cleaning *there*, they would invite the people to lots of maize and beans.]

The following example (24) consists of two correlative clauses, one of which functions as an accessory background description to the other one. Both verbs contain -*mu*- in its "action over there" meaning, even though the accessory verb is a verb of motion. It illustrates the absence of a clear-cut lexical division between motion verbs and non-motion verbs in Quechua (both verbs behaving like non-motion verbs):

(24) maypacham sieneguillaman hurayco*mu*nchic chay horcucta, chaypis poño-*mu*rca. (chap. 5, sec. 42)

[Where there is a mountain *which we pass when* we go down to Cieneguilla, *that is where* he slept.]

Example (25) is a clear illustration of the circular movement associated with the "action over there" reading. It is also found in present-day Quechua dialects and can be glossed as 'to go and act over there and then come back':[16]

(25) rarcactam picha*mu*ni, padre, taquecusac upiacusac. (chap. 7, sec. 95)

[We have *been to* clean the irrigation canal, father. Now we shall dance and drink.]

Of greater importance for the concept of speaker orientation and its fate in a written environment are those instances of -*mu*- (and *hamu*-) that indicate 'direction toward the speaker' in passages that are not part of a direct quotation. Logically, in such cases -*mu*- should refer to the place of writing, but this is not always the case because in narratives the orientation point for -*mu*- can be transferred to the principal site of action—that is, the place where the speaker wants his audience and himself to imagine themselves as being. Nevertheless, in the Huarochirí document, the author is still very conscious about his "place of writing" and seems confused as to which place should be chosen as an orientation point in individual instances. The use of -*mu*- in relation to shifting orientation points is in fact quite inconsistent and unpredictable. This is symptomatic of an incipient literary tradition in which the role of the narrator cannot yet be duly disposed of.

Writer orientation has as its domain the community of San Damián de Checas as opposed to other communities in the area, or it may be centred in the Huarochirí highlands in contrast to the coastal lowlands or the Anti (Huanca) region further inland. There is, however, an additional complication which originates from the mythical character of most of the Huarochirí narrative. Mythical places may be less well defined than concrete, geographically defined locations frequented by the author.

In chapter 2, the myth of Cuniraya, who follows Cauillaca from the meeting at Anchicocha to the ocean shore, contains no instances of -*mu*- until the ocean is reached. Anchicocha, situated in the highlands like San Damián, is used as the point of orientation. An alternative explanation would be that the author treats

Anchicocha and San Damián in the same way because both places are at equal distances from the sea. Sentences (26a–d) describe Cuniraya's arrival at the ocean shore and what happened subsequently. Instances of -*mu*- suddenly become frequent:

(26a) cocha patapi chayaspaca . . . pachacamacñicman cuti*mu*rcan. (chap. 2, sec. 27)

[Having reached the seashore, he turned back toward Pachacamac (*writer's direction*).]

(26b) chaymantas chay cuniraya viracocha ñiscaca miti*mu*rca cocha patañicta. (chap. 2, sec. 27)

[Then Cuniraya Viracocha fled along the seashore . . .]

(26c) ancha piñaspa cati*mu*rcan. (chap. 2, sec. 27)

[Being very angry she *came* running after him. (as 26b).]

(26d) cay llactacunaman ñatac miti*camu*rcan. (cf. 6). (chap. 2, sec. 28).

[He fled *toward these* communities . . .]

The inland movements exemplified in (26a) and (26d) have -*mu*-, whereas movements toward the sea remain unmarked. However, in the passage referring to the movements of the protagonists along the seashore away from the sanctuary of Pachacamac the author also uses -*mu*-. It appears as if, in search of a new orientation point, he imagined that he were looking at Pachacamac from a distance, seeing the heroes coming toward him. The "action over there" interpretation can be excluded because there is no reference to a definite location, no previous movement toward it, and no circularity.

In chapter 5, we observe a sudden change in the point of reference for speaker orientation, which is clearly selected on the basis of a shift in the focus of the narrative. Speaker-directedness is indicated by the lexical verbal expression *hamu*-, whose semantic value is similar to that of the affix -*mu*-. In (27a), the verb *hamu*- has the connotation of 'to appear on the scene' (invisible to visible), a semantic interpretation parallel to that of the affix -*mu*- in (16). First, people are said to come from different places to visit the semi-deity Tamtañamca at Anchicocha. The orientation point is Anchicocha, not San Damián:

(27a) cay runacta chica alli causascanta ricuspas tucoy hinantin llactacunamanta *hamu*spa yupaicharcan mucharcan. (chap. 5, sec. 40)

[Because they saw how well this man lived, people *came* from all communities to honour and worship him.]

Then, Huatyacuri approaches the site coming from the sea:

(27b) chaysi cay huatyacurica chay pacha ura cochañicmanta *hamu*spa . . . (chap. 5, sec. 42)

[At that time, Huatyacuri was *com*ing from the lowlands near the sea and . . .]

And, eventually, the orientation point is transferred to the spot where Huatyacuri is resting. Two foxes approach from either side:

(27c) huc hatocca uramanta *amu*sca hocri hanacmanta *amu*scatac, chaysi chaypi
pactalla tincuspas . . . (chap. 5, sec. 42)

A fox *came* from below and another one *came* from above. They met each other
there halfway and . . .

Chapter 6 describes Pariacaca's visit to the town of Huarochirí. In it, the author
takes care to indicate that Huarochirí is not his (the author's) location. Obviously, his
perspective is from San Damián, the place of writing. All motion toward Huarochirí
and, subsequently, to the village of the Cupara near San Lorenzo de Quinti is expressed
by means of verbs that do not contain -*mu*-. Interestingly enough, the avoidance of
-*mu*- is even maintained in the description of an irrigation canal that emerges from the
mountain at San Lorenzo de Quinti:

(28a) cay pucyum canan san lorenço hanacnin aton orcomanta llocsircan. (chap. 6,
sec. 81)

[This well now emerged from a high mountain above San Lorenzo.]

The verb *llocsircan* 'it emerged' is associated with an act of appearance, "invisible
to visible", by itself a sufficient ground for -*mu*- assignment. Apparently, the author
wishes to stress that the canal and its source are miles away from his own location. He
cannot see them from where he writes. Therefore, he leaves -*mu*- aside. On the
other hand, the author seems to know the place from his own observation, a fact
shown by his use of the sentential suffix -*m* (in *pucyum*). Its presence indicates first-hand
information.

Later on, the author tells us how the same canal is dug out by animals. At that
moment, his observation point shifts to the foot of the mountain from which the canal
takes its source. He now uses -*mu*- in every verb of motion in function of his new
imaginary perspective. The following sentences describe the fox's part in the digging
of the canal:

(28b) yna ñaupa*mu*spa ña chaupicta san lorenço hanacnin hurcucta seque*mu*ptinsi
concayllapi huc yutuca "pisc, pisc" ñispa pahuari*mu*rcan, chaysi chay atocca
"huac" ñispa muspaspa huraman hurma*mu*rcan. (chap. 6, sec. 87)

[As he [the fox] was leading onward and had proceeded halfway up the
mountain above San Lorenzo, marking out the course (of the canal), a partridge
suddenly flew up and said "pisk"! Then, the fox said "wak"!, lost his foothold
and fell to a lower level.]

A very unexpected change in the observation point of the narrator can be seen in
the following examples, taken from a passage in chapter 8. It tells the story of the
Pariacaca brothers meeting a man on his way to sacrifice his son to Huallallo
Caruincho. At first, the orientation point is the mythical place of the meeting, where
the Pariacacas are playing:

(29a) chaysi chay pacha huc runaca huacacuspa *hamu*rcan huc churinta apaspa. (chap.
8, sec. 99)

[At that time, a man *came* along crying, carrying one of his sons.]

(29b) mancharispa tucuy apa*mu*scanta corcan. (chap. 8, sec. 101)

> [Being scared, he gave them everything he had *brought* with him.]

Then, the orientation point is transferred to the village where the man lives (29c). The reason for this may be that the author feels a closer geographic association between that man's village and his own place than between the latter and the location of the mythical scene high up in the mountains to which he is referring. The association may be one of altitude or climatological conditions:

(29c) chaymantas chay runaca cuti*mo*rcan churinta apacospa. (chap. 8, sec. 101)

> [Then that man returned home (literally, *came back*), carrying his child.]

Subsequently, the man returns to the place where he had previously met the Pariacaca brothers. The verb is no longer marked with -*mu*-, showing that the real orientation point (place of speaker/writer) has ultimately prevailed over the mythical orientation point (place of main scene in narrative):

(29d) ynaspas ñatac pihcantin ponchaomanta ñatac chay pariacacap simincama cutircan. (chap. 8, sec. 102)

> [And so he returned (to that place) following the orders of Pariacaca.]

Conclusion

The way speaker orientation is dealt with in a text such as the Huarochirí document provides evidence of incipient adjustments to the requirements of writing. In the case of the proximal demonstrative pronoun, there are clear instances where proximity is established in terms of a location within the text. The use of the pronoun seems to obey a particular standard both for unmarked situations (location of the speaker/writer) and for specific text situations (location in the text, location in the thread of the narrative). On the other hand, the factors that dominate -*mu*-assignment to verbs of motion are much less well defined. There seems to be a conflict of tendencies between different perspectives that can be used. Either the place of writing may determine the presence of -*mu*- in a verb of motion or an imaginary observation point chosen by the author and liable to be abandoned at any moment may do so. Sometimes the author seems to be well aware of his present location and individual personality; at other times he forgets these and travels along with the heroes of his narrative to some place far away. It would not be correct to say that the orientation point for -*mu*- assignment in a narrative is always the location of the event in focus. Such may be the case for a moment, but there is a tendency for the author to shift his orientation point back to the place of writing. Since this can hardly be called functional in an anonymously written text, not intended to be place-bound nor person-bound, we may hold that -*mu*- assignment was still far from being well adjusted to the requirements of a written text. On the contrary, the contextual exigencies of actual speaking, in which the place of speaking is often highly relevant, seem to prevail. There is a discrepancy, then, between the degree of adaptation to text requirements of the pronominal system and direction marking in the verb. It is in the latter that the insecurity felt by the author becomes most conspicuous. That the pronominal system shows more advanced adjustments may be explained by the supposition that it is easier to manipulate and assign new meanings to lexical elements than to morphological categories.

To recapitulate, we may say that in early-seventeenth-century Quechua, a clear strategy for handling distinctions of speaker orientation in texts was not yet well developed. Yet, there existed tendencies that may have been indicative of possible future developments in case the language were to move toward a written tradition. One of these tendencies concerns the use of demonstratives for referring to parts of the text itself or to the thread of the narrative. Tentatively, another such tendency may have been the practice of temporarily replacing the speaker's location by the place of the event in focus as an orientation point for marking direction on the verb.

Notes

1. For a discussion of Quechua narrative discourse and some of its characteristics, see Howard-Malverde (1988, 1994) and Gutmann (1994).

2. It is not the case, however, of the theatre plays written in the seventeenth and eighteenth centuries (see Meneses 1983 and Mannheim 1991).

3. The document of Huarochirí has been published with an annotated English translation by Salomon and Urioste (1991). For a Spanish translation with a discussion of the historical background of the document, see Taylor (1987a) and Acosta (1987). The examples in this article were translated into English from the Dutch edition (Adelaar 1988).

4. In our view, the Andean inclusive plural must not be defined primarily in terms of its opposition with the exclusive first-person plural. More accurately, it refers to a sort of general group belonging as does *on* in French or "people" in English (Adelaar 1993).

5. For an analysis of the role played by Choquecaxa, see Kemper Columbus (1994).

6. In Quechua, hearsay is indicated by the presence of a sentential suffix *-s* or *-si*.

7. For a detailed discussion of evidentiality in the Huarochirí document, see Dedenbach-Salazar Sáenz (in this volume).

8. Huarochirí Quechua agrees with the northern Peruvian and Ecuadorian varieties of Quechua (corresponding to the Quechua IIB division in Torero's classification) in that it distinguishes only two degrees of distance in the demonstrative system (cf. Adelaar 1994d). Central and southern varieties of Peruvian Quechua distinguish three degrees, comparable to Spanish *este*, *ese*, and *aquel*. The demonstrative system of Pacaraos Quechua (Huaral, Lima) also encodes differences in altitude (Adelaar 1982).

9. For a more detailed treatment of quotations in Quechua and in other Andean languages, see Adelaar (1990).

10. Chapter 2, section 12: the section subdivision follows Salomon and Urioste's 1991 translation of the Huarochirí document.

11. The qualification of *-mu-* as a derivational affix follows an established usage of the linguistic literature on Quechua. From a strictly linguistic point of view, *-mu-* does not exhibit the characteristics of a derivational affix. For a discussion of this matter, see Adelaar (1994c).

12. The suffix *-mu-* and its functions have been discussed by Bills (1972) and by Van de Kerke and Muysken (1990). Virtually all reference grammars of specific Quechua dialects contain a section on *-mu-*. The most extensive one is found in Weber's (1989) analysis of

Huallaga Quechua. For a slightly different approach in terms of actant orientation and the centripetal-centrifugal opposition (*-mu-* being interpreted as centripetal), see Taylor (1990: 309–311; 1994: 60–61, 140).

13. In Huarochirí Quechua, the actual form is *amu-* (often written *hamu-*). In this respect, Huarochirí differs from most of the northern Peruvian and Ecuadorian varieties, which have *shamu-*.

14. The labels "cislocative" and "translocative" are frequently found in the linguistic literature on Quechua for the purpose of referring to the different uses of *-mu-*. Another possible label for the cislocative function would be "ventive", which is commonly used in Africanist studies.

15. *-mo* is an orthographic variant of *-mu-*.

16. At this point, not all occurrences of *-mu-* have yet been accounted for. The suffix *-mu-* may occur, for instance, with the verbs *ñi-* 'to say', as in *ñimuan* 'he says to me' (along with *ñihuan*, same meaning), or with *cu-/co-* 'to give', as in *cumurcan* 'he gave it to him' and *comuaspa* 'because (you) have given it to me'. It is not quite clear whether these instances of *-mu-* may be interpreted as 'action over there' or are due to lexicalised combinations of a particular suffix with a particular root. The combination of suffixes *-mua-* (*-mu-* + *-wa-*) could be an emphatic alternative for *-wa-* 'to me'. None of these possible explanations seems to account for all the attested cases.

9

SABINE DEDENBACH-SALAZAR SÁENZ

Point of View and Evidentiality in the Huarochirí Texts (Peru, 17th Century)

In this chapter, I shall look at some texts from the Peruvian seventeenth-century Huarochirí Quechua manuscript *Tradiciones de Huarochirí* (c. 1608). It is probable that these texts were narrated and written down by one or several Quechua speakers who had contact with Francisco de Avila or persons who knew him, but it is also possible that Avila himself copied and/or redacted these texts.[1] As we do not know much about the circumstances in which the texts came to be written down, an analysis of the discourse structure should help us get closer to the Quechua dialect used, to the narrators involved in their (re-)production, and to the quality of the texts as a collection of narratives and "ethnographic" and "testimonial" documents that originated in a non-literate society and yet became fixed in the written medium.

As the oldest known source on Andean culture written in an Andean language, the Huarochirí texts provide a starting point for the analysis of Andean verbal art. They date from a time when people first began to use the new medium of writing in order to express themselves and to convey information about their culture. As the author of these texts is unknown, the author-narrator-audience relationship has to be explored without a situational performative context, purely on the basis of the texts themselves.

Although at first sight they appear unique, these texts are in some ways typical of Andean traditional narrative: their content refers to ancient Andean beliefs, but already situated in a colonial setting; this is reflected in how language itself is used,[2] and in the very fact that the texts are written down. Thus these texts have methodological implications for the analysis and understanding of traditional Andean literature.

Here, I will concentrate on how the author-narrator(s) present(s) a certain point of view through the usage of evidential devices. Before entering into the discussion, I should like to look briefly at the state of research and clarify the concepts I use. With regard to the concept of "point of view", I have found Lanser's approach very stimulating, and her definition of the concept, as follows, useful for the present study:

> If we understand point of view to concern the relations between narrating subjects and the literary system which is the text-in-context, then we confront a complex network of interactions between author, narrator(s), characters, and audiences, both real and implied. At the very least, the notion of point of view subsumes those aspects of narrative structure that concern the mode of presenting and representing speech, perception, and event; the identities of those who speak and perceive; their relationships with one another and with the recipients of their discourses; their attitudes, statuses, personalities, and beliefs. Moreover, because narrative has the capacity to be multi-discursive . . . works of narrative often involve numerous subject/system relationships. In such cases, the textual perspective may become a superstructural synthesis of the various voices and perspectives—points of view—encoded in the discourse. (Lanser 1981: 13–14)

With respect to the relationship among the participants in the literary discourse, Lanser distinguishes "status", i.e., the relationship of the author with the literary act; "contact", i.e., the interaction between the narrator and the addressee; and "stance", i.e., the attitudes of the characters of the text toward the represented world.[3]

Whilst with respect to the Huarochirí texts virtually nothing is known about the status of the narrator(s), it is possible to study them as far as the contact between narrator and addressee and the position of the narrator is concerned. Besides style and content of the narrative, there are also certain morpho-syntactic devices that give information about the point of view. Thus the usage of the evidential suffixes, together with other morphological devices, such as tense and space markers, indicate the point of view adopted by the narrator. They also reveal something about the subjectivity of the information, the narrator's view, and his attitude toward the narrated account, as well as the position of the narrator in the cultural context.

Research carried out in the field of evidentials can best be judged on the basis of the book *Evidentiality*. In their introduction, the editors (Chafe and Nichols 1986: vii) say that evidentiality finds itself at a "stage of exploration", and although there have been several studies over the past years with reference to evidentiality in Andean languages, no new attempt at summarising and systematising has as yet been made.

In order to mark evidentiality, different linguistic means are used in different languages, as for example morphological affixes or lexical predicates. As to their exact function, some languages are described as having markers that exclusively refer to the expression of evidence; others show forms that have other functions at the same time. Anderson suggests the following criteria for the identification of evidentials:

(3a) Evidentials show the kind of justification for a factual claim which is available to the person making that claim, whether direct evidence plus observation (no inference needed); evidence plus inference; inference (evidence unspecified); reasoned expectation from logic and other facts; and whether the evidence is auditory, or visual, etc.

(3b) Evidentials are not themselves the main predication of the clause, but are rather a specification added to a factual claim *about something else.*

(3c) Evidentials have the indication of evidence as in (a) their primary meaning, not only as a pragmatic inference.

(3d) Morphologically, evidentials are inflections, clitics, or other free syntactic elements (not compounds or derivational forms). (1986: 274–275)

In two Andean language families, Quechua and Jaqi, evidentiality is marked grammatically. Verbal markers are essential for indicating an experienced or non-experienced action, and there is an interplay of these with discourse markers (traditionally called comment suffixes in Quechua and sentence suffixes in Aymara), which are also crucial for giving evidence of personal or hearsay knowledge (Hardman 1986; Weber 1986; Briggs 1994; Calvo López 1994; and others).

Weber (1986), in his essay on the so-called evidential suffixes in Quechua, points out, through examples from different dialects, that the suffixes which indicate the perspective on the information of a sentence are to be considered as evidential rather than validational—that is, they express *how* speakers came by their information, and not primarily the commitment speakers have toward the truth of what they say. Weber gives the different usages of the reportative suffix -*si*, one of which is its use when direct experience is unlikely and another is when the speaker wants to escape the implication of direct experience.

In her study "Talking about the Past: Tense and Testimonials in Quechua Narrative Discourse", Howard-Malverde (1988) describes the complex use of the suffixes that indicate the past tense in their interrelationship with the evidential suffixes in a Quechua dialect of the Peruvian central highlands. She distinguishes a "non-personalised" mode of description of events from a "personalised" mode that shows the participation of the speaker's subjectivity (Howard-Malverde 1988: 127–128, 133–134).

With similar intent I shall look at how the evidential reportative suffix -*si*, in comparison with the affirmative -*mi*, and the suffix of conjecture -*cha* are used in the Huarochirí manuscript.[4] I will focus—by means of analysing some chapters of the manuscript—on the usage of the evidential or commentary suffixes, the inclusive/exclusive verb plural, as well as the narrator's explicitly expressed opinion on the narrated account, and on how far he can be said to be an eyewitness of the narrated events. The interplay of these devices should help us in answering the following questions:

What was the situational context when the stories were told?

What is the attitude of the narrator toward the narrated text and toward the addressee?

Are there different text "genres" present in the manuscript?

Two genres easily distinguishable in the Huarochirí manuscript are narratives, on the one hand, and what I have termed "ethnographic descriptions", on the other, which I shall examine in turn.

Narratives

As one would expect in a narrative about events that occurred in a period of time that can be considered mythical (in Quechua marked by the time adverbials *ñawpa pacha* 'in former times' and *chay pacha* 'in those times'), the narrator uses the suffix *-si* to mark the narrated account as not witnessed by himself, combined with either the simple or the habitual past, sometimes changing to the present tense. The combination of the narrative past with the reportative suffix *-si* is widely documented in southern Peruvian Quechua narrative. However, in the case of the Huarochirí texts, there is a closer similarity to the pattern found in San Martín Quechua, insofar as consistent usage of the simple past with *-rka-* is found in the narrative structures of both.[5] Thus, in the chapters that relate a coherent narrative, usually of mythical character, we find the combination of the reportative evidential suffix *-si* and the *-rka-* past tense:[6]

(1)   § ñawpa pacha*s* inti wañu*rka*n /
chay*si* chay wañuskanmanta pichka punchaw tutaya*rka*n /
chay*si* rumikunaka paypura waktanaku*rka*n /
chayманta*s* kay mortero muhkakunari chaymanta kay maraykunapas runakta
    mikuyta kallari*rka*n /
llama urkukunari hinatak[7]—runakta ña katiri*rka*n /
(Comment:)
kaytam kanan ñukanchik christianokuna unancha*n*chik jesu christo apu*n*chik-
    pak[8]—wañuskanpi tutayaskantah /
kaykunaka riman
        ñispa "unanchanchik icha*ch* ari chay" / (chap. 4, fol. 66v)

[*It is said that in ancient times the sun died.*
Then—it is said—after its death it became dark for five days.
Then—it is said—the stones banged against each other.
After that—it is said—this mortar, the grinding stones and after that also these
    quern-stones *began* to eat the people.
And in the same way the llama and the mountains *began to drive* the people.
(Comment:)
This—I know—now we Christians *understand* as the *probable* darkness at the
    death *of our lord* Jesus Christ.
These people, however, say: "We believe that *maybe it was* that (what has been
    narrated)".]

But the reportative mode[9] is not only used in narratives with mythical character; it also serves to relate events that happened in a not very remote past connected with historical persons, but which were not witnessed by the narrator. Thus Chapter 20 starts with the account of the appearance of a *huaca*[10] in the past (*-rka-* and *-si*, *chaysi* [1]), then changes to the immediate historical past and to the present (*-rka-*/unmarked tense, *-mi*, *kaymi* [2]) in order to introduce the person who experienced what the narrator then tells in the reportative mode (*-rka-* and *-si* [3]) as he has been told about these events:

(2a) kay waka rikurimuskanta*s*, huk warmi lantichumpi sutiyuk alaysatpa ayllu
tari*rka*n
    chakrakta, uryakuspa /
chaysi
    huk mita ñawpak aspispaka
    "imah. kayka" ñispa*s*
pachallanpitak wischu*rka*n / (chap. 20, fol. 84–85r)

(2b) *kaymi* [don xpistobal] huk mita kay supay[11] llucllayhuancupa ñiskanchikta
rikurkan ñawinwan
    paypas yayan wañuskanmantaka ña ñiskanchik mana alli supay
    machukunap llullaykuskan kaspa /
    kay simiri *kay* hina*m* I / (chap. 20, fol. 86r)

(2c) huk tuta*s* don xpistobal, chay llocllayhuancupap wasinman ri*rka*n,
            chaypi sipasnin kaptin,
    chay wakaktaka, ña, hakispa
    mana ña asllapas chaytaka, yuyaspa, /
chaysi,
    ña chay wasipi chayaspa
    ispaykuypak
chay huchuylla rakay wasillaman yayku*rka*n, / (chap. 20, fol. 86r)

(2a) [*It is said that* a woman called Lantichumpi of the Alaysatpa ayllu *discovered
    this huaca that had appeared* when she was working the field.
    Then—it is said—once, when she was digging it out for the first time, saying—*it
    is said*—"*What could* this be", *she* just *threw it* to the ground again.]

(2b) [*This one* [don Cristóbal]—*I know* (it/him?)—once *saw* this "supay"[11] called
    Llucllayhuancupa with his eyes, being, after his father's death, also deceived
    by the ancestors' bad supay we have already mentioned.
    This story *is like this—I know it.*]

(2c) [*It is said that one night* don Cristóbal *went* to that Llocllayhuancupa's house—
    where his girl was—having already abandoned that huaca, almost not remem-
    bering it anymore.
    Then—it is said—after having arrived at that house, in order to urinate, he *entered*
    into that tiny derelict house.]

We can thus define the usage of *-si* in narratives as marking a temporal and often also
spatial distance of the narrator from the narrated events.

Whenever the narrator takes an explicit position in a story—that is, when he
comments on what he has told, he changes from the reportative *-si* to the affirmative
-mi, usually accompanied by the inclusive plural *-nchik*, maybe implying the wish to
include the addressee in his statements, which is understandable when he sets himself
off from the "pagan" content of the narrative, as, for example, in (1) above, that tells
about the rebellion of animals and objects against man after the death of the sun
(unancha*nchik* 'we understand'; apu*nchik*pak 'of our lord'). It is possible that this
commentator is not identical with the narrator, and at the current stage of my research
this hypothesis seems to be substantiated by the structure of the sentences and also by
the organisation of the chapters within the whole of the text corpus.[12]

The narrator also uses -*mi* when he refers to preceding or following chapters:

(3)   *kaytam kay kipanpi churasun* atinakuskantawan /
      ñam ari chay huallallo carvinchup kawsaskantaka runa mikuskantawanpas ima
          hayka ruraskantawanpas *ñawpak capitulopi rimarkanchik* /
      kananmi rimasun huarocheripi chay chay kitipi ruraskankunakta /
      chay simiri *kaymi* - / (chap. 6, fol. 70r)

   [*This—I know—we will put down later on* together with (the story of) their
       mutual fight.
   We *spoke already—I know it—in the first chapter* about that Huallallo
       Carvinchu's life and his eating human beings and all his deeds.
   Now—I know it—we will speak about all his deeds in Huarocheri and those areas.
   That story *is like this—I know it*]

Here the narrator uses the verb *rima*- 'to speak', which refers to the oral performance of a narrative, whereas the other verb used, *chura*- 'to put', implies writing and paper rather than oral transmission. The passage quoted does not seem to reflect a traditional device of oral art, although one might find similar references in performance cycles indicating, for example, that "yesterday we all have heard about the deeds of so-and-so". It is possible that these connective devices were created by the redactor. Here we have to consider that, when writing down myth cycles, they have to be ordered in a certain way, depending on the purpose of the work and on the supposed audience. This process of re-arranging myths in the written medium in a different or new, now "chronological", order is probably reflected in these texts; however, it cannot be verified because the original contextual situation is not retrievable. The redactor's composition and arrangement of the chapters seems to show an effort at chronological ordering from the most ancient events towards more recent ones, and within this one can see a "fieldwork" situation in which the narrator(s) first give the myths and then—maybe as they were asked to do so—give the "ethnographic" follow-ups, e.g., the myth about the goddess Chaupiñamca, followed by the description of the rituals carried out in relation to this same goddess. Just as with the conspicuous use of certain suffixes that reflect the writer's still imperfect familiarity with writing (Adelaar, in this volume), with respect to narrative structure there is a discernible effort at imitating European literary patterns on the level of chapter arrangement.

Going back to the usage of -*mi*, the narrator also uses it when he talks about geographical features and socio-political divisions of the region that occur in the story. He changes from -*si* to -*mi*, and sometimes to -*nchik*, and back to -*si* again:

(4)   chay*si* kay wakinnin wawkinkunaka |
          rispapas
      (insertion made by the narrator referring to the geographical position:)
          chay tupicochamanta wichaykuspa
      ñawpa ñanta ri*nchik* /
      chay*mi* quisquitambo sutiyuk /
      huk*mi* tumnacha sutiyuk /
      maymanta*m* limac ñiktapas riku*nchik* /
      (end of insertion)

chaymanta*s* ñan
>"tutayquirika tukuyta atiyta ña puchukan" ñiqta uyarispa*s*[13] kutimurkanku /
>(chap. 12, fol. 107r)

[*Then—it is said*—his other brothers, despite having gone on——(insertion:)
when climbing from that Tupicocha *we go* along the old path; *that one—I
know*—is called Quisquitambo; *the other one—I know*—is called Tumnacha,
from where—I know—we see what is called Limac (end of insertion)——*from
that* path—*it is said*—they returned, *having heard—it is said*—people say:
"Tutayquiri has already finished conquering everything".]

The narrator's familiarity or otherwise with the spatial location of the narrated events
influences the choice of evidential suffix in any given context. Thus space may be an
important dimension of the personal witness category at work in the use of evidential
suffixes (cf. Howard-Malverde 1990: 74–75).

The same device is used when a certain feature in the landscape (e.g., a stone) is
explained mythically, that is, the story that describes the persons involved is given in
the reportative past mode, whereas the stone that resulted from the petrification of a
character in the story is described as part of the here-and-now the narrator is living,
and therefore this account takes on the affirmative *-mi* and is told in the present tense:

chay*si* chay cauellacaka
>mana uyantapas payman tikrarichispa
kuchaman
>"hinallam chinkasak chika millay runap kachkasapap
>churinta wachaskaymanta" ñispa
chikacharkan
(insertion:) maypi*m kanan*pas chay pachacamac uku kuchapi *kanan*pas sutilla
>iskay rumi runa hina *tiyakun*
(end of insertion)
chayman /
chay*si*
>chay kanan tiyaskanpi*s* chayaspalla
rumi tukurkan. / (chap. 2, fol. 65r)

[*Then—it is said*—that Cauellaca, without even turning her face back to him,
disappeared toward the sea, saying: "Like this I will flee because I have given
birth to the child of such an ugly man, full of pock-marks",
——(insertion:) *where—I know*—even now in that Pachacamac Sea, *even now*
visible two stones like people are sitting (end of insertion)——in that direction.
Then—it is said——when arriving at what now *is said to be her seat*, she turned
to stone.]

These insertions of the narrator's experience, his space and time, are also often marked
by the usage of the directional verbal modifier *-mu-*, which reflects linguistically the
speaker's relationship with the location he refers to in the verb and allows conclusions
as to where the narrator was at the time he was telling the story or account—or at least
where he was not! In terms of Howard-Malverde (1988: 128), here the narrator gives
a personalised presentation of the events. According to Lanser's (1981: 192) sugges-

tion of a spatial axis, the narrator is here close to a fixed spatial frame, leaving the position of the narrator who looks at the narrated events from a quasi-outside, panoramic overview (cf. Adelaar, in this volume).

Ethnographic descriptions

So far we have seen a relatively clear usage of -*si* and -*mi* in what I call mythical texts with narrator's commentaries. Let us now turn to the type of text I call ethnographic description or account because it describes certain ceremonies and rituals related to the supernatural beings who act in the myths, normally narrated in the third person. Typical examples of this "genre" are chapters 7, 9, and 10, which describe the ceremony of cleaning an irrigation canal, the Auquisna ceremony for Pariacaca, and the ceremony held for Chaupiñamca.

In chapter 7, the narrator describes the celebration of the female Chuquisuso, who had managed to get a good irrigation canal for her community by negotiating and having sexual intercourse with Pariacaca (chap. 6). The ayllu that venerated Chuquisuso used to go to her seat and take offerings to her. After finishing this five-day ceremony and cleaning the irrigation canal, the participants come to the village, among them a chosen woman who represents Chuquisuso, and there is a great feast. While the narrator uses -*mi* to describe this, he switches once to -*si*, when he says that after finishing they come to the village:

(6)   chay*mi* ña chayta muchaspari . . . /
    chaypi tiyapayarkan /
        chay*si* ña chayta puchukaspa
        rarka pichaynintawanpas tukuyta ña puchukaspa*s*
    chaymanta
        takispa
    runakuna hamurkan /
    huk warmiktari
        "kaymi chuquisuso" ñispa
        payta hina alli manchaspa
    chawpipi *pusamurkanku* / (chap. 7, fol. 71v)

[*Now then—I know*—having adored that one . . . they stayed there.
Then—it is said—when they had already finished that, *when they had* already *finished* everything—*it is said*—also the cleaning of the irrigation canal, after that the people came singing.
And in the midst *they guided here* a woman whom they respected much, saying "This is Chuquisuso".]

There is another -*si* inserted later on, as if the narrator or scribe did not participate in this particular event or wanted to avoid being thought to know the narrated event through his own experience:

chaymanta*m* . . .
aswakta . . . kumuk karkan / . . . /
    ña kay rarkakta pichayta *puchukamuspari*
runakunakta anchapuni*s* combidak karkan

sarakta purutukta ima haykaktapas kuspa / (chap. 7, fol. 71v)

[*After that—I know—* . . . [a woman] used to give chicha.
After having already finished here cleaning this irrigation canal, she used to treat
people *certainly to a lot—it is said—*giving them maize, beans and other things.]

Yet the use of "pusa*mu*rkanku" 'they guided *here*' in (6) indicates his personal involvement, then he reverts to -*mi*. The same occurs in (7) "puchuka*mu*spari" 'after having already finished *here*'. Once again, when the narrator refers to Chuquisuso inviting
people to eat, he uses -*si* as if he had never witnessed that. He then mentions as
eyewitness (-*mi*) that this ceremony is still being performed in his days (unmarked
tense):

(8) chaytam kanan
        ña rarkakta pichaspaka
        musyaska[14] hinatak
     rura*n* mucha*n* / (chap. 7, fol. 72r)

     [After having already cleaned the irrigation canal, *that* now—*I know*—they do
        it as if confused, *they pray.*]

His final remark about how people tricked their parish priest in order to be able to go
on with their ancient customs is linguistically not quite consistent with the preceding
structure and diction—he uses Spanish *porque*:

(9) *porque* yallinrak*mi* paywan takin upyan machaskankama /
     padrektari
        "rarkaktam pichamuni padre * takikusak upyakusak" ñispa*m* llullachin /
        (chap. 7, fol. 72r)

     [Because *moreover—I know*—they dance and drink with them until getting
        drunk.
     I know that they deceive the Father *saying*: "I have cleaned the irrigation canal,
        Father, I will dance and drink".]

Possibly the narrator/commentator added these remarks afterward or as a response to
a question.

    The overall impression of the change from -*mi* to -*si* throughout the description is
that the narrator—although in his last remark he wants himself to be seen as a good
Christian—is still bound by ancient Andean beliefs and their practices. This is evident
in that he uses the affirmative -*mi*, which indicates that he is an eyewitness or has direct
knowledge, and also because, in the same affirmative mode, he describes how
Chuquisuso, who is a supernatural being, stems from a certain still existing ayllu:

kay [cupara] ayllumanta*m* kanan huk yumay chauincho sutiyuk /
kay chauincho ayllu*m* karkan chay chuquisuso ñiska / (chap. 7, fol. 71v)

[*From this ayllu* [Cupara]—*I know*—there is now a lineage called Chauincho.
[*From*] *this Chauincho ayllu—I know*—was the one called Chuquisuso.[15]]

In looking at the other two chapters mentioned, a similar picture emerges. In chapter 9, the narrator describes how ancient practices in honour of Pariacaca are still being performed in different villages and provinces. Whereas the first groups are presented with the affirmative -*mi*, later ones are described using -*si*, as if the narrator had visited and seen the first ones, but not the Checa, Sunicancha, and Chaucaricma, whose practices he describes as still existing in his time by using the unmarked tense. These peoples seem to have lived in the narrator's world, and he knew them, either by having seen them, or by having heard of them in his time. Toward the end of his account, he moves backward in time, indicated by his employing "ñawpa pacha" 'in former times', combined with the past tense and -*si* to enumerate the peoples of an earlier period and their veneration of Pariacaca (see table 9-1).

In chapter 10, after introducing Chaupiñamca and her kin relationship, the narrator describes her feast, which he seems to have witnessed because he uses -*mi* to describe the different dances. Only once does he switch to -*si*, when he mentions a dance performed with no clothing:

hukta*m* kanan casayaco sutiyukta takik karkanku /
    kay cassayacokta takiptin*si*
chaupiñamca ancha kusikuk karkan /
porque
    kayta takispaka
llatan*si* /
    wakillan wallparikunanta churaspalla*s*
takik karkan
    pinkaynintari huk wara utku pachallawan pakaykuspa / (chap. 10, fol. 77r)

[Now they used to dance *another one—I know*—called Casayaco.
It is said that when they danced this Cassayaco Chaupiñamca used to be very happy.
Because when they danced this one, *it is said* that they were *naked*.
They used to dance *putting on only* a few of their adornments—*it is said*—hiding their shameful parts only with cotton breechclouts.]

Table 9-1 The use of -*mi* and -*si* in the description of different groups who adore Pariacaca (chap. 9).

Comment and tense	Groups
-*mi* and past tense	Huarochirí province Chaclla province Mama province Colli from Checa *llakta*
-*mi* and unmarked tense	Surco *runakuna* Huayllas *runakuna* Concha
no comment suffix and unmarked tense	Sunicancha
-*si* and unmarked tense	Checa Chaucaricma; also the ones from Santa Ana and San Juan
-*si* and past tense; ñawpa pacha	a list of different Yunca groups

Might the influence of Christian education, or his knowledge of the church's morals, have moved the narrator to deny personal knowledge of such a "barbarian" custom (viz. his use of -*si*)? The usage of "pinkaynin", 'their shameful parts' also provides a hint of this. The narrator of the account may be identical with the one who makes this comment, but it is also possible that the comment was inserted into the text by the redactor who takes on the role of an "extrafictional voice" (cf. Lanser 1981: 124).

So far we have seen that, on the one hand, the narrator automatically uses the appropriate evidential suffix to testify his personal knowledge or ignorance of a phenomenon; on the other hand, he employs this linguistic means in order to deny or confirm his knowledge of certain events he relates, thereby conveying some information about himself and about how he wants to be seen by the addressee. Here, then, we notice a combination of the evidential aspect (how the narrator obtained his knowledge) with the validational aspect (the narrator's commitment with respect to the truth of the narrated account).

Special idiolectal or dialectal usages

While the examples I have presented here indicate a rather consistent and well-known usage of the Quechua evidential suffixes, there are also instances of unusual usages that are to be explained either as idiolectal or as a Huarochirí dialect feature which differs somewhat from the known application described.

In chapter 16 the narrator describes the expulsion of Huallallo Caruincho by Pariacaca to the lowlands. While he uses the reportative -*si* to this effect (and -*mi* is used to refer to other chapters of the manuscript), he also employs -*mi* when enumerating Pariacaca's brothers, although they definitely belong to the mythical sphere normally presented in the reportative mode:

(12) kaykunap sutin*mi* ñawpakninmanta pariacaca, /
     chaymanta*m* churapa, /
     chaymanta*m* puncho, /
     chaymanta*m*, pariacarco / (chap. 16, fol. 81r)

   [*The names of these—I know*—were, from their first one, Pariacaca.
   And after that—I know—was Churapa.
   And after that—I know—was Puncho.
   And after that—I know—was Pariacarco.]

Might the narrator actually be referring here to mountains called Churapa, Puncho, and so on, which would explain the use of the eyewitness evidential -*mi*?[16]

An interesting opposition of -*si* and -*mi* can be found in chapter 1, where the ancient time with its huacas is described in the reportative mode; but the changes caused by Pariacaca, who expelled the *yunca* (coastal population) and their god to the lowlands, as well as the more recent god Cuniraya Viracocha, are described using the affirmative suffix -*mi*. These gods' closeness to the narrator is demonstrated by the directional suffix -*mu*- in connection with Pariacaca:

(13) kipanpi ña may pacha*m* huk wakatak pariacaca sutiyuk rikuri*m*urkan/ (chap. 1, fol. 64r)

> [*I know that* afterwards already *at one time* another 'huaca' called Pariacaca appeared here.]

We also find the demonstrative pronoun *kay* 'this', and the time adverbials *kanan* 'now', and *ñahka* 'already', in connection with Cuniraya:

(14) chaymanta*m kanan* huk wakatak cuniraya sutiyuk karkan /
    (insertion:) kayta*m* mana allichu yachanchik,
        pariacacamantapas ichapas ñawpaknin karkan o kipanpas /
    ichaka *kay* cunirayap kaskanrak*mi ñahka* viracochap kaskanman tinkun / (chap. 1, fol. 64r)

> [*And after that—I know—now* there was also another huaca called Cuniraya—
> —(insertion:) we do not know *this one* well—*I know*—whether he was earlier
> than Pariacaca or after him (end of insertion)——but *I know that this
> Cuniraya's life* was *already* related to Viracocha's life.]

This, and the fact that the narrator quotes prayers to Cuniraya, which have a binary semantic structure (or "semantic coupling" as in Guaman Poma, Molina, and Pachacuti Yamqui) typical of the genre,[17] indicates, in my opinion, that he is very familiar with these gods; as "historical" beings, they may have to be presented in the affirmed knowledge mode, whereas ancient, mythical, supernatural beings, having already disappeared before the last pre-colonial gods, are connected with the hearsay evidential suffix -*si*. Such a hypothesis would also help explain the use of -*mi* in (12) when referring to Pariacaca's brothers and in (10) when speaking of Chuquisuso's descent. We may want to re-interpret the understanding of "eyewitness" to include religious phenomena that for the speakers seemed to have formed part of experienced life. Another instance of a special usage of grammatical devices is reflected in what Adelaar (1994b: 118) has termed the "complement of divine manifestation", which means that Huarochirí Quechua, or at least the variety used in this manuscript, made particular use of certain grammatical functions.

So far I have discussed the different types of text I consider to be distinct "genres" with respect to their narrator and his sources of information. Myth-like, coherent stories are usually told in the reportative mode—that is, with the evidential suffix -*si* and the simple past -*rka*-. Ethnographic accounts and descriptions tend to be related with the evidential (eye-)witness suffix -*mi* and either the simple past tense or unmarked tense, sometimes with the use of reportative -*si* in order to document the non-witnessing of an event and/or to deny having witnessed it. It would thus appear that when writing down myth-type narratives, the narrator(s) kept to the usage of the evidentials as practised in the oral narration of the myth. By contrast, with regard to ethnographic or testimonial accounts, the new medium of writing expresses and fixes personal experience versus hearsay perspective in a seemingly inconsistent way. This, however, may be explained by further studies of the texts in the light of the hypothesis that at least some of the manuscript chapters represent several voices, possibly joined together by a redactor. The written version of these accounts would then be revealing a context-performance-determined usage that is not yet adapted to a consistent employment of these suffixes in writing, an observation similar to that made by Adelaar (in this volume) with regard to the status of the suffix *-mu-*.

The expression of conjecture

Between the two poles of experienced affirmation and non-experienced secondary information, the Quechua language has another evidential area: of doubt, uncertainty, or conjecture, which in the Quechua II[18] dialects is expressed by means of the suffix *-cha* and its allomorphic variants. In the Huarochirí manuscript, *-cha* is found in conjectures in the reported speech of the characters and in conjectures made by the narrator. Especially in reported speech, *-cha* is often found together with the potential mode or future tense, which implies insecurity about the possible realisation of what is said. It can also indicate a warning or advice when it occurs in *pakta-ch* 'careful'!, 'rather . . . '. The narrator uses it when he expresses suppositions about beliefs and religious ceremonies of his time, about which he is not completely certain, and when he does not know exactly the date or the duration of a particular ceremony.

A comment made by the narrator with respect to the Christianisation of the ethnic groups whose ceremonies are described in chapter 9, refers to old beliefs that are in the process of disappearing:

> ichaka kananka ña kunkan kay pisi watallarak
>> kay doctor francisco de auila alli kunakiyuk yachachikiyuk kaspa I /
> chaypas manatak*cha* sunkukamaka iñinmanchu /
>> ñatak huk padreyuk kaspaka
> hinamantak*cha* kutinman I /
> wakin runakunaka
>> christiano tukuspapas
>> manchaspalla*m*.
>> "pakta*cha*. padrepas pipas yachawanman mana alli kaskayta" ñispalla*m*
> christiano: tukun / (chap. 9, fol. 75r–v)

> [But now they already forget [the old customs] within just these few years, because they have this doctor Francisco de Auila, a good person in charge and teacher.
> However, they do *not really seem to believe* with their hearts.
> If they had again a different Father, they might *probably* return *to these ways* [of old customs].
> Some people, after becoming Christians, *only because they are afraid*—I know—they become Christians, *just saying—I know:* "Careful! Maybe the Father or somebody might know of my bad life".]

Here the narrator/commentator clearly shows a great deal of scepticism with respect to the situation of Christianisation, and it becomes evident that only fear moves people to convert to Christianity. Whilst this shows the narrator's/commentator's detachment from the narrated events, a personal testimony is quoted in chapters 20 and 21. Here an artful usage of the evidential suffixes *-cha* and *-mi* is found in don Cristóbal's meeting with the old *huaca* Llocllayhuancupa from whom he wishes to distance himself. But as he is not completely sure whether Llocllayhuancupa has actually lost his power, he formulates his defiance using the suffix of conjecture *-cha*:

(16)   kayta puchukaptin*si*
            ña kasilla imapas kaptin
        don xpistobalka rimayta kallarirkan
            ñispa |
        (don Cristóbal speaks:)
        "yaw llucllayhuancupa /
            kamta*m* ari 'runakamak pachakuyuchik' ñispa
        ñisunki /
            'paytak*mi* ima hayka rurak' ñispa*m* ari
        tukuy runakunapas manchasunki /
        imapak*mi* kanan kayachimuwarkanki /
        ñukaka ñini*m*
            'jesu xpisto diospak churin kaytak*cha* chikan dios * paypak simintatak*cha*
            wiñaypas yupaychasak' ñispa*m* /
        ñini /
        kayri /
        pantanichu /
        kam kanan willaway
            'chayka mana*m* dioschu * ñuka*m* ima hayka rurak kani' ñispa
            chay pacha kamta manchankaypak / "
        ñispa /
        (don Cristóbal finishes speaking)
                ñiptin*si*
        chay supayka upayarkan / (chap. 21, fol. 88r–v)

    [*It is said that when* this *had finished* and there was already some stillness, don
        Cristóbal began to speak, saying:
    "Listen, Llucllayhuancupa; *I know* that they call *you* 'the one who has made man,
        the one who makes the earth tremble', *I know that saying* '*he is certainly* the
        one who made everything' all the people fear you.
    Why have you had me call here—*I am here*—?
    I say—*I know it*: 'Jesus Christ, the son of God, *this one is probably* the true God;
        and *his word* I will *probably* always respect'. This is it! If I am wrong, then
        tell me: 'That one is *not* God—*I know it. I know that I* am the one who makes
        everything', so that then I may fear you". *It is said that when he* [don Cristóbal]
        had said it, that supay was silent.]

The distribution of the evidential suffixes

Authors on Quechua grammar always suppose that the evidentials form one group of suffixes, which would also imply that they are used in the same morphological and syntactic structures. By studying the distribution of these suffixes, we learn something about the syntactic organisation in which these evidentials are embedded, and their distribution may be a clue as to different meanings or functions (cf. Jones 1992 on a

Papuan language). My brief presentation of the distribution should be seen as an initial step in this direction.

Despite a long tradition of Quechua grammar writing, detailed studies on a level beyond morphology are still scarce and mostly refer either to clause or to discourse analysis,[19] so that my observations are an incipient effort not only at understanding the evidentials in the Huarochirí manuscript but also in the general context of syntactic studies of the Quechua language.

In the manuscript, -si is used much more frequently than -mi, a situation which is easily explicable because of the story-character most of the texts have. But as can also be expected, in proportional terms -si and -mi are distributed equally. For the analysis of the distribution of the evidential suffixes -mi and -si, I have chosen to divide the sentence into units which, in my analysis of the discourse suffixes, have proved to be useful and meaningful sub-divisions:

author-action (the subject itself and the conjugated verb that includes the subject, also in its nominalised forms)

patient (the direct object and the nominal expressions with the other relational suffixes that mark what we traditionally call "cases"[20]—nominal forms as well as nominalised forms)

"circumstances" (above all time and space indicators)[21]

negations

In quantitative terms, both suffixes are distributed relatively equally with respect to the complex actor-action/patient, on the one hand, and circumstances and negations, on the other. However, there is a clear tendency for -mi to be used above all with nominal forms (subject and object), whereas -si is mainly combined with nominalised verbs (especially -spa and -pti-) when these incorporate the subject of the subordinate clause.[22]

This is only a general impression because my analysis does not take into account the difference in the usage of the evidentials by the narrator himself, as opposed to the usage in reported speech made by the characters. Syntactically, both -mi and -si tend to be used with the initial elements of a clause, a result confirmed by Rick Floyd (1994) in his study of evidential suffixes in Wanka Quechua.

The suffix -cha, which appears in the manuscript in different allomorphic forms ({-cha}, {-ch}, {-ch.}, {-h}, {-h.}, {-hc}), is used much less frequently than the other evidential suffixes. As has been mentioned here, it is mainly employed to mark a conjecture that the narrator/speaker expresses about the characters or about the narrated account, which is why it is generally found in the ethnographic descriptions and in reported speech. The suffix -cha is above all combined with nominal expressions, especially interrogative pronouns. It often occurs in the same sentence together with the future tense or potential mode, and sometimes with the verbs of supposition unancha- 'to consider, believe, understand as' and yuya- 'to think'. When comparing -cha with the other evidential suffixes, it seems that the usage of -cha is more easily captured and described.

A further area of study is the position of the evidentials in relation to the topic marker -ka and the other two sentence suffixes -tak and -ri (Dedenbach-Salazar Sáenz

1994). For the time being, after a global survey, there does not seem to be a fixed distribution rule, but hopefully a syntactic analysis will show certain patterns which may also allow the determination of different "styles" and different narrators.

Conclusion and prospects

On the whole, the usage of the evidential suffixes in the Huarochirí texts is very similar to their modern usage in Quechua IIB.[23] The reportative suffix -si, often together with the simple past tense, characterises a genre of story-like texts removed from the narrator in time and frequently situated in a non-defined space; the characters often belong to the mythical sphere. The suffix -si also serves to mark events that happened in a not very remote past connected with historical persons, or events not witnessed by the narrator.

The suffix -mi is typical of a descriptive genre of rituals and ceremonies, as well as personal accounts, and is most often used to show that the narrator has been eyewitness to an event or, for example, knows places from his own experience; this affirmative suffix is often accompanied by the habitual past tense or the unmarked tense and also by the verb modifying suffix -mu-. Moreover, -mi is used in connection with certain supernatural beings, probably marking their integration into human lived experience.

Conjecture or doubt as to the event referred to is marked with the suffix -cha, which shows that the narrator/speaker is not certain about his information. In complex narrative situations -si, -mi, and -cha are used in a deliberate manner that reflects both the actual evidential situation of the narrator and his attitude toward the narrated account—for example, whether he is or feels involved—and his attitude toward the addressee, that is, whether he wants to convey his involvement in or detachment from the narrated events. Thereby these suffixes also take on a validational aspect.

When reading the Huarochirí texts carefully and with one's mind on the standpoint adopted by the narrator, there is more than one voice to be heard; frequently the narrator of a story seems to be different from a commentator who puts the story into the overall framework of the collection, and may be different again from a redactor who may have been responsible for putting the texts together and writing them down. Thus parts of the texts may be understood as testimonies of an involved narrator who gives an account of his own culture and environment (in relating myths as well as personal experiences), other parts as ethnographic descriptions by a more detached narrator (in describing ceremonies and rituals), and still others as comments about the narrated account by a commentator who may or may not be identical with the detached narrator. All this is possibly woven together either by one of the narrators or by a redactor.

The present study has given us some suggestions as to how to differentiate narrators' attitudes, genres, and situational contexts; at the same time, it calls for new research, for example, in addressing the question of the voices and styles of different narrators. It is to be hoped that this kind of research will also be taken up with respect to modern Quechua tales so as to make more general statements possible, and perhaps such a comparative view could also shed new light on the Huarochirí texts themselves.

Notes

1. The meaning of the term *edit* and its derivatives normally refers to the preparation of a work for publication (e.g., Taylor's or Salomon and Urioste's editions of the Huarochirí traditions). The processes mentioned here are better described with the term *redact* and its derivatives, emphasising the meaning of reduction to literary form, revision, and rearrangement (cf. Oxford English Dictionary 1989). The manuscript was found among Avila's papers, but it is doubtful that he ever had the intention of publishing it—unlike his Spanish *Tratado*, which presents his own redaction (paraphrase and translation) of these texts, written in a very clear handwriting and provided with a proper title page, which may well have been intended for publication.

Trimborn (1967: 10) says that the handwriting of the Quechua manuscript and the Spanish *Tratado* is Avila's. However, a graphological analysis of the manuscript texts in comparison with texts attributed to Avila is still outstanding. This might help us in finding out how far he was personally involved in the (re-)production of these traditions.

2. Adelaar has studied several aspects of the Quechua structure of the Huarochirí manuscript: his analysis of the demonstrative pronouns and the directional suffix *-mu-* (Adelaar, in this volume), his study of reported speech (Adelaar 1990), as well as that of abstract and general concepts (Adelaar 1994a), suggest the complexity of the manuscript's discourse structure. On the formal linguistic level there is Urioste's morphological analysis (1973), and Salomon (1991) and I (Dedenbach-Salazar Sáenz 1994) touch on further textual aspects of the manuscript.

3. In Andean studies specifically, by comparison, Adorno (1989) has brought point-of-view analysis to bear upon the chronicle of Guaman Poma de Ayala, in terms of the construction of his ideological position through both written text and visual images.

4. Salomon (1991: 32–33), in his introductory essay to the new translation of the Huarochirí manuscript—which was published after I had written this paper—gives a brief discussion of the evidential suffixes, which shows similarities with my present analysis here.

5. With respect to the dialectal status of the Quechua used in the manuscript, Adelaar (1994d) and I (Dedenbach 1982) observed independently the similarity with Northern Peruvian Amazonian Quechua dialects. For example, the orthography of the manuscript suggests the non-existence of the post-velar /q/; this is reflected in my modernised transcription in which I use {*k*} exclusively for all the stops represented in the document as {*qu, co, cu*}. It can thus be assumed that the language of the Huarochirí manuscript belongs to the Quechua IIB dialect group (cf. footnote 18); however, this does not exclude the possibility that it was used as a "general language" incorporating basic and simplified features of Quechua IIB (cf. Adelaar 1994d: 149–150). With reference to the past tense forms, it is also possible that *-sqa-* as a verbal form ("tense") only developed toward the end of the seventeenth century (as I have argued in Dedenbach-Salazar Sáenz 1993).

Taylor (1987a: 21) finds Aru (Jaqi) influence at the lexical and morphological levels; here I should only like to observe that the texts obviously lack this influence at the syntactic level which I have been analysing. Perhaps this indicates that an Aru substratum had already been integrated into the Quechua vocabulary of this area without influencing the syntactic structure, or that the author of the manuscript was a Quechua speaker without local Aru influence in his syntactic structure. The question of dialectal classification is further complicated by the fact that we do not know which changes can be attributed to the narrator(s), commentator(s), or redactor(s).

6. I use a modernised transcription (see also note 5) based on a photocopy of the original manuscript, indicating chapters (*capítulos*) and *folios*, in which all names are spelled as in the manuscript; the different writings of the suffix *-cha* are kept in their original spelling because they represent sounds that are not easily reconstructable (Taylor represents them by *ĉ*). All sibilants, mostly written as {*s*}, and some as {*ss*}, {*ç*}, {*x*}, and {*z*} in the manuscript, are transcribed as {*s*}.

To make reading easier, the subordinate clauses are indented once when the subject of the main clause and the subordinate clause is the same; when there are different subjects, the subordinate clause is indented twice. The oblique stroke marks the end of a sentence; quotation marks are used to indicate reported speech, and within this, asterisks delimit sentences and clauses. All other punctuation marks (including the vertical bar) are kept as in the original.

For those who do not know Quechua, I translate the manuscript passages into English. The reader will notice the frequent usage of 'then' which reflects Quechua *chaysi*, a connective whose translation is also found in many modern Andean tales, and even Hillman's (1994) presentation of a narrative in Spanish shows many occurrences of *entonces*. My translation should be understood as a help for the reader, and at the same time tries to capture some of the diction and structure of the Quechua of Huarochirí, which is why the sentences are based very closely on the original text rather than stylistically elaborated and adapted to current English. As this essay examines the role of the evidential suffixes, these have to be translated into English, which—like other Indo-European languages—uses other devices such as lexical ones in order to express evidentiality (Anderson 1986). I translate the affirmative mode as 'I know', the reportative as 'it is said', and the conjecture as 'probably', 'maybe'. These expressions of comment and the word/phrase they are connected with in Quechua appear in italic type.

7. When comparing this construction with that of the preceding sentence, it might also be interpreted as an enumeration: 'the llama, the mountains', parallel with 'this mortar, the grinding stones'.

8. This is a possessive construction with *-paq*.

9. I use the term *mode* to describe not just the function of the evidential suffix itself but the whole affirmative or reportative context this suffix creates.

10. It is not easy to grasp the meaning of religious concepts which—since the Spanish conquest—have certainly undergone transformation. "Huaca" denotes an object, feature, or place that is special and different; untranslatable as it is, it implies the idea of something "sacred".

11. As with "huaca", it is difficult to translate "supay", interpreted by the Spaniards as 'demon' or 'devil'; in Andean belief it seems to have been related to the "world below", and may have referred to an ambiguous numen. It is interesting to observe that in chap. 20 the word "huaca" only occurs in the first part where its history is told; in the following part, that is don Cristóbal's report, only "supay" is used. Also in the next chapter, "huaca" is only used twice. Maybe this shows that it is really don Cristóbal's discourse which is represented here, and he has already adapted the Christian-influenced, now negatively connotated "supay" in order to describe Andean native gods (although he still shows traces of the original Andean use when qualifying supay as "mana alli"—that is, there can be 'good', "alli", and 'bad', "mana alli", supay) (cf. Taylor 1980; Crickmay 1994).

12. See also the discussion of the "ethnographic descriptions" for the interference of the commentator, and note 15.

13. There is a very thin final {*-s*} detectable in the manuscript. (The corrections made in the texts might also shed light on the process of redaction).

14. Perroud and Chouvenc: *musya-* "saber, conjeturar, adivinar, pensar, ver confusamente" 'to know, conjecture, prophesy, think, see confusedly'; Taylor: "confundidos [por el demonio]" 'confused [by the demon]'; Trimborn: "mit Vorbedacht" 'intentionally'. Taylor's translation seems to me the most acceptable one, although because of the broad spectrum of

meanings of *musya-* it might also imply divination or perhaps a state of trance during the ceremony.

15. Another possible interpretation of the shift from *-mi* to *-si* is the assumption that the narrator of the beginning and the end of the chapter is not identical with the one who narrates the ceremony itself. However, as this more complex narrative situation, which might also be related to the overall structure of the manuscript texts, is only emerging in my current analyses—after having finished this essay—it will have to be kept in mind, but cannot be dealt with in detail here.

16. So far, I have not been able to locate these names geographically (e.g., in maps of Lima and its surroundings from 1750, in *Mapas y Planos, Perú y Chile*, 33 and 33 bis, Archivo General de Indias, Sevilla; in a map from 1788 which is in the British Library, London; in Germán Stiglich, *Diccionario Geográfico del Perú*, Lima 1922; in the 1:100,000 maps of the province of Huarochirí by the Instituto Geográfico Nacional, Lima).

17. For studies of the poetic structure of colonial Quechua, see Husson 1984 and 1985, and Mannheim 1986a, and for a challenging view, Itier 1993.

18. For an overview of the dialectal subdivision of the Quechua language (according to Torero and Parker), see Dedenbach-Salazar Sáenz et al. (1994: XIII): Quechua I comprises the Central Peruvian dialects; Quechua II, the Southern Peruvian, Bolivian, Argentinian, and Chilean, as well as the Northern Peruvian and Ecuadorian dialects, with IIB including the dialects spoken in the Peruvian departments of Amazonas, San Martín, Loreto, Ucayali, and Madre de Dios; in the *sierra* and *oriente* provinces of Ecuador; in Putumayo and Nariño in Colombia; and in Acre in Brazil. The morphological differences between Quechua I and II are considerable; on the lexical level, there is a marked distinction between Northern Quechua and Central Peruvian Quechua on the one hand and the Southern dialects on the other.

19. On clauses, see Carlson de Coombs 1975; Cole et al. 1982; Costa 1972; Weber 1976. On discourse, see Levinsohn 1976 among others and Wölck 1979.

20. Except for the spatial and temporal expressions constructed with *-pi*.

21. In quantitative terms, with both suffixes (*-mi* and *-si*) the temporal indicators dominate, the reason for this being that I have included also the ones that mark the course of the narrative, as, for example, *chaysi* and *chaymantam*. In a further analysis it will be necessary to differentiate within this group of temporal markers the ones that refer to narrated time—thus establishing temporal relationships *within* the narrated events—and the ones that connect the sentences of the narrative itself in order to provide a chronological development of the narrative.

This group of "circumstances" also includes *hina-*, which when it occurs with evidential suffixes mainly has the function of connecting sentences or clauses, combined (a) with the nominalising suffix *-spa*, (b) with the connective *-tak*.

Another word included in the category "circumstances" is *imana-*, which occurs virtually only with the affirmative suffix *-mi* and frequently serves to introduce an insertion of personal knowledge about a phenomenon of the narrator's world; it can be translated as "as" or "like", and it tends to have an explanatory function. It may be convenient to consider it as a monolexeme in which *-mi* has become part of the word itself.

22. *-si* is also often connected with the deictic pronoun *chay* forming *chaysi*, and as such connects sentences.

23. Cf. notes 5 and 18.

ORALITY AND LITERACIES AS REFLEXES OF COLONISATION AND RESISTANCE

MARTIN LIENHARD

Writing from Within

*Indigenous Epistolary Practices
in the Colonial Period*

Before the European conquest, the autochthonous societies of the continent to the west of Europe carried out their basic semiotic practices within a communicative framework which—but only for the sake of contrast with those systems which privilege (even fetishise) writing—I shall call "oral". The colonial and modern groups made up of their descendants (direct or indirect), despite having reproduced a similar system for their own internal purposes, not only interiorised the writing fetishism (cf. Platt, in this volume), but succeeded in mastering writing for the purpose of dialogue with the "other".

Seemingly irreplaceable, the concept of "orality" in fact raises a whole series of problems. By virtue of its etymology, the term reduces the whole diversity of semiotic practices in an "oral" society to verbal expression, yet we do not know whether the spoken word fulfils the same function in "orality" as does the written word in the system based on written communication and its fetishisation. Amerindian "orality" always was—and still is—a complex semiotic system relying not merely on verbal ("oral") communication, but also on the most diverse media, including plastic, graphic, choreographic, gestural, musical, and rhythmical (cf. Rappaport, in this volume). Far from being ignorant of "graphic" communication, several Amerindian "oral" systems even countenanced the use of some type of "writing" for the notation of words or of whole speeches; consider, for example, the Mesoamerican glyphs or the Andean *quipu* system, tactile and visual at the same time. When I speak of Amerindian "orality", therefore, I shall be referring to an eminently multimedia system.

Before the European conquest, the setting for this multimedia Amerindian discourse was a part of the world characterised by relative cultural and linguistic homogeneity. In cultural, though not necessarily political, terms, communication took place between "equals". The arrival of the Europeans and, more than anything else, the fact that they took political control of the territory created the need for a new, intercultural type of communication between the groups who were marginalised by the conquest and the new masters. In this context, the defeated (basing their actions principally on the linguistic resources of their powerful interlocutors) produced a mode of discourse capable of serving them in their dealings, one that I shall call "indigenous discourse addressed to outsiders" (Lienhard 1992). Although traditional modes of expression, always bearing the stamp of "equality", continued to apply within the Amerindian communities on the inside, this new indigenous style came to govern communication, in both oral and written form, between the "conquered" and the "conquerors" and their descendants (Lienhard 1990).

This "indigenous discourse addressed to outsiders" manifests itself in two basic varieties: firstly, the testimonies of natives transcribed—as a general rule—by a representative of the opposing party, and, secondly, the letters and manifestos which the conquered themselves and their descendents addressed, from the very beginning of the colonial period, to their European or *criollo* interlocutors. In the following pages, I shall attempt to identify a particular type of discourse—the "indigenous letter addressed to outsiders"—and the communicative practice corresponding to it.[1] The texts themselves, the instruments of such a practice, will mostly be of interest in that they constitute the recognisable "traces" of a specific process of communication that is always highly politicised. Drafted in the context of latent or overt ethnic/social conflict, these indigenous letters manifest the fact, not only on the thematic level but also in the way in which they are written. The "indigenous letter addressed to outsiders" took on a role as part of a communicative system the basis of which was fixed in the sixteenth century: an asymmetrical system, dominated by the figure of the Spanish king. As I shall attempt to show, this system—whose "rules" were broken in all sorts of minor ways from the very start—steadily lost its validity until, during the indigenous insurrections of the eighteenth and nineteenth centuries, a radically new approach was formulated.

The basic process of communication

At the start of the colonial period, as borne out by currently accessible sources (see Lienhard 1992), indigenous epistolary practices took place in the context of a privileged relationship with the king or his representatives. Basing their terms on the feudal ones of the time, the authors of the letters—indigenous communities or individuals—regarded themselves as "vassals" of the king, their "lord", with the duties and rights that this entailed. In terms of the social hierarchy, then, the message was addressed from "below" to "above". But the native vassals were not only below the king: they were also, as colonial "vassals", far removed from the centre, at the "periphery" of the world. This meant that their messages to the king also had to cross the cultural and political chasm that separated the periphery from the centre. From the viewpoint of the indians, it was a case of movement from "within" (the indigenous community) to "without" (the world of the outsiders).

This asymmetry imposed two rules on the emergent discourse. Firstly, the situation of inferiority within the hierarchy dictated a rhetoric of respect; secondly, the movement from periphery to centre (or from "inside" to "outside") demanded the use of modes of expression with which the addressee was familiar. If the first of these rules was never openly infringed, the degree of enthusiasm brought to bear on the rhetorical simulation of feelings of respect enables us to gauge, up to a point, how genuine the natives' sense of affiliation to the colonial order was. As regards the second rule, any breach of it, whether minor or radical, gives us grounds for supposing a certain spirit of cultural resistance. Thus, the very form of the letters, sometimes more than their content, may be an indicator of the tension on the ethnic/social front at a particular time and place.

Judging simply by the body of evidence referred to, the authors of indigenous letters in the colonial period were recruited almost exclusively from the indigenous élite: native nobility, traditional authorities, local councillors. Only the members of this élite (and not all of them) actually had the opportunity to be introduced to written culture or, failing that, access to someone who could do them the favor of drawing up a letter while they dictated it. They were also the only ones with any degree of power or experience of dealing with it. However—and this is a feature that characterises the majority of the indigenous letters—the members of this élite were wont to speak, even when putting forward matters of concern to themselves as individuals or to their particular social group, in the name of the indigenous community as a whole.

Born out of a context of negotiation, indigenous letter-writing is therefore, in a broad sense, political. Its raison d'être is nearly always a desire to protest or to assert one's rights or claims, and the most diverse forms are deployed to this end. The integration of other discourses—historiographic, ethnographic, poetic, etc.—is subordinated to this primary aim. Any expression of feelings, when such appear, has nothing subjective about it and serves only to reinforce a political argument.

As I said earlier, indigenous letter-writing of the colonial period was characterised by a privileged relationship with the king (and his representatives). The ever deeper cracks that appeared in the whole social structure around the end of this period complicated this relationship. In the eyes of the indians, the legitimacy of the local representatives of the king in fact continually lost ground, and this fact was manifested, as we shall see, in a profound modification of the process of communication already outlined.

Once independence was won (though not by the indians), the epistolary relations between them and their criollo interlocutors ceased to be carried out within a stable framework. From the beginning, the rulers of the republics lacked—and not only in the eyes of the Indians—the "divine" legitimacy of the king. In this qualitatively different situation, the politics of the indigenous groups lost its relative coherence (which had never amounted to uniformity) and began, according to the new deals, to tend toward division, dispersion, and ambiguity when confronted by criollo political forces. In this context, indian-led letter-writing definitively abandoned its vertical relationship with the supreme authority and began to move in all sorts of horizontal directions.

The defence of "caste" interests

From the middle of the sixteenth century, certain groups of the Mesoamerican nobility, especially in the central area of Mexico (Mexico-Tlatelolco, Tetzcoco and Tlacupan), found themselves involved in intense letter-writing activity. These Mesoamerican groups were at that time the only sector of the Amerindian population with relatively easy access to an education equivalent to that of the literate classes in Rennaissance Europe, thanks above all to the work of the Franciscan missionaries. For this reason, their letters (written in Spanish, Nahuatl, or Latin) are models—at least on the surface—as far as respect for the conventions of letter-writing is concerned. An illustrative case in this regard is the letter in Latin addressed by don Pablo Nazareo and his wife, a niece of Motecuhzoma, to the king of Spain on 17th March 1566 (Paso 1939–1942, t. X, 89–129, translated into Spanish by Agustín Millares Carli, and reproduced in abridged form in Lienhard 1992: 44–53). In it, the "rhetoric of respect", or more precisely the praise of the king, is highly obsequious to the point of the obscene:

> It being, o most unconquered king, a distinctive property of kings and princes, by consequence of their divine power, that they enlighten all other mortals, just as the Sun [the Latin original has Phœbus] gives light to the whole world, whose splendours in this region of New Spain are spread by the more than sublime greatness of your majesty, so that if there were any light in us, far from shining it would be dimmed, and our feeble spirits, dazzled to their uttermost depths by the majestic brilliance of so much light, would be unable to bear it. (Lienhard 1992: 44–53)

What did don Pablo and his wife hope to gain from their letter? On the one hand, as they proceed to point out in between the quotations from Ovid and the Bible, a substantial income; on the other, the recognition of their "natural dominions" and "patrimony"—lands to which they had historical title. Their argument is based in the first instance on the right of succession, but the signatories also place emphasis on the assistance that members of their families had given to the Spanish during the conquest, along with the "disinterested" contribution of don Pablo himself to the cause of Christianity and of the Spanish. Don Pablo had been, amongst other things, rector of the College of the Holy Cross in Tlatelolco, a Franciscan institution which with its humanist education played a central role in the assimilation of the indigenous and mestizo élite of the central area of Mexico.

The recognition of seigneurial rights and titles, and the concession of a more substantial income by the Spanish crown, are amongst the claims most often voiced in the letters drafted in Mesoamerica by the descendents of the pre-Hispanic nobility. Even if their rhetoric is tailored—not always with the degree of excess of the letter from don Pablo and his wife—to the expectations of their interlocutor (the king), they tend also to incorporate certain modes of expression of pre-Hispanic origin. Don Pablo himself, abruptly interrupting his praises and his Ciceronian circumlocutions, introduces—in Latin—at least two discursive genres of recognisably Aztec origin: the "historical-genealogical-title" and the "frontier treaty". In recreating a traditional discourse, these sequences constitute, in the context of the letter, a sort of foreign body.

It is highly likely, in fact, that these insertions are basically the result of the "transcription" of some documents in pre-Hispanic style. The resulting cultural hybridisation that characterises don Pablo's letter is found again, in the most varied forms, in many indigenous letters.

As well as simply defending the privileges of the nobility, other Mesoamerican letters, based on a similar historical/genealogical argument, defend the interests of local indigenous autonomy. In such letters, the list of signatories sometimes includes, as well as the traditional lord or lords, other "*caciques* and principals", local indigenous government representatives of the "notables" and the "natives", and the scribe.

A sort of leitmotiv punctuates the majority of the letters emanating from the indigenous noble classes in the sixteenth and seventeenth centuries: the loss of economic and political authority which the traditional lords had suffered from the conquest onward. Expressed with varying degrees of pathos, this topos usually contains an attempt to demonstrate that the indians are utterly and completely incapable of paying the tributes or taxes demanded of them. In its letter of October 1554, the indigenous government of Cholula attempts to anticipate, with just such an argument, the expected introduction of tithes—a tax that "penalises" sowing and the growing of "things from Castile" (Paso 1939–1942, t. VII, 269–270, reproduced in Lienhard 1992: 36–38):

> They have told us that we are to give tithes, and we all feel very great pain about this, and the *macehuales* (peasants) become despondent and say that they shall flee. . . . We beseech Your Majesty for the love of God not to impose tithes upon us, because we are very poor and many ills would befall us. (Lienhard 1992: 38)

The plea is formulated with all the marks of respect, and the vindication is attenuated by the—albeit rhetorical—expression of Christian "feelings". The only discordant note, "the *macehuales* become despondent and say that they shall flee", is almost drowned out by angelic harmonies. In stirring up the spectre of rebellion and desertion, this veiled threat constitutes, nonetheless, the most forceful argument contained in the letter.

Complaints and disputes from the absolute periphery

If the letters written by the literate Mesomericans of the upper classes bear the stamp of a shared (and highly cultured) set of writing norms, others, emanating from the "periphery" of the colonial territory, or drafted by persons lower in the hierarchy or who had had a less mainstream education, evince a much more spontaneous approach to writing. Unlike those already considered, they are wont to refer (sometimes in rather excessive detail) to very concrete occurrences: episodes of ordinary everyday oppression suffered by the indians. Very remote from the archaising rhetoric of the more "aristocratic" letters, the style of this type of text comes closer, instead, to that of oral narration. The fragment that follows is from a letter (Anderson et al. 1976: 226–229, reproduced in Lienhard 1992: 77–80) written to the king in Nahuatl by someone referred to as the mayor of Jalostotitlan (Jalisco); the (contemporaneous) translation into Spanish was made by the Royal Audience of Mexico:

> Once again a sacristan lad, eight years old he was, in a big way (the curate) whipped him, in great measure did he flay his flesh: he fainted and was a week in bed, and as soon as he rose, he fled, and the priest asked his mother about him and to her did say: "What is become of your son"? And his mother answered him: "Great travail you gave him; for that reason he has fled". And at this the priest became wroth, and then on Sunday, when he began scattering holy water, "asperges" as he called it, in the midst of the church, as he walked around scattering this holy water, he hit the mother of the sacristan lad on the head with the hyssop, and drew from her much blood. (Lienhard 1992: 79)[2]

The written testimony of the indigenous intellectuals

Some indigenous letters freed themselves from the conventions of the epistolary tradition to take the form of an "autonomous" literary genre of unexpected dimensions. Firstly, I have in mind the lengthy letter-narrative (66 folios) which the Inka Titu Cusi Yupanqui, supreme authority of the rebel Inka state of Vilcabamba, dictated for his colleague, King Philip II of Spain, in the year 1570 (Yupangui 1985); secondly, the vast letter-chronicle (1189 folios), which the supposed Quechua cacique Guaman Poma de Ayala attempted to send to Philip III around the year 1615 (Guaman Poma de Ayala 1980).

Despite their proportions, these widely known texts display all the traits of the shorter indigenous letters. In particular, they share with them (although not in grammatical terms) a sense of speaking for the whole community. Their explicit addressee is the king of Spain himself, who is supposedly above all the concerns of colonial life. Their basic motivation, however, is still clearly the assertion of claims. Other indigenous chronicles, like that of Santacruz Pachacuti Yamqui (1968 [1613]) in Peru, or the "Historical Compendium of the Kingdom of Texcoco" from Ixtlilxóchitl (1975 [1608]), descendant of the lords of that place, come close, though not explicitly, to being an epistolary genre in the terms that we have been attempting to define.

Far from limiting themselves to a specific complaint or vindication of rights, such texts express with a high degree of literary elaboration the whole historical vision of their authors and the sections of society that they represent. Here, the indigenous signatories have ceased to be humble writers of supplicatory letters in the European style but have become authors entirely in their own right, individuals conscious of a radically new literary practice. In each case, it is difficult to be sure to what extent their highly unconventional mode of narrative expression belongs more to the European or to the indigenous tradition. The dominant feature of their composition, without any doubt, is hybridity: if the choice of form (the letter-chronicle or the narrative account) gives an outward semblance of European conventions, some of their linguistic/narrative resources and the sources on which they draw relate by contrast to an autochtonous oral heritage.

Reformist and revolutionary platforms

From the eighteenth century onward, the indigenous communities started from time to time to abandon the notion that the only person who could be explicitly addressed in the process of communication was the king of Spain or his representatives. Several of the epistolary texts of the eighteenth, nineteenth, and twentieth centuries, sometimes termed *memoriales*, are "open letters", or manifestos addressed to what would today be referred to as "public opinion". Their authors were the elected or self-proclaimed spokespersons of the indigenous communities.

The style of such manifestos, erudite in style and lacking all features of oral enunciation, ceases to allude to the oral tradition. They are perfectly geared to the cultural and linguistic norms of the interlocutor, but this does not imply any political submission to the colonial or criollo authority. It has ceased to be anything more than a tactical device designed to ensure the best reception of the message. Moulded in "acceptable" forms, the message which these texts transmit continues to be "indigenous" (although without the connotation of "pre-Hispanic"), because it relates to one of the political options that had been steadily forming within the indigenous world.

Written around 1749, the "True Representation and Humble and Lamentable Exclamation Made by the Whole Indian Nation to the Lord King of all the Spains' Majesty . . . " (Bernales Ballesteros 1969, reproduced in abridged form in Lienhard 1992: 241–254), was one of the early indigenous manifestos. Defended and disseminated by Fr. Calixto de San José Tupac Inca (descendent, on the maternal side, of the Inka Tupaq Yupanqui), this text—or one of its previous versions—came to serve in the 1740s as the political platform of a major neo-Inkan sector of the Peruvian population (Bernales Ballesteros 1969). Whilst it is, in formal terms, a "letter" or petition to the king, this manifesto was widely circulated—seemingly also in printed form—before as well as after its delivery to the official addressee (1750). Tired of having to petition the king and his council for everything, the "indian nation", sensing the breezes of reform then blowing, was attempting to reach the ear of all persons of goodwill.

Inspired, as the author points out at the beginning of the text, by the lamentations of the biblical prophet Jeremiah, the eminently literary form of this "lament" constitutes a sort of (superficial) concession toward the addressee:

> *Defecit gaudium cordis nostri. Versus est in Luctum chorus noster.* The happiness of our hearts has been lost. Our canticle has become a lament; because the joy of being Christians and vassals of a Catholic monarch has fallen from our hearts, on finding ourselves abased by Christians and affronted by Catholics. (Lienhard 1992: 248)

However, at heart, the argument of the text follows a rigorously autonomous logic. The endorsement of Christianity and the monarchy is accompanied by the emphatic condemnation of "real Christianity" and veiled criticism of a king who does not honour the undertakings contracted by his great predecessors. The whole text breathes the desire for greater political and religious autonomy for the natives. A precocious call to an incipient "public opinion", the neo-Inka *Representación* served at the same time as a platform for negotiation with the king and—thanks to the publicity achieved—as a means of exerting pressure upon the addressee and his government.

Voices of insurgency

Whether to defend the remnants of their autonomy or to strengthen their position in the process of negotiation, almost all Amerindian communities have taken up the armed struggle at one time or other in their history. War does not mean the interruption of letter-writing—on the contrary, from the eighteenth century at least, indigenous insurgency has tended to manifest itself in an intensification of the dialogue in letter form with the Spanish or criollo adversary.

The state of insurgency has deep repercussions on the communicative process underlying these indigenous letters. Instead of being addressed from a position of inferiority to an interlocutor considered superior (not to say "divine"), the subject that emerges in the writings of the fully mobilised communities is an "I" or "we" who addresses his adversary as equal to equal, or even inverting the relationship, as "superior" to "inferior".

The Guaraní War (1752–1756) and the Tupacamarist Rebellion (1780–1781)

According to the terms of the frontier treaty of 1750, Spain was to hand over to Portugal seven flourishing townships of Christian Guaranís in the area east of the Uruguay river. The governor of Buenos Aires was the person charged with executing the necessary expulsion orders in the name of the king. If for the Jesuits the prospect of the loss of seven of their *reducciones* was difficult to accept, for the Guaranís it was a frontal attack on their very existence, physical, economic, and cultural.

In the series of letters in Guaraní (Mateos 1949;[3] four reproduced in Lienhard 1992: 330–346) which they addressed to the governor in 1753, opposing the handover of their ancestral territory to Brazil, the elements of an autonomous indigenous mode of expression emerge amid the protestations of fidelity to the king and the gospel. The seven indigenous responses to the threats of the governor offer, with formal variations as well as more fundamental ones, the same type of argument: the Guaranís were never conquered by the Spanish, rather they "gave themselves" to God and "chose" the "holy king", God's representative on Earth, as their protector. The king confirmed them their possessions, in the name of God. Immutable, like God, the king cannot have changed his mind; it is inconceivable, therefore, that he should wish to expel them from lands that he himself—or one of the earlier royal "incarnations"—entrusted to the care of those under his protection.

"Immutable in his will" and not linked in any way to Spanish colonialism, this king is a mythical figure, a product of the Guaranís' imagination. In recognising solely the authority of a "mythical" monarch, they divorce themselves not just from the colonial power of Río de la Plata but from that of the historical Spanish king—who, of course, was "mutable in his will".

"Masters" of the king, the Guaranís are equally so of God, of a God imposed on them, historically, by the Spanish. Secure in this certainty, the caciques of the town of Santo Angel address the governor:

> Even if you bring your cannon, we shall not fear. God Our Lord alone, we being poor indians, shall help us greatly, and the holy Angel also shall be our aid and protection. It may be that God Our Lord will place you in our hands. . . . you trust in your cannon and artillery. May it serve you well, being that in which you place most trust. All that you say to us is in vain. . . . It will all avail you nought. (Lienhard 1992: 342)

The insurgents, the "we" of the letter, now place themselves at the centre of the world, ready to take any measures whatsoever to defend their autonomy, and arrogate to themselves alone the interpretation of the values which the agents of the universal monarchy claimed to defend: Christianity and the idea of royalty. The style of the Guaranís' dialectic, particularly when we take into account the sense of holy war that appears in some of their letters, suggests the messianic character of their movement.

Far from being the precursor of criollo emancipation which some historians have made him out to be, José Gabriel Condorcanqui Túpac Amaru, leader of the great Andean Uprising of 1780–1781, in the letters which he addressed to his adversaries (in elegant Spanish) used a discursive logic reminiscent of that of the Guaranís. Indeed, in his plea-letter to the *visitador* Areche (5th March 1781), a sort of political testament, Túpac Amaru portrays himself as embodying, with no possibility of contradiction, the "will of the king" (Durand Flórez 1980–1982, t. III [1981], 204–222, reproduced in Lienhard 1992: 258–272). According to his virtually irrefutable argument, not only is the violence deployed against the local functionaries of the king himself deserving of no punishment whatever, it is even worthy of a royal reward: "And if killing those guilty of lèse-majesté is rendering a great service to the crown, we, by killing the chief magistrates and their minions, are rendering great service to Your Majesty and are worthy of reward and gratitude" (Lienhard 1992: 269). If the Guaranís knew that they could count on God against the outsiders, Túpac Amaru is, as can be gathered from his letter to the visitador Areche, the very instrument of divine justice:

> For as in the holy church of Sangarará, being there lodged the Most Holy Sacrament, they slaughtered women, which drew God's wrath down upon them straightway: for just as they did not venerate the Holy One, neither did the Holy One avail them, and as abusers of clergy they perished without assistance of clergy. Although I sent a pair of lads around the streets proclaiming that they should return to Christian ways (for my mind was not to kill them but rather to take them on one side, give them the benefit of my reason and set them on the road to salvation), Heaven in its lofty judgement closed the opportunity to them, and with their own hand they gave themselves up to la Parca (Death), being thus the authors of their unhappy fate. (Túpac Amaru refers doubtless to his victory at Sangarará, on 18th November 1780; Lienhard 1992: 266–267.)

The self-proclaimed representative of God and king in Peru, Túpac Amaru seems in fact to subscribe to an Andean code of values and norms of behavior, as embodied in the header that appears on his letters and manifestos: "Indian of royal Inka blood". Speaking with the authority conferred on him by, inter alia, his seventy thousand indigenous soldiers, Túpac Amaru addresses himself to the criollos with the intransigence that the Inkas were wont to display in the face of their adversaries ("Warning of Túpac Amaru to the Criollos of Cusco", 20th November 1780, in Durand Flórez 1980–1982, t. III [1981], 97–98; reproduced in Lienhard 1992: 257):

> If spurning this my warning you do the contrary, you will experience your ruin, my gentleness will turn to fury, and, just as I can say it, so have I strength to do it, as I have at my disposal seventy thousand indians, and other provinces which have offered themselves to me and which I have at my orders; so do not make light of this my warning which is born of my love and clemency. (Lienhard 1992: 257)

The unqualified respect for the "will of the king", and the free interpretation of the will of God, is obviously a cover for a different political reality: that of the rebirth, under the powerful impetus of the "indian of the royal stock of the Inkas", of Andean autonomy.

The process of recovery of a measure of autonomy on the part of indigenous societies in the colonial period is, beyond a doubt, the common denominator of the uprisings led respectively by José Gabriel Condorcanqui (Peru) and Nicolás Ñenguirú (Paraguay). In the letters just referred to, not only is the theme one of restoration of freedom, but the desire for this restoration also brings about a profound modification of the communicative process which until then had governed indigenous letter-writing habits. This transformation of the process gives rise to a new phenomenon, the "manifesto addressed to and against the outsiders", which is not bound in any way by the system of "feudal" rules that originally applied. In appropriating for themselves the "divine" authority of the king, the insurgent indians do not address themselves to a superior, nor do they speak from the periphery to the centre. They are, rather, on the point of inverting the roles, and making themselves the centre of their own world.

Yucatán Caste War, 1847–?

It is in the letters of the rebel Mayas of Yucatán (mid-nineteenth century) that the inversion of roles—and the rejection of all the traditional rules and conventions of communication by letter between the Indians and their adversaries—reaches its culmination. As a clear example of this we may cite the letter that Juan de la Cruz, prophet and "messiah" of the "speaking cross" movement, sent on 28th August 1851 to Miguel Barbachano, the governor of Yucatán (Bricker 1981: 208–218; reproduced in abridged form in Lienhard 1992: 129–135). Carrying the indigenous appropriation of universal religion and royalty to its logical conclusion, the author presents himself from the very outset as the Son of God the Father himself, as the creator of the *dzules* ('outsiders, whites'), the indians, the Negroes, and the mulattos. In his capacity as divine authority, situated—like the king in the ideology of universal monarchy—

above both opposing groups, Juan de la Cruz orders that an end be put to the "mutual slaying" between indians and dzules, that his dzul "children" free the Mayan prisoners, quit indigenous territory, and celebrate thirty high masses in his honour. Here, we are very far indeed from a simple assertion of rights. Should his commandments, inspired only by love of his "children", not be obeyed, the prophet promises a truly "divine" punishment:

> Don Miguel,
>> All these my commandments
> that I am sending to thee,
>> Those here,
> It is necessary
>> That thou obey them.
> Because [if] I see
>> That thou art not obeying them,
> I will place a great punishment
>> On the city of Mérida
> And over thy land. (Bricker 1981: 216)[4]

If the inversion of the roles of "vassal" and "lord" is, in this text, truly spectacular, the rejection of epistolary conventions is no less obvious. Like the other insurgent authors who emerged during the course of the "caste war", Juan de la Cruz insists in his dialogue with the chief of the dzules on using the Mayan language (a language which Barbachano doubtless understood). In itself, the choice of the indigenous language did not necessarily imply a rejection of all European rules of discourse. Juan de la Cruz, however, far from simply conceiving the letter in Spanish and putting it into Mayan, adopts the prosody—parallel distichs—of Mayan ritual language (Bricker 1989: 341–343) and presents us, in short, with a text totally rooted in Mayan verbal culture.

The peasants' struggles against spoliation: Mexico (1856) and
Peru (the 1880s)

Already anachronistic by the second half of the nineteenth century, the values that the rebel Mayans defended, whilst at the same time subverting them, still referred to the colonial experience. In the same period, other insurgent native factions claimed, in opposition to the "national" landowning oligarchies, to represent certain values which are in themselves properly criollo, such as "patriotism", "democracy", the "nation", the "people", "civilisation", and "progress". Frequently, rejecting their marginalised status, they claimed for themselves the role of vanguard of the "people" or of the "nation" in defense of a republican order which was, in reality, highly unfavourable to them (Anti-landowner proclamation of the indians of Zacoalco and San Cristóbal, Jalisco, 30th September 1856, in Reina 1980: 148–150; reproduced in Lienhard 1992: 139–143):

> The indigenous people of the town of San Cristóbal, in union with those of
> Zacoalco and the white notables . . . , in common accord recognise no other type
> of government but the representative, popular, federal type with no restitution
> [restriction?] whatsoever, upholding it with weapons in hand until the last drop
> of blood shall have been spilt. (Lienhard 1992: 142)

The peasant and indigenous notion of liberalism was quite distinct, of course, from
that of the liberal classes who wielded power. For the peasants, "emancipation" meant,
above all, the recovery of their lands:

> The predecessors of the indigenous peoples took up arms in eighteen ten, serving
> under the orders of the illustrious leader of Independence, don Miguel Hidalgo
> y Castilla, in the firm belief that with the Spanish government overthrown, they
> would recover the vast possessions which the latter had usurped from them with
> bloodshed to the detriment of all the other neighbours; an episode which was
> witnessed with pleasure by the landed classes, who more than any others are to
> blame for the misery and the backwardness in which our unfortunate fatherland
> finds itself. (Lienhard 1992: 141)

This (conditional) deference to the republican government, in this case that of the
liberals, does not signify the abandonment of indigenous autonomy, but rather its
suspension. If the government does not comply with what the indigenous communities
expect of it, they will indeed return to defending their rights for themselves: "[We
beseech the higher government to] be so good as to examine the contents of the
enclosed, and to lose no time in giving its higher verdict on the matter, to avoid the
peoples having to reconquer by arms their usurped properties and reclaim them as
property of the Indians" (Lienhard 1992: 143).

The claim to an indigenous "patriotism" also appears in the language of the
Peruvian *montoneros* who fought against Chilean occupation in the early 1880s. The
native guerrilla fighters of Comas, in the central mountains of Peru, wrote as follows
to a collaborationist landowner (Letter from the guerrilla leaders of Comas, 16th April
1882, in Manrique 1981: 393–394; reproduced in Lienhard 1992: 284–286):

> We know that you, along with other traitors of our beloved Fatherland,[5] are in
> this Province, communicating with, and giving instructions as to how the
> Peruvians can be ruined, to those perfidious Chilean bandit invaders, traitors,
> like yourself, of their country. . . . Do not include us in the ranks of the barbarians
> . . . , as we, with right and justice on our side, unanimously rise up to defend our
> Fatherland: we are true lovers of the land of our birth.

The "fatherland" of the Comas guerrilleros has, to be sure, little in common with that
of the criollo oligarchy. Once again, as in the case of the Tupacamarist Uprising, it is
a utopian "fatherland" constructed not from the perspective of criollo Lima, but from
the standpoint of the ex-Inkan highlands.

Here again, the inversion of roles in the letter-writing process is signalled by the
fact that the sender does not defer to the values of the addressee, but rather subordinates
those values to himself, making of them values of his own. In appropriating the idea

of "fatherland" from their criollo adversaries, the authors of indigenous or peasant letters such as these constitute themselves—in political and communicative terms—at the very centre of that "fatherland", relegating their adversaries to an ignominious "periphery". In the letter from the Comas *guerrilleros*, native speakers of Quechua, one can also observe the appropriation (and the equally radical transformation) of Spanish, the language of their adversaries.

Conclusion

As regards the terminology employed, the "indigenous discourse addressed to the outsiders" is dressed up, almost inevitably, in the values—or the former values—of their addressees: Christianity and monarchy, republic and fatherland, people and nation, progress and civilisation. As evidenced by the texts of the indigenous letters, the political significance of such terms depends, nonetheless, on the specific place that the interlocutors occupy in the process of epistolary communication. During the "consolidated colonial period", with the indigenous sender still in a position of inferiority and on the periphery with respect to the "centre" (the king), the official meaning of these terms was not questioned—at least not openly. As we are dealing here with eminently "diplomatic" texts, it is difficult at times to gauge to what extent the indigenous people actually subscribed to the cause of the "outsiders".

At the moments of indigenous counter-offensive, which occurred continually throughout the eighteenth and nineteenth centuries, on the other hand, the indigenous authors of letters, manifestos, and proclamations, occupying—for the moment at least—the "centre" of the process of communication, do not hesitate to invert the official semantics of these terms to give expression to the persistence of an indigenous, autonomous, interpretation of society and history. Masters of their destiny, the rebel indians appropriate to themselves the values—or ex-values—of their adversaries; they subvert them and fling them back at their former masters, just as they return blow for blow. The subversion consists, in fact, in interpreting them completely literally and carrying them through to their logical conclusion. If God is universal, any human community may appropriate him. If the king is king by divine right, there is no reason why the colonial power, which is merely temporal, should arrogate to itself the role of being His exclusive representative; the king belongs to all those who follow God's law. If the Republic guarantees equal rights for all citizens, the war against discriminators and despoilers is a just war. The Fatherland does not belong to those who proclaim themselves its owners, but to those who defend it against its adversaries, and so on. Stripped of the ideological content that they had acquired through their use by the Spanish or the criollos, the values introduced and abused by the "outsiders" are converted, in the indigenous texts, into forceful arguments against those who falsely claimed to uphold them.

ACKNOWLEDGMENTS   Translated from the Spanish by Christy MacHale.

Notes

1. Epistolary communication of a horizontal kind (i.e., between the members of an indigenous community themselves), a different phenomenon from that dealt with here, is the subject of the work of Sarah Lund (in this volume).

2. "4° oc cepa ce piltoni sachristan 8 xihuitl quipia cenca miec oquimecahuitequic cenca oquixipehuac ynacayo oçotlahua ce semana huetztoc omoquetzac niman otzoloc auh yn totatzin quitlatlania ynantzin quilhuia catia moconeuh quitoa ynantzin oticmacahuitequic otzoloc auh yca oqualanic totatzin auh yn iquac ypan domingo ya teteochihua yca tlateochihualatl yquac mitoa asperges oncan nepantla teopan yahui teteochihua yca ysopo oquihuitequic cihuatzintli ynantzin pilton sacristan quiquatzayanac yxquich esti oquiquixtilic". (Anderson et al. 1976: 168)

3. Mateos (1949) does not provide the Guaraní originals, but only a contemporary translation of them, presumably the work of one or more of the Jesuit missionaries in the area.

4. Dn. Miguel

> tulacal lein Val mah than
> Cin tuchitic techá
> ha lo
> tzá
> Cah aɔocbesic
> tumen Cin Vilic
> mah tan aɔocbesice
> Cin ɔaic humpel unohochil Castigo
> tu noh cahil Cansihoó
> ẏokol alumil. (Bricker 1981: 216)

5. The use of the term *fatherland* in translation, here and in the ensuing discussion, is deliberately chosen to reflect the patriarchal connotations of the original *patria* (translator's note).

SARAH LUND

On the Margin

*Letter Exchange among
Andean Non-Literates*

In this essay, I am concerned with examining the meaning of written forms of communication for a largely non-literate[1] Quechua-speaking society. My particular focus in exploring this question rests on the interrelationship between the spoken word and the written text in communication between close family members living far apart. In such exchanges, memory plays an essential role in the oral delivery of the message content, while the written form has the role of legitimator and potential source of sorcery. Thus, the personal letter takes on the characteristics of an epigraphic phenomenon, placing on record the names and identity of persons connected with the physical object.

The preoccupation with the oral/literate dichotomy has a long tradition in the Western history of ideas. Rousseau, in his essay "On the Origin of Languages", brought to our attention the inherent conflict between orality and textuality. His views of literacy emphasised the enslaving impact of that medium on the natural spirit of man, an idea which was to later influence Lévi-Strauss, McLuhan, and finally Derrida (Havelock 1986: 36). Jack Goody's earlier writing on literacy (1963, 1977) was also firmly placed in this sequential tradition, the consequences of literacy concerning "The Domestication of the Savage Mind". According to Goody, literacy made possible the growth of knowledge and the shift toward the objectification of the individual (cf. Harbsmeier 1984: 78; Havelock 1986: 113–114). Most of these arguments give primacy to the irreconcilable contradictions between the oral and the literate; the contrasts in the communicative media creating in themselves distinct kinds of societies with different kinds of conscious citizens.

In my opinion, the view of orality and literacy as mutually exclusive stems from a far too rigid typological distinction between oral and literate society. In the former, communication is seen to be exclusively acoustical. In terms of the latter, literacy is equivalent with phonetic writing only. Certainly this dichotomy is far too severe, and we are forced to wonder whether there was ever a purely oral society untouched by the use of some system of signs to communicate.

In our preoccupation with difference, we have neglected the powerful ways in which these interrelated forms of communication articulate. Recently this oversight has been drawn more fully to our attention as we experience our own literate tradition being powerfully transformed by a form of secondary orality (Havelock 1986: 31). The written preparation behind all of the oral presentation in contemporary media confronts us with the dramatic interplay between the oral and the written. It is the dynamics of this interchange which I wish to explore here, not in terms of confrontation, infiltration, or forced progression along a scale of complexity, but as a kind of dialogue between interdependent media. This articulation and interchange has no doubt always been a part of human experience.

This study must also be placed in the particular ethnographic context of the resettlement of highland villagers (Quechua-speaking *runa*)[2] both to the east and to the west of the Andes.[3] I have been preoccupied with experiential aspects of this mobility in the hopes of attaining insight into runa views on the process of separation and the essence of unity. Initially, I focussed on rituals of departure and arrival, treating them as essential rites of passage that mark the important thresholds of transforming experiential worlds. One of the obvious themes that arose from this discussion centres on villagers' confrontation with literacy in three very specific contexts: that of acquiring identity papers; of signing work contracts; and finally, of writing letters as part of ritual exchange between families residing in the highlands, the coast, and in the eastern jungle. In a largely non-literate village setting, these three contextualities seem to me to provide a particularly latent opportunity in which to explore wider theoretical issues concerning the interface, as opposed to the contrasts, between orality and literacy and between text and context. Further, the interplay between personal consciousness and social domination in the context of emerging literacy can be seen as particularly enlightened within the context of these relatively contained ethnographic situations.

Letter-writing in particular is one of the situations that Walter Ong (1986: 156) has characterised as forming a margin between the oral and the textual. As John Salisbury said: "'Letters speak voicelessly the utterances of the absent'" (quoted in Clanchy 1979: 204). Thus, I have chosen of the three possibilities for this chapter to focus particularly on letter-writing between villagers from Matapuquio. I will be dealing with letters authored and witnessed by wider family constellations, written down by local scribes, and delivered by travellers who are either departing from or returning to the village. It will become apparent that this courier takes on the role of the ultimate interpreter of the message in a situation in which both the author and the addressee communicate through a medium that they do not master and in a foreign language only poorly understood. In this communication maze, it will also be appreciated that letters are viewed with great suspicion, as media of sorcery.

My choice of letter-writing as a point of departure rests on several important considerations. First, while identity papers and work contracts are textual components in relationships between individual villagers and the wider socio-cultural universe of Peruvian society, letter-writing is an internal communication between closely related villagers living at a distance, a kind of communication that struggles with a general lack of knowledge about respective contexts. Further, much of the dynamic of this communicative exchange either struggles to impose the ascendency of a certain set of collective values over individuals removed from the collective pressures of life in the village, or they form part of the verbal assurances that such responsibilities are still respected despite lengthy absences. Thus, I find letters and letter-writing a particularly poignant example of the complex shiftings between shared meanings and disparate appreciations, between collective memories and divergent expectations, between the fear of witchcraft and the longing for a genuine message.

The written oral interface

Before turning to the specific instance of letter-writing, let us take the opportunity to discuss in a more abstract sense the contrasts and similarities between orality and literacy. A seeming consensus lies in the importance given to the free-floating nature of the written word, disassociated as it is from the context of its production. Some authors have gone so far as to argue that, more than any other invention, writing has changed the parameters of human thought in striking ways (Goody 1986; Hallpike 1979: vi; Havelock 1986; Ong 1982: 14–15). The role of literacy has been seen to have powerful liberating effects fundamental to logical analytic modes of thought, a sceptical and questioning attitude, and the recognition of the important distinctions between time and space, myth and history. A literate people have the wherewithal for innovative, democratic, and socially humane thinking, essential to economic development, the process of urbanisation, and the rise of complex government (Gee 1988: 196). To be literate is to be civilised (Havelock 1986: 35–36).

This obvious idealisation masks the historical complexity of literacy in society (cf. Graff 1979). By addressing a particular written practice of a people poised on the margins of a literate tradition, I hope to address some of the ambiguity inherent in the role of literacy. I will emphasise how literacy is embedded in certain social settings, thus implying that the process of interpretation is an integral aspect of the practice of literacy. Further, the basis for interpretation is essentially bound up with socialisation, with the social groups and institutions that form the context or the conditions of the text's production (Gee 1988: 209).

Plato has been given the distinction of being the first writer to record his scepticism toward writing, and some of the doubts he expresses about the literate mode certainly hold relevancy for our discussion here. Plato held the written mode as suspect because he saw it as undermining the role of memory, especially in the process of acquiring knowledge. "For Plato, one knew only what one could defend in face-to-face dialogue with someone else" (ibid., 197). The written text was suspect because of its quality of seeming completeness, giving it an illusive authority. In a contradictory way, Plato also points out the great weakness of writing in that it cannot stand up and defend itself. For Plato, true knowledge comes when one person makes a statement and another asks, "What do you mean"? Such a request forces the speaker to "re-say", that is, to say in different words, what he or she means. In the process he sees more deeply what he means, and responds to the perspective of another voice/viewpoint. (p. 197).

In contrast to the written word, orality presupposes dialogue. It is from the context of communicative exchange that one can say that authorship as we know it does not exist in a non-literate society (Foley 1986: 8). The oral narrative is collectively fashioned, and the context must be appreciated to grasp the meaning. As opposed to the universalising nature of the written word, such discourse is particularistic, taking into account the conditions of performance and the various roles of oral forms in the culture as a whole. From an oral tradition, the immediacy of the audience is an inherent aspect of the performance, allowing as it does for an ongoing assessment of what can be taken for granted as shared understanding (Todorov 1984: 34). This is one of the most difficult transitions to be overcome, when someone from a largely oral tradition assumes a literate mode of communication. There is no first-hand experience of interaction by which to judge the posing of the message. As we shall later come to appreciate more fully in the particular case of letter-writing, it is with difficulty that the orally oriented writer, who is basically delivering a monologue in the form of a letter, can imagine the reader and anticipate her/his reactions to the words. An oral orientation presupposes an active interlocutor (Sweeney 1987: 178–179).

Within the historical context of colonialism, indigenous peoples of the Americas frequently hold the belief that their languages cannot be written down (e.g., Brotherston 1979; Perrin 1986: 211). For them, learning to read and write involves assuming a foreign language with unfamiliar vocabulary and grammar, a language that is strongly associated with their subordination. The power of élites is held to be inseparably bound up with their power of writing; their exclusive source of a kind of materialised and infinite knowledge. Here, too, Christian missions have been active for centuries, evangelising through the medium of the written word in a holy book. These foreigners are assumed to be in the possession of special powers of divination by means of which they can communicate with their gods. As opposed to indigenous means of supernatural communication based on the personal intermediary of the shaman, the external nature of the written word is held to be particularly potent and of another order, making shamans of all outsiders (cf. Perrin 1986).

Seen in this light, literacy is a part of the yawning gap between an indigenous world and that of outside domination. Thus, for many indigenous peoples, learning to read and write implies putting aside an entire way of life, accepting the premises of an élite society, and ultimately embracing foreign gods. In such a situation, literacy implies far more than the "technologising of the word" (Ong 1982), the additional accumulation of technical skills. Far from being part of an inevitable process, this perspective on literacy rather poses a complexity of problems laden with normative ambiguity.

Matapuquio/Chanchamayo/Lima:
The letter circuit

Keeping these brief comments on a complex field in mind, let us turn our attention to the specific instance of letter-writing between Matapuqenians. That this simple exchange is fraught with tensions and ambiguity can be suspected in terms of what has been said so far, but first let me develop the background to this situation more fully.

Matapuquio is a runa village in the southern highlands, in one of Peru's poorest departments, Apurímac. Though holding their own territory, the villagers have been under the influence of the local hacienda for centuries, by working on the estate to gain access to vital pasturelands, additional agricultural fields, and more recently to cash income (cf. Skar, H. 1982). Neither wages nor any form of formal education were available to the villagers before the mid-1960s. The change occurred when the local *hacendado* (land boss) began to offer money in payment for work and built the village school at his own cost on hacienda property bordering the village. The school curriculum is limited to the first three years of primary school. The teachers come from the surrounding mestizo towns, but they hold their posting with a degree of disdain, and their attendance and efforts are sporadic. Village children have many family responsibilities, and schooling in general, coupled with the teachers' attitudes in particular, are viewed by parents as highly questionable. While all instruction is carried on in both Quechua and Spanish, the goal of teaching is to learn to read and write in Spanish. In fact, none of the teachers that I have known in the village were able to write Quechua, and they were fascinated to see my books in that language. With no books, and few of the students having paper and pencil with which to work, the school is woefully hampered in being able to teach reading and writing skills. On completing three years of "compulsory" education, the vast majority of village children have learned to speak some Spanish, and they can write and recognise their names.

There are villagers who know how to read and write, however. Young men and women who have left the village for the coastal city of Lima have often, and at considerable sacrifice, gone to night school. When these young people return to the village to marry and settle down, they begin to serve as scribes, writing down the many letters which are composed in the village and sent with travellers leaving for the coast or to the eastern jungle.

From a village perspective, the two groups of non-residents in Lima and Chanchamayo form what they would call colonies (*mitmaqkuna*). Those living outside are subordinate to their families and ultimately their village in the highlands (*ayllu*). This hierarchical relationship of mitmaq to ayllu is fundamentally associated with the continuing rights to village land, irrespective of long absences. One of the main expressions of this subordination can be found in a fairly complex system of exchange between village and jungle and between village and city. The letter forms a part of this exchange. Though this is not the only context in which letters circulate, nevertheless, it is one of the main situations in which villagers are compelled to communicate in writing.

Let me be more concrete. When someone is leaving Matapuquio for the jungle or for Lima, they take with them agricultural produce to give to their families living outside. This food is considered an important medium by which physically to bind the non-resident villagers with the substance of their lands and their kin in the highlands. It is a kind of pledge that village rights are being maintained for the ones that are away. In return when someone travels up to the highlands from the coast, dry goods, clothing, and money are sent along as the appropriate response to the agricultural gifts. People living in the jungle send fruit, coffee, and money. In this way, produce and objects associated with one region are exchanged with those from the other, thus becoming important anchors in reproducing patterns of kin-based socioeconomic relations between ecological zones.[4]

The letters accompanying such commissions are mainly a kind of inventory. They are a recognition of what has been previously received and a declaration of what is enclosed. They serve to keep a check on material possessions and as such are evidence of the power relations between villagers, and over worldly possessions, all bounded within the system of exchange. This exchange has close associations with the Incaic and colonial *mita* system, a kind of work tribute which also had as an aim to acquire resources unavailable in the home environment (Murra 1982; Wightman 1990: 86–88). If we see these exchanges of produce and letters of inventory between mitmaq and ayllu as tribute, in the sense of a testimonial of respect with an urgency of cohesion, we can more easily appreciate how closely literacy is associated with the exercise of power at a distance. The bulk of the letters I have available at this time seek to keep a check over the movement of material possessions and human beings. They serve as a control mechanism within the dynamics of a local tribute system in which pre-eminence of the highland community is constantly seeking reaffirmation from its mitmaq. The role of the written document becomes that of authoritative voice checking, comparing, and demanding accountability.

Letters exchanged between Matapuqenians are concerned with accountability, and in this role they have a definite connection with contractual agreements. They are documents with evidential value linking writing with units of wealth, particularly money. From this perspective there are many similarities between the role of the letter and that of the contract and the identity papers mentioned in the introduction, as being the initial encounters with literacy for departing villagers. All three of these kinds of documents can be interpreted as demonstrating the qualitative shift from status to contract, the long-term implications of which are the disassociation of law and custom (Goody 1986: 144).

The three texts all bear the mark of strong legal undercurrents which play off the tension between an abstracted legal position with the specificity of individualised agreement. In the example of the personal letter reproduced below, we see that acceptable standardised form limits the particularised message at the same time giving expression to the essential particulars of a specific transaction completed in the past.

Matapuquio, el 21 de Setiembre 1985

Estimados compadres,
    Reciben de Esteben Quispe y Epifania Cotarma sus compadres, asi como de Victor su ahijado y de Evardista Cotarma los más calurosos saludos.
    Les agradecemos del dinero que nos han mandado; Este agradecimiento viene de todo corazón.

Epifania ha estado mal de salud pero con el favor de Dios ya esté bién.
Sin otro particula me despido en el nombre del Señor.

Abrazos
Epifania
Nota: Cuando van a venir para aqui?

[Matapuquio, 21st September 1985

Dear Compadres,

Receive the warmest greetings from your compadres Esteban Quispe and Epifania Cotarma, as well as from Victor your godchild and from Evardista Cotarma.

We thank you for the money you have sent. This gratitude comes from the bottom of our heart.

Epifania has been ill but with God's grace now is well.

With no other news, I will close in the name of the Lord.

Abrazos
Epifania

P.S.: When are you going to come here?]

The collective orality of letter exchange

There is another side to letter-writing and exchange between Matapuqenians that remains to be explored, one that gives us an opportunity to take into account the many aspects of a letter's production and delivery. I would move away from the generalised institutional effects of literacy, in this particular case letter-writing, toward an exploration of the indissoluble links between literacy, context, and meaning. Here we are concerned with a type of text, the letter, and the various ways of both producing and reading those letters as social and historical creations.

For the majority of Matapuqenians, a kind of collective orality is the single most important aspect of creating and receiving letters. This is true of the inventory letters described here, as well as letters with a more intimate content. There are so few who can take on the role of the literate in the communication so that letter writing and reading is a group effort. Someone is leaving for Chanchamayo, and a woman, newly widowed, will try to reach her son with the news of his father's death. She wants her son to come home to help her. It is arranged that a scribe will come to her house to write the letter. The courier/traveller is also present, as are several married children, and one of their spouses. The deceased man's brother is specifically asked to come. People perch around on the low walls of the patio and the letter is begun, the scribe labouring over a piece of lined notebook paper with a small pencil stub lost to view in his large fist.

At the top is entered the place and date of the letter and the complete name of the addressee. Without further introduction, the text begins with a progress report on the welfare of those present, and continuing in this formulaic vein inquires into the health of the long absent son from whom they have not heard for a very long time. There are no capital letters or punctuation to mark sentences, but if read orally the meaning is clear enough. The main point of the letter follows: the father is dead, and the son is needed at home. In very brief terms, the mother insists that the son return and promises to find him a wife and provide everything he needs to begin his own family. Again in a very stylised manner, the letter is closed 'for lack of more to say' ("sin mas que decir te despido"), with greetings also from the father's brother, as well as sisters, brother, and brother-in-law being specified. Another piece of paper is folded into a kind of envelope, and the name of the son is written on the outside with only one indication of address, Chanchamayo. No one really knows where the son is in Chanchamayo, which is a huge territory, but maybe someone amongst the other villagers residing there will have word of him.

This is a summary of the letter's text, but is no indication, whatsoever, of the lively discussion carried on in conjunction with forming the letter. The father's brother is the youth's godfather (*padrino*), and he confers with his sister-in-law about which family they should approach in asking for a wife. It becomes apparent that the courier is not leaving for Chanchamayo by chance, but is being sent by the widow to find her son. The courier is the widow's younger half-brother, and there is much discussion as to whom he shall seek out to ask for help when he arrives. The siblings and brother-in-law, much older than the absent youth, obviously feel strongly that their brother must return to take up his responsibilities as youngest child—that is, the support of his mother and the cultivation of the remaining fields that have not already been divided out between them. Their presence, in addition to that of the mother and father's brother, adds authority to the letter. Long after the scribe is finished with the brief epistle, and the widow has put her thumbprint at the bottom of the letter over her name, the courier is being coached as to what must be said to truly convince the son to return.

Eventually, the traveller departs for the jungle, and finally he does manage to find his nephew who is working with four other youths from Matapuquio on a coffee plantation at Santa Inita. The letter is delivered, but none of them is sufficiently literate to read it through, though they recognise the name written below the fingerprint and can decipher the village name, the date, and the boy's name. Eventually they ask for help with the reading, but long before the actual text is read and the content of the letter delivered, the uncle has been telling about the father's death and how the boy must come home. He can relate how the elder siblings are committed to his return to take up his inheritance and that the mother and father's brother are already concerned with finding a wife for him. Questions and answers, problems and solutions as to how things can be arranged are being aired long before the formal message is ever received. In fact, the letter itself is almost forgotten in the oral discussion about its content, or rather the complex message behind its content.

In writing about rituals of travel, Van Gennep (1960: 37) describes the letter as a kind of sign that wins recognition for the traveller, automatically incorporating the courier into the receiving group. Through the letter, the traveller is able to identify himself with others he meets. As I have learned to appreciate among Matapuqenians, the letter really serves as an object of trust, authenticating the oral message which the courier delivers. In many cases, I would go so far as to say that the letter is the authenticating symbolic object and helps solve the problem of communication at a distance. For many, the tangible letter conveys the views and feeling of the writer's wishes, far and beyond what the written content actually communicates. The letter is a physical reinforcement of what is being said (Clanchy

1979: 245–246). In fact, though the youths scrutinised the letter's headings and signature, they failed to show any interest in critically examining the written contents of the document. The letter becomes simply a subsidiary to the memorisation of the message and not its replacement.

Every text is of a type. When considering the interface between literacy and orality, the letter, the type of text under discussion here, poses requirements in terms of our expectations of both form and content. "One always and only learns to interpret texts of a certain type in certain ways through having access to, and ample experience in, social settings where texts of that type are read in those ways. One is socialised into a certain social practice" (Gee 1988: 209). Within a highly literate social practice, the familiar letter as a type is associated with intimate conversation. In the eighteenth and nineteenth centuries, it was cultivated as a literary art form within the context of an intimate relationship. The essential texture of this genre gave ascendency to the conversational paradigm, favouring the speaking tone of voice (Redford 1986: 2).

For the runa, interpretation of a letter involves an entirely different practice. As depicted in the case above, the letters consist almost entirely of formulae, listing titles and epithets of sender and addressee. They confirm relationships, but do not express a one-to-one kind of intimacy between individuals. Sentiments are generalised to the extent that one can wonder at their impersonal tone. However, it should be recalled that one of the biggest barriers of literacy for an orally oriented person is to imagine the audience. The audience postulated in many of the letters written by Matapuqenians would seem to be pure stereotype.[5]

The runa letter generates meaning on its terms above and beyond the written meaning on its page. I would venture to say that the burden of meaning within the practice of letter exchange rests on the experience of the letters as presence (Foley 1986: 16). One integrative theme in my research (Skar, S. 1994), which has allowed me to place ethnographic elements in new relationships, discusses the total identification runa often assume between the sign and the object represented.[6] Many of their beliefs in magic are founded on assumptions about sympathetic and contagious links in the sequence of cause and effect. Letters are held to be very forceful objects in this sense and are almost always received with suspicion and fear, as well as joy and anticipation. The most disturbing letters are those exceptional ones actually received through the post. In one instance, the addressee actually kept the letter and the envelope of such a posted letter in separate places. The envelope was obviously very disturbing to him with its stamps and elaborate address. It was the envelope he took out to show me first, asking in a conspiratorial tone: "How could they possibly know me, know my identity number"? He did not appreciate how an address worked with its levels of inclusiveness. Nor did he realise that that which we call a postal service is not a limited group of people who know you intimately, but rather a relay of de-personalised links from periphery to centre to periphery again. That the post was able to deliver a letter to him on the basis of what was written on an envelope obviously gave them some kind of power over his person. In this medium, total strangers knew him too intimately, and the thought was disturbing. There was a possibility that the letter, especially the envelope, could have some malevolent power over him since it came to him via strangers.

Among Matapuqenians there is a strongly held belief that letters are objects of sorcery (*wiñapi*). Félix Cárdenas, a village outsider who keeps a simple shop in his house, is known to specialise in written sorcery. It was claimed that he once wrote such a letter for his wife who was unhappy with her daughter-in-law for accusing her, by letter, of neglecting the cow left in the mother-in-law's care. In the process of writing the reply, don Félix took three lighted candles and turned them upside-down saying the full name of the daughter-in-law, then proceeding to write a letter. I was assured that one could kill an entire family in this way. At any rate, in this case, the mother-in-law was writing to her son, but the sorcery was meant for the daughter-in-law, who is named. The bewitched letter caused the son to beat his wife for no apparent reason. But the daughter-in-law's family knew that it was the misunderstanding over the cow left in Matapuquio which was ultimately behind the beating. The vindication of the mother-in-law was made possible through the letter, which was sent by a different courier from the one who delivered the original accusation.

It is a dangerous thing to receive a letter too open-heartedly because it may not be what it seems. Loss of fortune, abandonment by spouse, or the fact that one never returned to the village have all been attributed to bewitched letters. Through the letter as object, the malevolent attitudes of the sender are placed right at the heart of the receiver. No matter what the tone of the written words might be, the contagious effect of the evil intent is what becomes communicated. The letter has a kind of organic identity with the sender. When received by the addressee, the link is not broken. Once put into contact with the receiver, powerful objects such as letters of sorcery continue to exert an influence.

Conclusion

Largely hampered in their movements earlier, it is mostly during the course of the past twenty-five years that Matapuqenians have moved out of their village to establish permanent settlements in the jungle and on the coast. This separation has stimulated the use of literate forms as a means of communication between villagers at a distance. However, the use of writing in the letters exchanged between villagers takes on meaning in terms of other forms of communication. Problems of authenticity, of trusting what is written, continue to rest largely on the persuasive powers of the courier. Memory, instead of written content, still comprises the main medium of the message relayed between groups. An intimate one-to-one conversational tone associated with the familiar letter-writing has no place. The letter's set phraseology and physical format reflect links with techniques of memory and oral tradition as well.

It seems paradoxical that, within written tradition, the letter is a literary genre/type which strives for the oral tone, the writing down of intimate conversation, and as such might be characterised as a literate form at the margins of orality. From the standpoint of a non-literate tradition such as that of Matapuquio, letter-writing has nothing to do with conversation. Rather, it is characterised by formulaic ingredients: an elaborate focus is placed on devices of authentication such as the signature, seal, dates and place, and identified witnesses. The physical document is scrutinised, while the written contents are given little or no critical examination. Letters for Matapuqenian readers serve as important signs of recognition, legitimising the accompanying oral message.

Our discussion of the role of letter-writing in a non-literate society has thrown into relief the ambiguity and complexity in the dynamic relationship between the written and the spoken. The limited use of literate forms relates at many levels to social processes and structures, an appreciation of these being necessary to reveal the full significance of the written. The role of letter exhange is a complex reality with contradiction and discontinuities arising out of the social setting of which it is a part. Thus, the letters exchanged by Matapuqenians become a convincing example of the inextricable link between text, context, and meaning.

ACKNOWLEDGMENTS   My research has been funded by the Norwegian Research Council for the Social Sciences and the Humanities (1976–77), by the Swedish Social Science Research Council (1984, 1986), and most recently by the Institute for Cultural Comparative Research (1991–92). I am grateful for their generous support.

Notes

1. I use the term *non-literate* in the title and the text as opposed to *illiterate*. The former emphasises the acoustic character of successful oral communication; the latter is couched in the negative image of failed communication in a medium not mastered (cf. Havelock 1986: 119).

2. Quechua-speaking villagers in the southern sierra refer to themselves as *runa*, or 'human beings'. I have chosen to use their term of self-reference in this chapter, out of a sense of respect for their community and in recognition of the many difficulties involved in using other terms of reference such as "indian".

3. *Lives Together Worlds Apart. Quechua Colonization in Jungle and City* (S. Skar 1994) explores in a more comprehensive way the uses of literacy in the context of migration.

4. This dynamic economic interdependence between contrasting ecological areas is referred to as "vertical economy" (Murra 1982) and has been a crucial factor in interregional relationships for centuries.

5. See Sweeney (1987: 180) for a discussion of Malay letter writing and the difficulties posed in communicating a piece of news.

6. Another powerful example of this is found in Allen's contribution to this volume. There the discussion focuses on the use of *inqas* in the context of pilgrimage, while in this case letters bear the qualities of their authors. In both cases the aspect of movement in space is important and seems clearly associated to more generalised ideas about the flow of life energies.

TRISTAN PLATT

The Sound of Light

*Emergent Communication through Quechua
Shamanic Dialogue*

For Norman

Ⅰt is becoming increasingly difficult to interpret Andean oral testimonies in isolation
from the wide range of visual memory techniques (including forms of "writing")
which they invoke and presuppose (Arnold et al. 1992; Condori and Ticona 1992). In
a previous article (Platt 1992), I argued that even the oral performances of modern
North Potosí shamans are grounded in a deep historical belief in the authority of
graphic inscriptions (*qillqa*) which can, in principle, be "made to speak" (*parlachiy*).
The experience of the Spanish invasion led much of this graphic authority to be
resituated in the alphabetic code and representational aesthetic of the invaders—as,
classically, in the work of Waman Puma (Adorno 1986). The authority of the
alphabetic code developed particularly in the context of the catechetical and notarial
discourses reproduced through the administrative and archival practices of the colonial
church and state (Mannheim 1991), while the new representational aesthetic emerged
above all in the wealth of sacred art aimed to skew native perceptions of the divine in
the direction of a Christian body of iconographic conventions (Gisbert 1980; Fraser
1982; MacCormack 1991). Further, our awareness of different forms of literacy
among colonial Andean populations (e.g., Adorno 1982; Itier 1991; Duviols and Itier
1993; Lienhard 1992) has grown to the point where it is becoming necessary to ask to
what extent the existence of mass alphabetic illiteracy during the Republic is not itself

a relatively recent product of a process of modernisation which, at the same time, has created for purposes of its own reproduction the image of a "purely oral" Andean culture.

The oral text here presented belongs to an Andean shamanic tradition that has also been marked by the great imperial bureaucratic revolution introduced into European statehood by Spain, where the most elaborate documentary and archive-based methods of government thitherto known in Europe were developed in the sixteenth century (González Echevarría 1990). The result is, in the first instance, a form of textuality that seeks authorisation on both oral-performative and scriptural grounds. In the séance I shall present, the mountain spirits, or *jurq'u*, are summoned by the shaman to answer questions put to them by a small domestic congregation, but their speech and identity are marked by the scriptural context within which they act. The political and religious context is constructed through dialogue by incorporating references to the literate practices present in the wider society, which both legitimate and are legitimated by the oral procedures of the séance.

For within this inscriptional context, where Andeans recognise "writing" as a major instrument of colonial authority, while at the same time seeking to domesticate it, the shamanic séance manages to keep open an oral and dialogic space within which contexts, frames of interpretation, and truth conditions are up for negotiation (cf. Duranti and Goodwin 1992). This has various consequences for Andean approaches to the construction of knowledge: (1) alphabetic metaphors may be used creatively to authorise other forms of graphic inscription; (2) the "dictates" transmitted by the mountain spirits through the shaman to the congregation can be discussed and reinterpreted according to local perspectives; and hence (3) "the letter of the law" is seen to be at least minimally flexible and modifiable in relation to local realities.

Finally, the transcript allows us to analyse the way in which communication is constructed over an evening made up of a sequence of short conversations between the shaman, the congregation, and the mountain spirits that serve a powerful local St James known as "Father Pumpuri" (*Tata Pumpuri*)—who himself remains off-stage. From hesitant beginnings, dialogue becomes gradually more fluent, until the antiphonal affirmation of speech in the last section allows the séance to be recognised as a success by all parties. Attention to the wider aural context allows us to see this collective recognition of communicative competence emerging from a rich tilth of supporting noise: whistles to summon the jurq'us, the clinks of bottles during libations, the crackle of coca-leaves being handed round, the sighs and invocations of the shaman in trance, the semi-audible murmurings of the congregation, and finally the rhythmic beating of wings that announces the arrival and sustains the presence of the mountain spirit in the form of a condor-messenger from the lofty frontiers between earth and sky.

Communication with unknown sources of sacred power is an inescapable aspiration for the ethnographer who wishes to write about religion. When Evans-Pritchard said that only believers could do so, he meant that otherwise the vital connections, perspectives, and *chiaroscuro* of the believers' truth will inevitably escape one. While my own faith is insecure, volatile, and often vanishes, I have tried to write as a believer to help represent the "reasons for faith" that underlie these acts of communication with the personalised forces of the cosmos. In support of this, I can at least claim to have felt the other side of faith in Father Pumpuri's power, which is fear. However, it will be useful here also to invoke that suspension of disbelief which is expected of the audience at any dramatic performance. The relation between the development of Andean shamanism and that of Andean drama is clearly a fruitful avenue for future research.

Meeting Tata Pumpuri

Geographically, Santiago (St James) de Pumpuri is a tiny hamlet of a few straggled houses surrounding a small adobe chapel, situated on a high plateau above 4000 metres above sea level near the northwestern borders of Macha territory. Looming over it, on the borders with the altiplanic Department of Oruro, rises the mountain range known as the Cordillera of the Friars. Pumpuri has been one of the rural annexes of the indian parish of San Pedro de Macha at least since the seventeenth century. This parish (*doctrina*) was founded by Viceroy Francisco de Toledo in the 1570s as an administrative and evangelical focus for the highland segment of an important dual society, Macha, which had been the ethnic "capital" (*cabecera*) of the pre-Hispanic "federation" (*señorío*, or *nación*) of Qaraqara. Today, the hamlet falls on the borders between two *cabildos* (rural tribute-paying groups), each belonging to one of the five minor ayllus into which each of the two moieties of Macha have been divided since pre-Hispanic times.

The old white-washed and thatched chapel of Pumpuri can be seen from far off, at the ceremonial entry (*ch'isiraya*) to the sacred plain where the cult of St James is centred. Here pilgrims pause to chew coca and pour libations before approaching the tiny village. The appearance of the tower of the old chapel made me uneasy when I first saw it in 1971:[1] with only one turret surviving the summer rains like a peaked hat, and two bells that seemed almost like eyes, its whitewashed adobe base was stained until almost halfway up its height by the blood of sacrificed animals. Inside, the shadowy reredos (*retablo*) was full of clustered images, with that of St James dismounted in the middle, his aquiline face black-bearded and crowned with a hat, the sacred heart of Jesus suspended over a crescent moon with its horns upturned, and the Bolivian tricolour over one shoulder.[2] Today, the old chapel is flanked by a modern church roofed with corrugated iron, where the image of Father Pumpuri has been relocated by priests aiming to "clean up" the Pumpuri cult, although his devotees say that he still prefers the old adobe chapel (Figure 12-1).

The power of St James of Pumpuri is recognised over much of the southern Andes: pilgrims arrive for his feast on 25th July from northern Argentina,[3] Chile, and southern Peru, as well as from distant parts of Bolivia—La Paz, Oruro, Potosí, Sucre, Santa Cruz, the coca-growing Yungas of Chapare, and the eastern lowlands. The strength of the faith he inspires is visible in the strong emotions aroused in his devotees: unconditional adoration and obedience, pride, anguish, weeping, fear and trembling. He is known for his medical powers: he can kill and he can cure, and he is sometimes invoked as the Angry Doctor (*phiña miriku*). His treatments are perceived either as disasters (*disgrasya*), with which he can punish ritual neglect and moral misdemeanours, or as good fortune (*surti*), with which he rewards the devout. Health; fertility of humans, animals, and crops; and economic prosperity are offered as the reward of religious faith.

SR. SANTIAGO DE BOMBORI

Figure 12-1 Tata Santiago de Pumpuri: a photo sold to pilgrims during the fiesta.

As doctor,[4] St James is patron of curers and shamans, but he does not tolerate black magic or devil worship (something of which his church critics are not always aware). However, neither does he belong exclusively to the realm of the High God (*altu dyus*), as does another "miracle", Tata Killakas, who is based in an altiplanic shrine near Lake Poopó. Tata Pumpuri partakes in the Glory of the Upper World (*janaj pacha*), but he also has "roots" (*saphi*) of Glory in the Inner World (*ukhu pacha*). He is therefore a clear expression of the need to "offer to both sides" (*purajman jaywayku*), to the powers of Without and those of Within, characteristic of Andean Christianity, which recognises the essentially creative role of the chthonic powers in generating new life in tense coexistence with the Upper Deities and the High God (cf. Platt 1987).[5]

The Tata goes to battle raised above merely human foot-soldiers on his horse: his most terrifying weapons are lightning (*glurya sintilla*, the Flash of Glory), thunder, and thunderbolt (*rayu*), which are imagined as the flash, rumble, and bullets of his arquebus.[6] The thunder also represents the sound of his horse's hooves as he gallops through the clouds. His metallic bullets (*walas*, from Spanish *bala*) streak to earth with the lightning—*k'aj!* in Quechua onomatopoeia—and fulminate animals, houses, church towers, people, and especially those fated to be a shaman, or *yachaj*. For these, the experience is an initiation: they die, but are reassembled at a second flash and resuscitated at a third. The triple imagery of Easter, as well as of the pre-Hispanic cults of Charcas, is thus reproduced in their death and resurrection. In their new vocation, they will communicate with Father Pumpuri and place their indian clients in living contact with him, either channelling his voice directly or through the medium of the condor-mountain spirits which are his servants.[7]

At the spot where the initiation took place, now sacralised as *surti parisirun* (the place where the Luck appeared), the future yachaj finds one of Santiago's bullets, still smoking with sacred energy, and nurtures it with dishes of sacred foods (*glurya jampis*) while learning to become a shaman. The best way to neutralise its dangerous energy is, indeed, to channel it into a shamanic session, or Council (*kawiltu*).

Spirit possession

The shaman's effort to construct the conditions for communication between congregation and spirit messenger is a difficult and risky undertaking. The bullets themselves must be taken to hear Mass in a Christian church from time to time, to prevent their "eating" the initiates by draining them of energy till they die. My friend Santiago, one of the main actors in the text that follows, had been struck by lightning, but resisted the call to become a shaman. He suffered from a long-drawn-out illness, one symptom of which was the arrival of a condor in his bedroom while he was asleep, eager to occupy his body. The experience left him frightened and shaken, and in 1977 he eventually died. As so often in South Andean thinking, inherently dangerous sources of sacred power can only be tamed partially for the benefit of human society if they are placed under the aegis of the Christian church; in Andean Christianity, this includes the obligation to accept the rôle of shaman if one is nominated by the lightning bolt of St James.

Spirit possession is itself dangerous and exhausting: the spirit enters in the shape of a bird—generally a condor[8]—and possesses the shaman, giving him extra intelligence (*aswan intilijinti*) and changing his voice to the point where the audience can hear him and the spirit conversing as two separate people. To reach this pitch of spiritual susceptibility, he must chew quantities of coca leaf, smoke tobacco, drink neat alcohol and grape spirit, and pour libations for the sacred sources of power while approaching the state in which he can suddenly fall into a state of trance and spirit possession.

The séance (*kawiltu*, from Sp. *cabildo* 'council') I attended and taped in August 1971 consisted of six separate sessions, divided into one group of four and one of two. Before they began the candle was extinguished, and the spirit was heard to enter and speak in complete darkness. Within each group, there were pauses between the sessions when people talked in the darkness, commenting on the answers given by the spirit and phrasing new questions. These "intervals" are a valuable commentary on the form and content of the preceding session of shamanic dialogue. The candle was relighted during the central "intermezzo", which separated the two groups, and then again at the end. The overall frame for the event was therefore given by this oscillation between light and darkness, establishing an elementary visual code within which the aural experience was inscribed.

Most of the elements that contribute to the global signification of the event are aural, and have therefore been caught on the tape, though they cannot include smells, touch, and the intimate feeling of familial warmth shared before the invisible "action" on the altar table. Gesture is only available in aural form: actions are etched on the darkness. Intonation, murmurs and rustles, hesitations, the clinking and blowing of bottles, the "whistle" of the shaman's bullet, the slurps of the condor drinking alcohol offered by the yachaj, and especially the rhythmic flapping of his wings as he perches invisible on the altar table—all combine with distant background noises to make up an overwhelmingly aural field of meaning that dispenses with all visual cues beyond the basic opposition between the candle and the dark.

Setting the scene

The yachaj we asked to hold the council was a compadre of my friend Santiago and his wife Feliciana, the couple I was staying with in Liq'unipampa. His name was Ignacio Mosques.[9] One bright winter's morning in August 1971, we went to the little mill house on the river nearby where he was grinding wheat flour. The water glittered beneath the sunlight as it streamed through rocks and pebbles down from the distant salt mines and licks at Salinas. A turf-lined canal threw a heavy flow of water on to the wooden water wheel beneath the mill, and the sound of the stone mill wheel could be heard rumbling inside the house. Upstream, over a bed of tumbled stones and boulders, lay the hot baths of Phutina, and further on—out of sight from the mill house—the gold and antimony mines of Churiña. The world smiled.

We entered, and Santiago began to explain things while I watched the flour dusting the edge of the lower millstone as the upper stone turned ponderously on its vertical shaft. At first Ignacio was reluctant; he said his bullets had been playing up, making him ill, and he had had to take them to the Sanctuary of Tata Killakas to hear mass. But the tape recorder clearly interested him, and he liked the idea of taping a session. Finally he relented and agreed to come that very night. We promised him 15,000 bolivianos (August 1971 rates).

During the rest of the day all the children in the hamlet were full of excitement. They played in the sunlit patio at being the jurq'u who would be summoned by the yachaj, imitating his first greeting—*winas nuchis wawas kristyanus*! 'Good evening, my Christian children'!—and laughing at their own efforts. But when that evening, well after dark, Ignacio finished his meal of liver with hot sauce (but no Christian salt) and entered the little room where we were going to hold the council, the children fell silent.

From the moment the yachaj entered, the dramatic performance had begun.[10] Laughter was wiped from every expression. By candlelight, the altar table (*misa*) was prepared behind the door: an old wooden box, on it a woman's weaving (*ajsu*), folded, then a smaller rations-cloth (*inkhuña*), then another folded cloth. The yachaj accepted quantities of coca leaf which he covered in the folds, along with his two bullets. He began to take coca leaf continuously, offering it round regularly to the congregation who received two handfuls at a time, seated, between two cupped hands (*yanantin*; see Platt 1986). An empty aspirin bottle was filled with pure alcohol and given to the yachaj: this was the *uña*, the 'offspring' of the bigger bottle (*wutilla*) full of diluted alcohol, which was passed round for all to drink.

We discussed with the yachaj the questions we wanted to ask and who was going to put them to the mountain spirit. The yachaj continued drinking and taking coca leaf, combining tranquil courtesy with a certain reserve, as if he were saving his strength, or was simply allowing himself to enter the state of increasing stupor produced by the combination of coca leaf, alcohol, and cigarettes. Sometimes he heaved a sigh and murmured barely audible invocations—to Holiest Father (the Sun), Holiest Mother (the Moon), Father St James of Pumpuri, etc.—while he drank pure alcohol and libated with drops of the diluted alcohol. One of his bullets had a little hole in it, which he filled with neat alcohol as an offering for the jurq'us; then he blew a libation with a long-drawn-out spluttering whistle that the jurq'us would hear and respond to. As the evening wore on, the whistle became less diffuse and shriller. Finally, he asked us to extinguish the candle.

We were now in complete darkness. At first there was barely a sound, except for the dogs barking outside, or a distant child crying in the night. From time to time we heard the yachaj blow into the bottle and the uña, and in the little orifice of his bullet (*wala*), which now emitted an acute whistling call to the distant jurq'us.[11]

Then he began to speak in a normal manner, asking us what we wished to know, laughing at my questions about Inka and Chullpa. Everyone began to converse again, unseen. We went on taking coca leaf, and I continued to feel a growing stupor, the darkness wrapped me round, the bullet continued whistling and the bottles huffing and puffing, and I heard dimly the clinking of glass and the rustle of coca leaves from the direction of the altar table. The murmurs of the yachaj as he poured libations alternated with conversation; he communicated a sensation of relaxed dignity. He ventured a question—and at that moment the sound of violent flapping broke out high up against the wall behind him; we were compelled to silence as it descended toward the floor, hitting the box on which the altar was laid out, and striking my knee and the microphone. And a loud, authoritative voice greeted us: "Good evening, Christian children"!

THE COUNCIL[a]

Liq'unipampa, August 1971
Macha, Moiety Alasaya, Ayllu Alaquyana, Cabildo Phichichua.

Scene: A small square room, thatched and plunged in darkness, in the hamlet of the Carvajal patrilineage on the low puna region of Macha. Throughout their visit, the mountain spirits continue beating their wings in a regular flapping as they sit balanced, invisible, on the altar table (misa).

Session 1
Enter jurq'u with wings flapping

Jurq'u
winas nuchis, wawas kristyanus!
i "chunkaiskayniyuj chakullani" niwaychij, kristyanus;
"jisus maria waqaychiri" niwaychij, kristyanus;
ima ofrisisunkichij, wawas kristyanus?

> [Good evening, Christian children!
> And call me "Twelve[b] Chakullani"[c] say to me, Christians;
> "Jesus Mary Protectress"[d] say to me, Christians;
> what is your problem, Christian children?]

Santiago
kunan "kay chimpapi kanman", nin, "uj chullpa santus kanman", nin.
kanmanchu tatay? chayta watukúy munayku.

> [Now, he says, "over there might there be a Chullpa saint",[e] he says;
> might there be, my father? That's what we want to ask.[f]]

Jurq'u
asi ti pikaru pis!
awir, kay wirjintachu parlachíy munankichij, awir, kristyanus?
o sinu kay uj qullutachu, wawas kristyanus, awir?

---

[a]*Kawiltu*, Sp. *cabildo* (municipal council), is used to designate the dramatic speech genre I refer to as 'council' or 'shamanic session'. The text was taped in Liq'unipampa, hamlet of the Carvajal patriclan, in August 1971, and transcribed and translated in the days immediately following the session.

[b]For the importance of the number 12 in Northern Potosí, which is libated to as 'Father Twelve' (*tata chunka iskayniyuj*), see Tristan Platt (1983). Pre-Hispanic duodecimality has probably converged with such Christian expressions as the Twelve Apostles. Here the sacred number functions as an honorific.

[c]The name of a neighbouring hill.

[d]*waqaycha-* 'protect'; + *-iri* (Aymara agentive nominaliser) 'protector'.

[e]The Chullpa are the pre-Inka people who lived before the rising of the sun. The name is also given to the house-like burial tombs that are often found at archaeological sites. These tombs all face east, according to modern Macha, because the Chullpa thought the sun was going to rise in the West. When the sun rose most were burned up in the holocaust, except for a few who dived into the water and became the modern ethnic group Uru-Chipaya. 'Chullpa' therefore refers to a pre-Inka culture, whose traces are to be seen in their archaeological remains, which exert dangerous forces on the living and whose pre-solar time persists in a shadowy form within the earth, manifesting itself above all at the new and full moons. Andean time is therefore not linear like an arrow but cumulative like the layers of a cake.

This question arose from an experience a few days before. Santiago and I had gone to Milluri to see whether the legend of a chullpa saint's altar and cross located inside a neighbouring hill was true. We had found a tunnel entrance, and I had crawled in to find a parting of the ways, one going down but silted up, the other emerging on another part of the hillside. The question had remained unresolved, so I had asked for it to be put to the jurq'u.

[f]In Potosí Quechua, final syllable stress indicates loss of a suffix, whose identity must be inferred from the wider sentential and discursive context. Cf. Cerrón-Palomino 1987 for the same process in Cochabamba Quechua. In this text, the missing suffix is the object-marker *-ta*, unless otherwise indicated.

[What a rascal, then![g]
Let's see,[h] do you want to have this virgin speak, then, Christians?
Or else one of these peaks, Christian children, let's see?]

Santiago

"kanmanchu chaypi santus"? nispa kay wiraquchi watukúy munan arí.

[This *wiraquchi*[i] wants to consult, please, he says "might there be saints there"?]

Jurq'u

isu pikarus! winu, awir, pusarqamusaj, winú?

[That's it, rascals! Well, let's see, I'll go and bring it here,[j] okay?[k]]

Santiago

awir . . .

[Let's see . . .]

Jurq'u

a siñur santyaku miriku glurya istrilla nasimyintu!
awir, tata santisimu mustramu!
ima niwasunchus, wawas kristyanus, winú?

[Ah! Lord St James Doctor Glory Star Birth![l]
Let's see, Father Holiest Our Lord![m]
I wonder what he'll tell us,[n] Christian children, okay?]

[g]In some forms of this greeting, the derivation is clearly from Spanish *sin pecado* 'without sin', as an epithet of the Virgin Mary. For example, in another council I taped with a different yachaj in 1978, we heard *sin pikaru kunsiwira* 'sin pecado concebido' (conceived without sin). See Solá 1969 for similar greetings formulae in use in Chinchero (Cuzco): A. *awmarya* 'Ave María! B. *simpikaru* 'sin pecado', 'without sin'. However, I am grateful to Rory Hamilton for pointing to another possible derivation from Spanish *pícaro* 'rascal', which would be adapted to the Quechua vocalic, consonantal, and accentual system in exactly the same way as *pecado*: 'pikaru'. Here my translation hazards a derivation from *hazte pícaro, pues* 'be a rascal, then'! In general, I take *pikaru* as deriving from *pícaro*. Those who wish can always try substituting 'sin'; it is even possible that a conflation of the two meanings may have occurred: 'sinful rascal'.

[h]"awir", Sp. *a ver*; translated throughout as 'let's see'.

[i]I.e., the anthropologist, Tristan. *Wiraquchi* is the standard term for translating *gringo*; cf. *kawalliru*, from Sp. *caballero*.

[j]*pusarqamusaj*: note the combination of suffix *-rqu-* (*-rqa-* before *-mu-*) indicating the jurq'u's sudden exit, with the cislocative *-mu-* indicating his expected movement of return to the altar table. The object of the verb is unclear: it may be simply the answer, or it may be the chosen peak or virgin itself.

[k]Final syllable stress here indicates missing interrogative suffix *-chu*.

[l]*istrilla nasimyintu* was glossed by participants as 'born up in the tempest'; a derivation from the Star of Bethlehem seems probable.

[m]A string of Spanish-derived epithets for St James: "médico, gloria, estrella, nacimiento, santísimo, Nuestro Amo"... 'Doctor, Glory, Star, Birth, Holiest, Our Lord'... 'Holiest Father Our Lord' refers to the Sun and also to the Christian Host; see Platt (1987).

[n]Note the frame-indicator *niwasunchus*, made up of *ni-* (say) + *-wa-sun-* (directional 3ps 1ppl inclusive) + *-chus* (dubitative): deictic reference is to speech from outside the immediate spatial context. The jurq'u

Exit jurq'u with wings flapping

Yachaj
bay tata santyaku tata!
a "chay wirjintachu munankichij, qullutachu? mayqintá wajachíy munankichij"?
"chay wirjin wajachíy munayku,
kanchus imachus awir chay a chullpaj santun a"? ninaykichij a.

[There,[o] Father St James, father!
So (he's asking you:) "do you want that virgin, or that peak?
"Which[p] do you want to call on"?
"We want to call on that virgin you must say then,
"is that Chullpa's saint there or what, let's see then"?]

Santiago
a chayta mana asirtaykuchu a.

[Yes, that's what we're not certain of.[q]]

Yachaj
"kanchus imataj chaypi"? nispa ninkichij a.

[You must say (to Jurq'u), "I wonder what's there" . . . ?]

Santiago
aaaaa . . .

[Ahhhh]

Yachaj
bay tata santisimu mostramu!
mana nuqanchij jinatajchu parlanku, ratu, tatáy, paykuna parlanku.

[There, Holiest Father, Our Lord!
(*pouring libations and chewing coca*)
They don't speak like we do, they speak very fast, my father.]

---

here groups himself with the congregation over against Tata Pumpuri, who is expected to reveal a mystery to all (including the jurq'u). The session shows a constant process of frame-shifting, which may include distant participants outside the immediate speech situation, such as Tata Pumpuri himself. See Figure 12-2.

[o]*bay* Sp. *vaya*! A common interjection in Northern Potosí Quechua.

[p]Here stress probably indicates the absent discourse-marker *-taj*. Note that, rather than indicating the relationship between the sentence in which it occurs and the sentences immediately preceding and following it (as is usual with such discourse markers), the suffix must itself be inferred by the listener—on being alerted to its absence by stress—in the light of his/her understanding of the wider context. Compare the study of the discourse-markers used in the Quechua narratives of Huarochirí in Dedenbach-Salazar Sáenz 1994.

[q]Again Santiago focusses on the content of the question rather than on the way in which it should be put, as the yachaj invites him to do. The whole of this interlude is taken up with the yachaj's comments on the nature of jurq'u speech, the constraints it places on human speech, and the best way to establish dialogue with it. Not until his own confusion is invoked (*mana nuqanchij jinatajchu*) does Santiago connect experientially with the yachaj's drift (*ratu a turwachikun*), whereupon metalinguistic dialogue is at last under way.

Santiago

ratu a turwachikun chaytaj . . .

> [Yes, very fast, that's what confuses one . . .]

Yachaj

chayta tata Griguryu, allinta tapuriy, tapurinkichij a.

> [That question, father Gregorio, ask it right, all of you ask it then.]

Gregorio

awir tatay . . .

> [Let's see, my father . . .]

Yachaj

sinu "yasta kawiltu"! nipullawasunchij a payqa, i? ujta apaykamuytawanqa.

> [Otherwise , he'll just say to us[r]
> "*Cabildo's* over"![s] no? as soon as he's brought in another one.[t]]

Santiago

arí a.

> [Yes, indeed.]

Yachaj

kuntistajtin atintiwasun,
mana kuntistajtinqa ratu chay "yasta kawiltu"! nispa phinksupullanqa payqa a.
bay maria kunsiwira bay!
parlakuychij, tatay, parlakuychij, parlakuy tata Griguryu, imallatapis . . .

> [If there's an answer he'll attend to us,[u]
> if there's no answer, at once he'll say "*Cabildo's* over"! and just rush
> out.[v]]
>
> (*Whistles with his bullet and libates*)

---

[r]Note the incorporation of Sp. *ya está*! 'okay, it's finished'! as Quechua complement. Alternatively from Sp. *basta*! 'enough now'!

[s]*nipullawasunchij*: here the frame-indicator *-wa-sun-chij* groups the yachaj with the rest of the human congregation and excludes the jurq'u and his speech as external to that group (frame B, Figure 12-2).

[t]The use of *-yku-* (*-yka-* before *-mu-*), with a paradigmatic meaning of gentle entry into an enclosed space, complements the jurq'u's expansive use of *-rqu-* above in *pusarqamusaj* (cf. note j). The object of the action is similarly unclear.

[u]The subject of *kuntistajtin*—from Sp. *contestar* + *-jti-* (switch-reference) + *-n* (3ps possessive)—may be Gregorio: 'if he answers'. In *atintiwasun* (Sp. *atender*) the frame-indicator *-wa-sun-* again situates the jurq'u's speech outside the human speech-community (which includes the yachaj) (frame B, Figure 12-1).

[v]From Quechua *phinkiy* 'leap, jump' (glossed as Sp. *brincarse*). The Aymara suffix *-su-*, equivalent to Quechua *-rqu-* (see notes j and t), is preceded by vowel-deletion according to the Aymara morphophonemic rule. Although Aymara influence is strong among these Quechua-speakers (some of whose great-grandparents spoke Aymara as their first language), the choice here may be motivated in part by the Quechua predilection for assonance and onomatopoeia (after *nispa* lit. 'saying', citative framing); cf. Mannheim 1991.

There, Mary of the Conception, there!

(*To the others*)

Talk, my father, keep talking all of you, talk, father Gregorio, just
anything . . . ^w

Gregorio
bay tatay . . .

[There, my father . . .]

Session 2

Enter jurq 'u with wings flapping

Yachaj
misaman, tatay!

[To the altar table, my father!]

Jurq'u
winas nuchis, wawas kristyanus!

[Good evening, Christian children!]

All
winas nuchis, tatay!

[Good evening, my father!]

Jurq'u
a "chunka iskayniyuj chakullani awugaru" niwaychij, wawas kristyanus

[And say to me "Twelve Chakullani Lawyer",^x Christian children!]

Santiago
chunka iskayniyuj chakullani awugaru!

[Twelve Chakullani Lawyer!]

Jurq'u
a "jisus maria anjilawarta waqaychiri" niwaychij, kristyanus.
wa! ima okasyun tiyan? wa! awir, dun santyaku, awir pis!
a dyus pagarasunki muchachu!

---

^wThis key utterance shows the importance of unsemanticised sound, murmuring, as the aural ground
upon which the jurq'u's intervention can be constructed. It is swamped by the swishing wing-beats of the
arriving condor.

^x*awugaru*, from Sp. *abogado* 'lawyer'. Here the jurq'u adds a further honorific to his title that
demonstrates his participation in the construction of a legal discourse.

> [Ah, Say to me "Jesus Mary Guardian Angel Protectress"! Christian children!
> Wa! What's the problem? Wa! Let's see, don Santiago, let's see then!]

(Drinks alcohol. To the Yachaj)

> [Ah, thanks, boy![y]]

Yachaj

jina, tatay, wirjinta waturikuyta munashan,
chayta kawalta waturipuy, tatay a.

> [That's so, my father, he's wanting to consult the virgin,
> so ask her correctly for him, my father.[z]]

Jurq'u

wa! "jisus maria" niwaychij, wawas kristyanus!

> [Wa! Say to me "Jesus Mary", Christian children!]

All

jisus maria!

> [Jesus Mary!]

Jurq'u

winu kunan, qan, imatá munanki, awir, dun Griguryu?
awir, imataj asuntusniyki, awir, waway kristyanu?

> [Well now, you, so what[aa] do you want, let's see, don Gregorio?
> Let's see, so what's the matter with you, let's see, my Christian children?]

Santiago

chay . . . chay qullapi kanmanchu, tatay, chay chullpaspata santusnin?

> [In that . . . that peak, might there exist, my father, Chullpas' saints?]

Jurq'u

isu ti pikaru! piru, waway, mana kasqachu.

> [That's it, rascal! But, my child, it seems there isn't.[bb]]

---

[y]Note how the yachaj here channels the speech by which the jurq'u constructs him (the yachaj) as a dependent of some kind—possibly the door-boy or clerk who shows the lawyer into the courtroom.

[z]The yachaj has decided for Santiago which divinity to choose, and asks the jurq'u to 'consult the virgin correctly' (*kawalta*, from Sp. *cabal* + *-ta* [adverbial marker]). But it turns out that the jurq'u has already got the answer. The display of independent actions and intentions help establish the yachaj and the jurq'u as two entirely different actors in play.

[aa]Stress here indicates loss of final suffix *-taj*.

[bb]Another "shamanic flight" of virtuosity: after inviting Santiago to put his question again, the jurq'u reveals that he has already made the consultation during his absence, and produces the answer like a rabbit out of a hat. Note the use of the reportative suffix *-sqa*, indicating that the jurq'u has received the information indirectly from another with certain knowledge; for the implications of Quechua evidentials for the epistemoiogical status of Andean history, see Howard-Malverde 1990.

Santiago
manachu kasqa?
>[There isn't?]

Jurq'u
mana kanchu, waway, chayqa mana kaj chullpa, inkalla.
>[There isn't, my child, and it's not Chullpa, just Inka.[cc]]

Santiago
aaaa . . .
>[Ahhhh . . . !]

Jurq'u
ri timpumanta pacha rumi t'ujyarishajta ruwasqanku, nara mas,
qhuya jinallamin kasqa,
mana imapis kanchu chay ukhupiqa.
>[They set the stone exploding,[dd] from the time of the King, that's all,[ee]
it seems it's just exactly like a mine,
there's nothing inside there.[ff]]

Santiago
aaaa yasta tatay.
>[Ahhh . . . That's it, my father!]

Jurq'u
isu pikaru!
>[That's it, rascal!]

Santiago
ujta tapurikuyta munallaykutaj kay ripimanta,
imamantataj kay wiraquchista disgrasya qhatíy munan?
kay ripisitunta p'akikukunku ari.
>[There's another thing we'd like to ask you, please, about this jeep,
why does misfortune wish to follow these wiraquchis?[gg]
This jeep of theirs is very badly broken.[hh]]

[cc]In this and the following speech, the jurq'u invokes the widespread Northern Potosí conflation of the Inka with the King of Spain, and contrasts the period of colonial mining with the pre-social ('wild', jurq'u) Chullpa.

[dd]*rumi t'ujyarishajta ruwasqanku*: the impression of explosive immediacy created by the onomato-poeic *t'ujyay* is reinforced by the use of the inceptive *-ri-*, the suffix of continuing action *-sha-*, and the transformative suffix *-ya*; the explosion *-t'uj!-* was, so to speak, perpetually in the act of becoming.

[ee]From Sp. *nada más*, an example of the jurq'u's heavily hispanised Quechua.

[ff]Not a chullpa saint, perhaps; but local mines do contain ogres such as *Wari*, *Satanás*, or Lucifer, *dyawlus* ('devils' Sp. *diablos*), *supay*, *tiyu-tiya*, *pachatata-pachamama*, and other semi-colonised, but still subversive goblins; cf. Platt (1983).

[gg]The plural *wiraquchis* here includes my assistant, Wagner Oporto, a mestizo from the valley town of Micani.

[hh]This refers to an occasion following a visit to the shrine of Pumpuri, when my jeep had a puncture on the return journey. The tension between causality and chance presents itself—particularly as, with one

Jurq'u
isu pikaru pis!
"jisus maría anjilawarta waqaychiri" niwaychij, kristyanus!
winu, dun santyaku, glurya miriku istrilla, waturimusaj waway, awir,
imachus jucha kasqan waway, winú?

> [That's it then, rascal!
> Say to me "Jesus Mary Guardian Angel Protectress" Christian children!
> Well, don Santiago, Glory Doctor Star! I'll go and consult, my child,
>   let's see!
> what the fault[ii] would have been, my child, okay?]

Santiago
awir tatay ...

> [Let's see, my father ...]

Jurq'u
isu pikaru pis isu! patrún waturimusun waway, winún?

> [That's it then, rascal, that's it! We'll go and ask the boss,[jj] my child,
> okay?]

Santiago
yasta tatay.

> [All right, my father.]

Jurq'u
wa! sumaj ura, wina ura kashaykichij, wawas kristyanus, winún?

> [Wa! Let it be a fine hour, a good hour for you,[kk] Christian children,
> okay?]

Santiago
yasta tatay.

> [All right, my father.]

Jurq'u
wa! tukuy sunqu tukuy alma kashankichij, wawáy, winú?

> [Wa! Be with a whole heart, a whole soul,[ll] my child, okay?]

---

spring bound up with cowhide, the vehicle appeared to be almost limping. We wanted to find out *why* the puncture had happened *then*, and to *us*.

[ii]The concept of *jucha*, chosen by early catechisers to translate 'sin', more correctly denotes any moral misdemeanour or fault of ceremonial omission.

[jj]I.e., Tata Pumpuri. Final stress on *winú* indicates missing interrogative suffix *-chu*.

[kk]*kashaykichij*: the 2ppl imperative + *-sha-* of continuous action: lit., 'be being (all of you) good time fine time'!

[ll]Imperative has become affirmative (*-nki* replaces *-yki*): 'you are being whole heart whole soul, no'? The phrase was contrasted by participants with *iskayriyay*, lit. 'to become two', i.e., 'to be undecided'.

Exit jurq'u with wings flapping

All

ya tatay ya . . .

> [Yes, my father, yes . . . !]

Santiago

"mana kanchu" ninqa.

> ["There's nothing", that's what he says.]

Wagner

"Santos no hay" dice, "mana kanchu" nin "chay jusk'upi".

> ["There are no saints", he says, "there's nothing in that hole", he says.]

Yachaj

"mana kanchu, ri timpupi urqusqanku" ninsina, manachu?

> ["There's nothing, they took it out in the time of the King,"[mm] I think
> he said, no?]

***

From Session 3

Santiago

kunan, chay chullpa santusqa unay timpu kanmanchu? manachu kanman karqa?

> [Now, would Chullpa saints have existed long ago? Wouldn't there
> have been?]

Jurq'u

a tiyan a, kay santuariusmanta kayqa a, tata ri, tata ri lisyinsyamun, . . .
u- algun riya, algun timpu a chaymanta kashan waway,
jurq'uspi piru jurq'uspis kashanpunitaj kashan.

> [There are, from these sanctuaries,[nn] father King,[oo] father King gave a
> license . . .

[mm]The phrase could be taken to refer to the removal of a pre-Christian mining huaca by Christian
authorities.

[nn]The "sanctuaries" are the sites of major regional miracles and are the foci for great pilgrimages, or
romerías. There are said to be twelve miracles, of which one is Tata Pumpuri himself.

[oo]The persons of the Inka and the Spanish monarch are conflated in Father King, *tata ri*. As the source
of moiety organisation and early modern civilisation, he is contrasted—as the Sun with the Moon—with
the earlier fecund time of Chullpa society. Here he is credited with incorporating the Chullpa into his New
Dispensation as licensed sources of ancient sacred power. The image of an earlier time of superabundant
fertility combined with demographic pressure is found in many other parts of the Andes; compare the age
of Wallallu Qarwinchu in the early seventeenth-century tales of Huarochirí (Salomon and Urioste 1991).
Macha and Huarochirí agree, too, that there was a yet older age, that of the *lumas* (Sp. *lomas* 'mountains';
Macha) or of Black and Night Ñamca (Huarochirí), which was characterised by total darkness before the
rising of either Sun or Moon.

Another, another day, another time, then, that's when they're from, my child,
but in the wild places too they're there right enough.PP]

Santiago
may jurq'upitaj kashan?

[In which wild places are they?]

Jurq'u
santuarius kashan, chullpa q'asapi kashan, waway kristyanus. . . .

[They're (in) the sanctuaries, they're in Chullpa Pass, my Christian child. . . . qq

Santiago
aaa! chullpa q'asa . nin. . . . !

[Ahhh! (*To the others:*) He says Chullpa Q'asa . . . !]

Jurq'u
isu pikarun!

[That's it, rascal!]

Santiago
chayllapichu?

[Just there?]

Jurq'u
chullpa q'asapi kashallantaj a, altu qullun,
chunka iskayniyuj tanka achachilapi, chaypi kallantaj, wawas kristyanus.

[They're at Chullpa Q'asa, all right then, its high peak,
and at Twelve Grandfather Tanka,ʳʳ they're there, too, Christian children.]

PPThe Chullpa represent the ancient pre-Christian ancestors who continue to exist in the Inner Dimension (*ukhu pacha*), like the other pagan dead (*sajras*). Some sanctuaries, such as Killakas, may become wholly absorbed by the High God (*altu dyus*); others retain a partial (Pumpuri) or total (Tanka-Tanka) affiliation with the Inner World.

qqThe Road of the Dead (*alma ñan*) to the Western Ocean (*la mar, mar qucha*) is said to go through Chullpa Pass, overlooking the salt-lick of Qharata, which leads up from the low puna where I was living to the high pastures of Macha and K'ulta. There is an important unexcavated archaeological site at the pass, with Chullpa tombs and settlement remains.

ʳʳTanka-Tanka: one of the highest peaks in the Cordillera de los Frailes, from whose "devils" Santiago came fleeing, according to the origin myth collected by José Luis Grosso. The title of "Grandfather Twelve Tanka" evokes an ancient pagan huaca with a triple personhood which awoke priestly paranoia in the sixteenth and seventeenth centuries. His legendary treasure was said to lie beneath the Franciscan monastery known as La Recoleta in Sucre. The trinitarian dimension recurs in the fact that Tanka-Tanka marks the boundary between three maximal ayllus—Macha, K'ulta, and Qaqachaka—according to the *Composición* and *Amojonamiento* of Macha in 1646, published in Platt (1982: app. 1). The name persists at several other sites in modern Potosí and Chuquisaca (information from Verónica Cereceda and Olivia Harris).

***

Session 6

Enter jurq'u with wings flapping

Jurq'u
winus nuchis wawas kristyanus!

> [Good evening, Christian children!]

All
winas nuchis, tatay

> [Good evening, my father!]

Jurq'u
a "sus maria anjilawarta waqaychiri" niwaychij, wawas kristyanus,
a "chunka iskayniyuj", wawas kristyanus,
a "chunka iskayniyuj chhankaquru" niwaychij, wawas kristyanus!

> [Ah, say to me "Jesus Mary Guardian Angel Protectress", Christian
> children,
> Ah, "Twelve", Christian children,
> Ah! say to me "Twelve Chhankaquru", Christian children!]

All
chunka iskayniyuj chhankaquru!

> [Twelve Chhankaquru!]

Jurq'u
a "sus maria anjilawarta waqaychiri"
niwaychij, wawas kristyanus,
wa! tukuy sunquchu kankichij, wawas kristyanus?

> [Ah, say to me "Jesus Mary Guardian Angel Protectress", Christian
> children
> Wa! Are you wholehearted, Christian children?]

All
ari, tukuy sunqu, tatay.

> [Yes, wholehearted, my father.]

Jurq'u
a sumaj ura wina ura, wawas kristyanus!

> [It's a fine time, a good time, then, Christian children!]

All
sumaj ura wina ura!

> [A fine time, a good time!]

Jurq'u
a winu, kay kawalliruykijtapis walijllamin wasin kashan, wawas kristyanus.

> [Well now, this *caballero* of your family is perfectly well, Christian children!]

***

Jurq'u
salur, wawas kristyanus, a surtirisunchij kay chiqan kawiltu, sumaj kristyanus!

> [Your health, Christian children, We'll be lucky with this well-made Council, fine Christians![ss]]

All
bay tatay.

> [There, my father!]

Jurq'u
"quri chuqi qullqi chuqi kawiltu" niwaychij, wawas kristyanus.
a, ni tiyanchu, waway? salur, bay a muchachu!

> [Say to me "Gold gold, silver gold Council" Christian children.
>
> (*Drinks noisily*)
>
> Isn't there any more then, my child? (to the yachaj) Your health, there then, boy!]

Yachaj
misaman, tatay, misaman!

> [To the altar table, my father, to the altar table!]

Jurq'u
a parlakuychij, wawas kristyanus!

> [Well, speak, Christian children!]

All
parlakushayku, tatay!

> [We are speaking, my father![tt]]

Jurq'u
a sumaj ura wina urachu kankichij, wawas kristyanus?

> [Is it a fine moment for you, a good moment, Christian children?]

[ss]Good Christians of the jurq'u's persuasion can expect to be blessed with good luck.

[tt]A collective affirmation of communicative competence.

All

sumaj ura wina ura kayku, tatay!

> [It's a fine moment for us, a good moment, my father!]

Jurq'u

sinu, kunan, kay walijllamin kay kawalliruyki[j]tapis tatan maman.

> [But now, this caballero of yours, his father and mother are just fine.]

Wagner

imamanta, tatay, chay chullpa qullus surujcháy munawayku?

> [Why, my father, do those chullpa peaks want to give us altitude
> sickness?]

Jurq'u

imaraykutaj chay q'uwitata asarpawajchij karqa, wawas kristyanus, awir, ichari, dun
santyaku?

> [Because you should have roasted a little *q'uwa*[uu] Christian children,
> let's see, isn't that right, don Santiago?]

Santiago

ari, tatay.

> [Yes, my father.]

Wagner

awir, imataj?

> [Let's see, what was that?]

Jurq'u

awir, insyinsyitun asarpariyman, q'ushñirichikuyman, wawas kristyanus, wawas
kristyanus,
kay wina ura allin timpu, awir—
algun riyamanta paykuna kanku, wawas kristyanus, awir, ichari, dun santyaku?

> [Let's see, I'd have quickly roasted a little incense, I'd have made some
> smoke, Christian children, Christian children,
> at a good and fine time like this, let's see—
> they are from another age, Christian children, let's see, isn't that so,
> don Santiago?]

Santiago

ari, tatay.

> [Yes, my father.]

Jurq'u

a chaypi chullpa wayra, sanju wayra, wak'aj wayran, sullu wayra tiyan,
wawas kristyanus,

[uu]A resinous plant burnt as incense for the earth deities.

kapas chaywanraj tinkunkumanraj karqa,
piru ura uralla pasan, wawas kristyanus.

> [Up there you find the Chullpa wind,[vv] the Trench wind,[ww] the huaca's
> wind,[xx] the Fetus wind,[yy] Christian children.
> They would probably have met with that,
> but in a little while it passes, Christian children.]

All

ari a, tatay.

> [Yes, my father.]

Jurq'u

ichapis kaymanta jina . . .
di ripinti, awir, pilutata jina tukuykuchinman, awir,
nuqanchij imanasunman, wawas kristyanus?

> [Perhaps then like. . . .
> perhaps, let's see, it'd leave us like a football,[zz] let's see,
> and what would we do then, Christian children?]

All

ari a, tatáy.

> [Yes, my father.]

Jurq'u

asi pikaru a!
sumaj ura wina ura kachun, wawas kristyanus.

> [So rascal, then!
> Let it be a fine time, a good time, Christian children.]

[vv]'Up' supplied: the chullpa (Late Intermediate) settlements and terraces are generally found on fortified hilltops. The chullpa wind is closely related to the fierce Altiplanic winds described by Cobo in the seventeenth century, which attack the traveller in Lipez with such force that they freeze-dry him in one gust. His mouth-muscles tauten, making him smile, so that later travellers meet a smiling mummy on their road, which no doubt (although no source says it) demanded its own offerings from the passer-by. It is this power of assimilating the living to the state of mummies that characterises the winds emitted by the Chullpa, unless they are shown respect and placated. For a fine contribution to the study of Andean winds, see Cereceda (1993).

[ww]*sanju*: a deep ditch where the Inner Glory from the Inner Dimension (*ukhu pacha*) has struck as lightning; the place may become an object of individual devotion. It, too, can emit a fierce and deadly wind.

[xx]In Macha today, *wak'a* are human-shaped rocks that come alive during the period of intense fertility that characterises the full and new moons.

[yy]The wind that blows from the place where an aborted fetus or unbaptised placenta is buried. Without the Christian salt of baptism, they grow into a 'naked baby' (*q'ara wawa* or *q'ara uña*) or 'goblin' (*twinti*, Sp. *duende*), which kills its mother by returning to eat blood in the womb and continuing to eat until it consumes the heart (*kurasun* Sp. *corazón*).

[zz]Glossed as 'we'd crouch and clutch our head to our knees [to protect ourselves from the wind], like a ball of yarn (*muruq'u jina*)'. The risk is that 'you'd end up like a stone shaped like a ball of yarn (*tukuwaj muruq'u rumi jina*)'.

All

sumaj ura wina ura.

>   [A fine time a good time.]

Jurq'u

kunan yastañamin kawiltu kashan, ijus.

>   [Now the Council is really over, sons.]

Santiago

yastachu?

>   [Is it over?]

Jurq'u

yastamin kawiltu wawas kristyanus, winún?

>   [The Council is really over, Christian children, okay?]

All

bay tatay.

>   [All right, my father.]

Jurq'u

awir kunan rugamyintu supliku kaywan chunka iskayniyuj kuka sink'an,
jinataj winu, singanitun, q'uwita, dilantiruntawan chuqarparichinkichij,
dun santyaku, winú?

>   [Let's see, now a plea, a supplication, and with it Twelve Perfect Coca
>   Leaflets,
>   and likewise you sprinkle right away wine, *singani*, q'uwa, with its
>   Lead Llama,[aaa]
>   don Santiago, okay?]

Santiago

yasta tatay.

>   [All right, my father.]

Jurq'u

awir kupiarichinki kay chullpa wayramanpis, waway, winún?

>   [And do make a copy[bbb] for that Chullpa wind, my child, okay?]

All

bay a tatay.

>   [There then, my father.]

[aaa]The noblest form of animal sacrifice. The *delanteros* lead the llama troops on their long journeys to the distant valleys.

[bbb]*kupiyarichinki*, from Sp. *copiar* 'copy'. The phrase further confirms the presence of a notarial vocabulary in the jurq'u-lawyer's discourse.

Jurq'u

chaymanta tarillanman, wawas kristyanus.

> [Afterward he'd just find it, Christian children.]

All

bay a tatay.

> [There then, my father.]

Jurq'u

asi pikaru a!
jinalla, wawas kristyanus.

> [So, rascal, then!
> That's it now, Christian children.]

All

bay tatay.

> [All right, my father.]

Jurq'u

ari, yastamin kawiltu kashan, yastamin kashan, wawas kristyanus, ijus,
a ratukamaña, wawas kristyanus, iju,
yasta wilá jap'ichikuychij . . .

> [Yes, the Council's really over now, it's really over, Christian children,
> sons,
> till soon, Christian children, son,
> right now, light the candle . . .]

Exit jurq'u with wings flapping

Wagner

ratukama, tatay!

> [Till soon, my father!]

Yachaj

wilá jap'ichiychij, tatay!

> (to Santiago)
> [Light the candle, my father!]

Commentary on the Text

The condor's speech can be analysed into types of speech act—greeting, self-introduction, formulaic repetition of sacred names or liturgical phrases, incitation to consult, terminating remarks, etc.—which are repeated in a regular sequence from one session to the next. For example, the self-presentation is generally followed by the formulaic repetition of sacred names, which in turn leads to the incitation to consult. There is also a significant catechetical element—invitations to the audience to repeat his words with the phrase *niwaychij, wawas kristyanus* 'say to me, Christian children'!—and the development of the whole séance across six sessions reflects the audience's increasing confidence and ability to join in the responses. This gradual emergence of the capacity to make easy verbal exchanges is part of a process by which the relationship between spirit and congregation is progressively achieved.

One feature that merits comment is the way in which inter-person directionals (person subject + object marking) and the Quechua distinction between exclusive and inclusive first-person plural, are used at different moments to shift between sub-groups of speakers and addressees. I call these features of deictic reference "participant frame-indicators" because they specify the bounds of the relevant speech group(s) at different moments in the conversation.[12]

For example, participant frame-shifting allows the jurq'u sometimes to group himself reassuringly with the congregation in opposition to Tata Pumpuri, and at other times to group himself more loftily with his master Tata Pumpuri, as against the yachaj and the congregation. Thus, *ima niwasunchus, wawas kristyanus, winú?* 'what do you think he'll say to us, Christian children, okay'? is analysable as *ni-* (root 'say') + *-wa-sun-* (directional 3 p. sing. > 1 p. pl. inclusive) + *-chus* (dubitative), with the *-wa-sun-* ('to us') establishing the jurq'u's membership of the group (congregation plus yachaj) to be addressed by Tata Pumpuri (frame C, Figure 12-2). On the other hand, in the phrase *imatachus dijtawanqa?* 'I wonder what he'll dictate to me'? (not included in the selection presented here), the replacement of *-wa-sun-* with *-wa-nqa* (directional 3 p. sing > 1 p. sing + 3 p. sing. future) leaves the jurq'u alone as the sole recipient of Tata Pumpuri's message in a separate, off-stage, speech situation, from which the yachaj and the congregation are excluded (frame E, Figure 12-2).

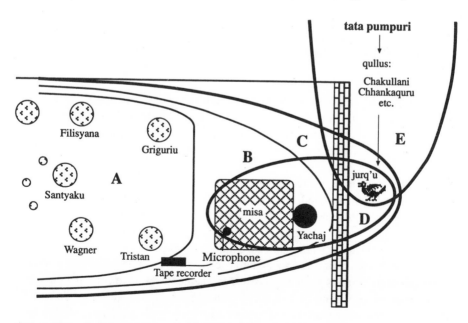

Figure 12-2   Participant frames (A–E) in play during the Council.

On other occasions the use of the pragmatic resources of Quechua allows the yachaj to group himself, now with the jurq'u as opposed to the congregation, and then again with the congregation as against the jurq'u. Thus, when the yachaj and the jurq'u exchange messages (e.g., *misaman tatay*! 'to the altar table, my father'! or *dyus pagarasunki muchachu*! 'ah, thanks, boy'!), they are instantiating a frame that embraces them both in a clearly hierarchical relationship, but excludes everyone else (frame D, Figure 12-2). Again, the phrase *kuntistajtin atintiwasun* . . . 'if there's an answer, he'll attend to us' can be analysed as *kuntista*- (root < Sp. 'contestar', 'answer') + -*jti*- (switch-reference nominaliser) + -*n* (3 p. possessive), followed by *atinti*- (root < Sp. 'atender,' 'attend, pay attention to') + -*wa-sun* (directional 3 p. sing. > 1 p. pl. inclusive), where the 'to us' (-*wa-sun*) on this occasion refers to the yachaj and the congregation as the group to be "attended to" by the jurq'u (frame B, Figure 12-2).

The result of such manoeuvres is that, rather than a static set of participants established in a fixed set of relationships, the internal structure of the groups in interaction is constantly being modified according to the communicative requirements of the moment. The ability to manipulate these features of the Quechua person system is an important rhetorical resource in the negotiation of the emerging communication between the parties.

Session 1

The first session shows both the failure to construct a connected exchange of sentences and initial efforts on both sides to correct the failure. The jurq'u first appears with the sound of wingbeats descending from the roof and repeatedly striking the improvised altar table (misa). Blowing and whistling, the spirit greets his "Christian children" and instructs them to address him as *chunka iskayniyuj chakullani* 'Twelve Chakullani'. 'Twelve Chakullani Lawyer', to give the spirit his full identification (see session 2), is therefore giving audience to his Christian children in council (perhaps modelled on a court of session).

But people are still taken by surprise; they do not respond to the spirit's instructions or answer his questions directly. He tells them to pray to Jesus Mary Protector, and repeats his own sacred name, but they still do not answer. Then, to bring them to speak, he asks them directly: *ima ofrisisunkichij, wawas kristyanus*? 'What is your problem, Christian children'?

My friend Santiago now stutters out the question prepared beforehand. A few days before we had visited a chullpa church (*chullpa inglisya*), a hole in a hill which was said to date from the time of the pre-Inka *gentiles* called Chullpas and to contain an underground altar with a cross on it belonging to a chullpa saint. We had resolved to ask the jurq'u whether there might be a chullpa saint inside.

The jurq'u then enunciates a standard exclamation, and asks whether we want to make one of the Virgins speak the answer, or whether we want to consult a mountain peak. Without answering him directly, Santiago repeats the question. The jurq'u thereupon announces that he will go out and bring back something unspecified, probably the answer.

A torrent of sacred names precedes his parting shot of "What will he tell us, Christian children, well"? The sacred names make it clear to all what sort of a spirit they're dealing with: he cites his patron, Lord St James of Pumpuri, the Doctor associated with the Glory, the Star, and the Birth, and thus with the Holy Sacrament and the body of Our Lord as incarnated in the Sun and the Host. We know, therefore, that the speaker is a messenger from the Realm of Glory (*glurya parti*) and from the patron of shamans and curers, St James of Pumpuri.

Interval 1

This includes a revealing discussion of how to talk to mountain spirits. The shaman gives the congregation some quick indications on the correct way to address the spirit, in preparation for the second session. These comments include a key passage of "speech about speech", indicating the rules of linguistic behaviour which the congregation must follow for communication to be achieved.

As the wingbeats fade away toward the roof of the house, the shaman goes over the spirit's questions and tells the audience what they should have said. He instructs them to be on the ball, to put their questions with promptness and clarity. After all, "they don't speak like we do, they speak all in a moment". "Yes", answers Santiago, "so quickly that one gets muddled (*turwachikun*)". The shaman insists that the questions must be well formed (*allinta tapuriy* 'ask well'), or else the spirit will put an end to the council right away. He continues: "If there's an answer he'll attend to us, if there's no answer he'll stop the council". Then, blowing a long-drawn-out poignant whistle with his bullet, he calls the spirit back, saying first to all present, "Talk among yourselves, talk among yourselves, anything . . ."

The most important thing of all, then, is to keep talking. While questions must be clear, it is also essential to keep up a to-and-fro hum of conversational sound if the spirit is not to abandon the council. And the spirit can only appear if there already exists an expectant buzz of conversation, a formless murmuring, with no specific semantic content at all. The condor-lawyer has to be able to interrupt, to compel the audience to silence by the swishing wingbeats of his poncho.

So the raw material of speech—sound—must be present as the crucial support upon which the dominant voice of the spirit-lawyer can construct itself in order then to elicit the form of dialogue. His liturgical repetition of his own and other sacred names is itself a ploy of the same order: the names are repeated in a continuous stream to constitute the relevant universe of sacred referents, but also to give the audience a clear model which they can repeat and thus generate the dialogic text of the council.

Session 2

The second session is more successful. Santiago gives the jurq'u back his name "Twelve Chakullani Lawyer", the jurq'u sips noisily the little cup of alcohol offered him by his "boy" (*muchachu*, i.e., the shaman), and everyone responds finally with "Jesus Mary" at the spirit's invitation. More expansive, the spirit again asks his Christian children what their problem is, and Santiago repeats the question.

Now at last comes the answer. There is no chullpa saint inside the hill. The hole belongs to what we may call (following the mythic conflation of the Inka with the King of Spain) the "Inka-Hapsburg" period: it is "just a mine from the time of the King".[13]

Santiago quickly moves on to his next question, also discussed previously. On returning shortly before from Pumpuri, my jeep had broken a spring, and Santiago wanted to know why misfortune (*desgrasya*) was pursuing us. Again the spirit says he will leave to find out what fault (*jucha*) we have committed, this time by asking his patron directly; and out he flaps.

Interval 2

An interesting feature (of which there are other examples in later sessions) is the way the condor's answers can be glossed, expanded, and reinterpreted in discussion between the yachaj and the congregation until a consensus is arrived at. There is room here for members of the congregation to feed in their own views, and the conclusion may differ from what the condor originally said. In this case we find a significant modification: the yachaj suggests that the jurq'u had said that the chullpa saint was taken out in the time of the King (*ri timpupi urqusqanku ninsina* 'They took it out in the time of the King, I think he said'). This implies that it used to be there but was removed in the Inka-Colonial period. The phrase *urqusqanku* implies deliberate action to remove the chullpa sacred materials, which would fit very well with what is known of priestly efforts to "extirpate idolatries" in the region, where the retrieval of the idol was necessary before it was formally disposed of.[14] In fact, the jurq'u's actual words were that the stone had been blasted out (*rumi t'ujyarishajta ruwasqanku*) during colonial mining explorations (*qhuya jinallamin kasqa*),[15] which refers to a more profane aspect of the colonial exploitation of Charcas.

In the relation between these two types of speech—shamanic dialogue and "interval"—we can observe, therefore, a reflection of the way in which state and ethnic hierarchies were themselves founded on the consensual ethic of the local community. Vertical enunciation from positions of power (shamanic dialogue) is contrasted with the communal chewing over of the pronouncements of authority and their reinterpretation through local debate (intervals).

Session 3

In the selection here published, a short section is included from the third session on the same subject. After hearing that there was no chullpa saint in the hole I'd entered, I asked for a further question on whether there were such beings as "chullpa saints" at all. Although I had already been told of certain chullpa saints (e.g., St Gabriel, St Jerome, and St Philip), I was curious to hear what the jurq'u would say.

He obligingly brought into play another important legal term: *lisyinsya* (<Sp. *licencia*). The King Inka was said to have given a "license" (*tata ri lisinsyamun*) for some chullpa saints to continue receiving cult in the sanctuaries, places where a miracle has appeared, or in the "wild places" (jurq'us) above the level of cultivation,

where the archaeological remains of chullpa settlements are situated and where the mountain spirits live.[16] The term suggests the projection of an Hispanic legal discourse onto the relationship between Inkas and Chullpas.

Session 6

We now jump forward to the last session, which is by far the most successful. This can be seen by the way everyone joins in sending back the responses to the new spirit, Chhankaquru: first the greeting, then his name with formal title, and then two formulaic phrases which recur constantly. In this session, we find fluent and courteous exchange reaching a metalinguistic level. The jurq'u repeats the phrase used at the end of the first interval by the yachaj: 'speak'! *parlakuychij*! But now it does not elicit a formless muttering in preparation for the spirit's arrival: rather, the reply is nothing less than an affirmation of communicative competence, 'we are speaking'! *parlakushayku*!— and with this the success of the council is formally affirmed (cf. note tt).

From then on, the rest is plain sailing. A few additional questions and answers are taken as the pretext for some ritual advice on how to deal with the effects of the chullpa peaks today (*surujchi*, wind, etc.), who had provided the point of departure for the whole council. The jurq'u announces that the council is now really over, and this is accepted without demur. Finally, the spirit gives some general ritual advice to Santiago, and suggests he "copies" it (*kupiarichinki*) for the chullpa wind as well. The similarity with the *traslado* of a legal document again supports the hypothesis that legal language and ideas provide a literate framework within which the oral procedures of the council are inscribed. It also suggests that when we analyse the structure of ritual offerings as a text, there are good Andean reasons for doing so, rather than simply those pertaining to a particular academic fashion.

Conclusion

We have observed various techniques by which the participants in the séance negotiate their relationships and collaborate to create the preconditions for successful communication. The notes to the transcription merely indicate the wealth of context evoked and negotiated by native speakers in the course of constructing dialogue. Throughout the séance, it is the task of the yachaj to enable the congregation to communicate with the jurq'u, while that of the jurq'u is to provide a bridge between the congregation and Tata Pumpuri. The first is the pre-condition for the second. Emergent communication with the jurq'u is therefore a way of smoothing people's relationship with the most powerful local representative of church and state. While Tata Pumpuri is the divine doctor who carries life and death in his hands, the jurq'u combines the rôles of notary, parish priest, and family practitioner: he elicits speech and relays it to the great regional specialist in Pumpuri, returning with words of knowledge, comfort, and practical advice.

We can see the council, then, as being modelled to an important degree on the consultation by indian clients with a local mestizo lawyer (*abogado*), who is in touch with the higher levels of the judiciary (Pumpuri). These higher levels dictate their messages to the condor-lawyer as their intermediary.[17] And the whole structure is embraced by the form of the state: hence, when the spirit has to go to England to find out if my family are well, he says he will be going to talk with *uj istaru*, 'another state', who as representative of all those residing in its jurisdiction will give audience and a reply to the condor's question.

The underpinning of the Bolivian church and state with the medical authority of Tata Pumpuri and his messengers is coherent with the theocratic nature of the state in which Andean *runa* conceive themselves to be living. It also legitimises the existence of this state in a way that provides a touchstone with which to judge the performance of any real, existing government. For the unifying concept that relates the different aspects is that of Law—natural, human, and divine. Creating a chain of communication with these ideal forms of church and state can compensate in part for the deficiencies of those concrete beings who incarnate local government and religion at any given time.

Our analysis has led us, therefore, to appreciate the powerful forms of legitimation that could be constructed for the colonial and creole States: the colonial order could even penetrate and occupy Andean creative and imaginative spaces that might be thought to be immune to such domination. But, at the same time, domination is legitimised through negotiation during sessions and reformulation during intervals. This phenomenon confirms—at the levels of oral performance and the interactive construction of communication—the existence of an ideal "pact" between communities and state, which established the normative context for coexistence and mediation within a multi-ethnic political order.

In fact, of course, these mechanisms of legitimation have broken down repeatedly during the long and agitated history of Northern Potosí. To take just one example, we have evidence that in 1927 the mountain spirits supported the indians in their rebellion against hacienda penetration, and one mountain peak called Condornasa was even fed the remnants of a particularly abusive *hacendado* who had been killed by the indians (Platt 1982; Rivera Cusicanqui and THOA 1992). Further study of Macha shamanism could therefore include an oral consultation with Condornasa, among other important peaks. This would lead us to understand better the points of rupture and inversion in these oral and literate forms of social legitimation, which emerge at key moments of economic crisis and political unrest.

ACKNOWLEDGMENTS   Parts of this text were presented at the 1991 conference "Textuality in Amerindian Cultures: Production, Reception, Strategies" held at the Institute of Latin American Studies, University of London; at the 2nd International Conference on Ethnohistory (Coroico 1991); at the conference on "Andean Music and Cosmology" (Berlin 1992); and at the St Andrews conference on "Context" (1994). My thanks to the other participants in these meetings for their comments. The text discussed was transcribed and translated with the help of Santiago Carvajal and Wagner Oporto. My thanks to Primitivo Nina, Quechua language assistant at the University of St Andrews, and to Spanish honours students taking Amerindian Studies during Martinmas Term 1991 for much stimulating discussion of both text and translation.

Notes

1. This first visit was part of a more extended series of visits to other parts of Macha, beginning with a year's residence (June 1970–June 1971) in the valley parish of San Marcos de Miraflores and three months on the Puna near Castilloma in June–August 1971. Later brief visits to Pumpuri were made in 1982 and 1985.

2. Studies of the Pumpuri cult are currently in preparation by José Luis Grosso, Universidad del Valle (Cali), and Virginie Royer de Véricourt, Institut des Hautes Études de l'Amérique Latine (Paris). The loss of St James's horse is a feature in the origin myth of the cult: St James appears in Pumpuri fleeing from the "devils" of the great mountain of Tankatanka; see Grosso (1995).

3. In Jujuy, Bolivian migrants have formed confraternities dedicated to the local cult of Tata Pumpuri.

4. Grosso (1995) has shown convincingly that Tata Pumpuri's composite formation includes San Cosme, patron saint of doctors, as well as San Bartolomé and Santiago.

5. As well as "devils" of various classes (*dyawlus*, *supay*, *sajras*, *tiyu-tiya*, *sanjus*, *lugaris*, *q'ara wawas*, etc.), the Inner World contains Chullpas and Inkas; the Roots of Tata Pumpuri as of other Mountains and Towers; and the Holy Spirit, which is about to emerge—some say in the year 2000—to initiate a new age after the overturning of the present world. In some ways, Tata Pumpuri seems to be holding the fort for believers during the present age of the neo-liberal Anti-Christ (Platt 1988). Grosso (1995) reports that the relation between Inner and Outer is also present in Tata Pumpuri's image, which is said to consist of an original miracle in stone later covered in stucco and wood "by a painter" so that St James should not leave Pumpuri. The power of the miracle is thus concealed within the visible image, and Grosso rightly compares this practice with the concealment of *huacas* within Christian images denounced by the Second Council of Lima in 1567, as well as by the Synod of Charcas in 1773.

6. The Jesuit lexicographer of Aymara, Ludovico Bertonio, translates 'arquebus' as *illapa*, elsewhere the name of the pre-Hispanic lightning god (Bertonio 1956 [1612], 1:66). In pre-Hispanic times, the lords of Qaraqara went to war on litters (*lampa* or *anda*) carried on the shoulders of their vassals, and bearing a sling with which they dispensed bolts on the model of Illapa. See Tristan Platt, et al., in press; especially the presentation to part 1.

7. For a description of the formation and linguistic practices of an Aymara shaman, see Huanca (1989).

8. The flights of Andean shamans, in the forms of condors, falcons, swifts, and other birds, are known from pre-Hispanic times; see Salomon and Urioste (1991: 88–89).

9. Ignacio Mosques, now dead, was from moiety Majasaya, minor ayllu Wakhuata, minimal ayllu or cabildo Milluri, whose territory begins on the other side of the river and is visible from Liq'unipampa.

10. This passage, from the beginning of the paragraph to the entry of the mountain spirit, is based on a Spanish version (Arica 1975) of my notes written down in English the day after the council (August 1971).

11. In another council I attended in 1978, a different shaman summoned the jurq'us by ringing a hand bell like an altar boy at mass.

12. For discussion of the various types of frame and sub-frame invoked by speakers in the process of negotiating different interactive relationships, see Kendon (1992). In the Macha council, Quechua linguistic resources that can be heard in the darkness stand in for the visible and gestural manoeuvres referred to by Kendon.

13. For Andean approaches to the periodisation of historical time, see Platt 1988 and 1992 and, most recently, Harris 1995.

14. See, for example, the activities of padre Hernán González de la Casa, priest in Macha, Toropalca, and Quilaquila in the 1570s; in Platt et al., in press (primera parte, documento 1).

15. Both yachaj and jurq'u use the reportative past -*sqa*, indicating the indirect nature of the evidence for their different opinions, although once proposed the opinion may quickly become treated as established fact, and the more positive form of the verb adopted (e.g., the jurq'u's *mana imapis kanchu*).

16. *lisinsya* 'permission' may also be used to address the altar table when asking permission to make libations—e.g., *misa, lisinsyaykiwan, ch'allarisun* . . . 'altar table, with your permission, we will pour libations' . . .

17. In another council (1978), not only does the condor at one point say, *imatachus dijtawanqa* 'I wonder what he will dictate to me'!, he even refers to St James as *dijtatur* 'dictator', a technical term from sixteenth-century notarial vocabulary (cf. González Echevarría 1990). Other suggestive terms in modern Macha Quechua include *convenio* or *acuerdo* to describe the "legal" relationship between Pumpuri and his devotees.

GLOSSARY

Symbols and abbreviations

Qu.	Quechua
Ay.	Aymara
Sp.	Spanish
var.	variant form
pl.	plural
<	derived from

apu (pl. *apukuna*) Qu.   Mountain deity (cf. *jurq'u*; *awki*).

artefacto Sp.   Handmade miniature goods used in ritual.

awaq mamacha Qu.   Female saint patroness of weavers.

awayu Ay.   Woman's mantle.

awki Qu.   Hill spirit (cf. *jurq'u*; *apu*).

ayllu Qu., Ay.   Unit of social organisation (cf. *saya*).

ayni Qu.   Principle of reciprocity in labour and ritual obligations.

bayeta (*wayita*) Qu., Ay. (< Sp.)   Homespun plainwoven woollen cloth.

cabildo (*kawiltu*) Sp., Qu.   Municipal council; rural tribute-paying group; séance during which the *yachaj* consults the mountain spirits.

cacica Sp.   Female political leader (cf. *cacique*).

cacique Sp.   Male political leader (cf. *cacica*).

ch'isiraya Qu.   Space where rituals are conducted, located at entry points to shrines and settlements.

chicha Sp.   Maize beer.

chinu Ay.   Warp threads on the loom; knot-string record (cf. *kipu*).

chullpa Ay., Qu.   Pre-Hispanic ancestors; burial places of pre-Hispanic ancestors (cf. *gentil; machu*).

compadrazgo Sp.   Ritual kinship.

criollo Sp.   Inhabitant of Spanish America of European descent (cf. *mestizo; runa*).

despacho Qu. (<Sp.)   Burnt offering to the gods (cf. *misa*).

gentil Sp.   Spirit of ancestors (cf. *machu; chullpa*)

huaca (*wak'a*) Qu.   Sacred object or site.

inqa (var. *inqaychu*) Qu.   Small stone with powerful supernatural properties.

istrilla Qu. (< Sp.)   Star that guides the individual's destiny.

janaj pacha (*hanaq pacha*) Qu.   Upper world (cf. *ukhu pacha; kay pacha*).

jurq'u Qu.   Mountain spirit (cf. *apu; awki*).

juturi Ay.   Hollows in the land thought to lead from the inner world (cf. *ukhu pacha*).

kancha Qu., Ay.   Animal corral.

kay pacha Qu.   This world, this place; the domain of the living in the here-and-now (cf. *ukhu pacha*).

kipu (*quipu*) Qu.   Inka knot-string record (cf. *chinu*).

laceadores Sp.   Horsemen practised in the use of the lasso.

lista Ay.   Stripe in woven poncho (cf. *saya; pampa; salta*).

machu Qu.   Spirit of ancestors (cf. *gentil; chullpa*).

mallku Ay.   Male.

mamacha (var. *mamita*) Qu.   Female deity; female saint (cf. *awaq mamacha*).

memorista Sp.   Community historian.

mestizo Sp.   Person of perceived mixed European and Amerindian descent (cf. *criollo; runa*).

misa Qu. (< Sp.)   Ritual table; ritual offering (cf. *despacho*).

misal Qu. (< Sp.)   Quartz crystal used in ritual.

mita (*mit'a*) Qu.   Labour tribute under the Inka regime.

mitmaq Qu.   Colonist from the Andean region.

nación Sp.   Community delegation to the pilgrimages in Southern Peru; confederation of indigenous peoples.

pachakuti Qu.   World turning; cataclysmic moment when a former order ends and a new one begins.

pachamama Qu.   Female earth deity (cf. *wirjin tayka*).

pampa Qu., Ay.   Flat area of land; unpatterned area of woven cloth (cf. *salta; saya; lista*).

paqo (*paqu*) Qu.   Ritual specialist (cf. *yachaj*).

pukllay Qu.   To play or act; also used to refer to bullfights and ritual play.

puna Qu., High moorland typically 3,600 metres above sea level in the Southern Andes.

reducción Sp.   Colonial population resettlement.

resguardo Sp.   Indigenous land legitimised by colonial-era titles.

runa Qu.   Quechua-speaking person of indigenous cultural origin (cf. *mestizo*; *criollo*).

salta Ay.   Patterned area of woven cloth (cf. *pampa; saya; lista*).

saya Ay.   Single-coloured area of woven poncho (cf. *pampa; salta; lista*); unit of territorial or social organisation (cf. *ayllu*); lit. 'standing up'.

t'alla Ay.   Female.

tata Qu.   Term of address for adult male; male saint (cf. *taytacha*).

taytacha Qu.   Icon representing Christ (cf. *tata*).

tierrakuna (var. *tirakuna*) Qu. (< Sp. + Qu. plural suffix)   Powerful, animate places in the landscape.

toqapu (*tocapu*) Qu.   Abstract design in pre-Columbian textiles.

tullqa Ay.   Brother-in-law; a ritual role in fiestas in Northern Potosí, Bolivia.

ukhu pacha (*uku pacha*) Qu.   Inner realm; the underworld; domain of spirit beings (cf. *juturi; kay pacha; janaj pacha*).

ukuku Qu.   Bear figure in Southern Peruvian fiestas.

uywiri Ay.   Herder; provider.

visitador Sp.   Colonial inspector of population and taxes.

wayno (var. *waynu*) Qu.   Type of song with characteristic rhythm (cf. *wayñu*).

wayñu Ay., Qu.   Term designating an animal marking ceremony; type of song with characteristic rhythm (cf. *wayno*).

wirjin tayka Ay.   Female earth deity (cf. *pachamama*).

yachaj (*yachaq*) Qu.   Shaman; ritual specialist (cf. *paqo*).

yumbo Sp.   Lowland indian (idiomatic).

BIBLIOGRAPHY

Archives

Avila, Francisco de. 1608. Tratado y relacion de los errores, falsos Dioses, y otras supersticiones, y ritos diabolicos en que viuian antiguamente los yndios de las Prouincias de Huarocheri, Mama, y Chaclla...MS. 3169. Biblioteca Nacional, Madrid.

Notaría Primera de Ipiales (NP/I).

Notaría Primera de Pasto (NP/P).

Tradiciones de Huarochirí. c. 1608. Runa yndio ñiscap Machoncuna ñaupa pacha...MS. 3169. Biblioteca Nacional, Madrid. [See also Trimborn 1967; Taylor 1987; Adelaar 1988; Salomon and Urioste, 1991].

Primary and Secondary Sources

Abercrombie, Thomas. 1986. The Politics of Sacrifice: an Andean Cosmology in Action. Ph.D. thesis. University of Chicago.

Acosta, Antonio. 1987. Francisco de Avila Cusco 1573–Lima 1647. In Taylor, Gerald. 1987a, pp. 552–616.

Adelaar, Willem F. H. 1982. Características del quechua de Pacaraos. In Aula Quechua, ed. Rodolfo Cerrón-Palomino, pp. 19–33. Lima: Ediciones Signo Universitario.

———. 1988. Het boek van Huarochirí, Mythen en riten van het oude Peru. Amsterdam: Meulenhoff.

———. 1990. The role of quotations in andean discourse. In Unity in Diversity: Papers Presented to Simon C. Dik on His 50th Birthday, ed. Harm Pinkster and Inge Genee, pp. 1–12. Dordrecht: Foris. Also in (1991) Past, Present and Future: Selected Papers on Latin American Indian Literatures including the VIII International Symposium, ed. Mary H. Preuss, pp. 161–66. Culver City, Calif.: Labyrinthos.

———. 1993. La categoría del plural inclusivo en las lenguas americanas: interpretación y realidad. In España: ¿Ruptura 1492? ed. Maximiliaan Kerkhof, Hugo de Schepper, and Otto Zwartjes, pp. 207–216. Amsterdam: Rodopi.

————. 1994a. La expresión de conceptos abstractos y generales en quechua: visión diacrónica. *In* Andean Oral Traditions: Discourse and Literature/Tradiciones orales andinas: Discurso y literatura, ed. Margot Beyersdorff and Sabine Dedenbach-Salazar Sáenz, pp. 1–20 (Bonner Amerikanistische Studien, 24). Bonn: Holos.

————. 1994b. A grammatical category for manifestations of the supernatural in early colonial Quechua. *In* Language in the Andes, ed. Peter Cole, Gabriella Hermon, and Mario Daniel Martín, pp. 116–25. (Occasional Monographs in Latin American Studies, No. 4). Newark: University of Delaware, Latin American Studies Program.

————. 1994c. ¿Hasta dónde llega la inflexión? Criterios para una clasificación interna de los sufijos verbales en quechua de Tarma/norte de Junín. *In* Estudios de lengua y cultura amerindias I, Actas de las II Jornadas internacionales de lengua y cultura amerindias, ed. Julio Calvo Pérez, pp. 65–83. Universidad de Valencia: Departamento de Teoría de los Lenguajes.

————. 1994d. La procedencia dialectal del manuscrito de Huarochirí en base a sus características lingüísticas. Revista Andina 12(1): 137–54.

Adorno, Rolena. 1986. Guaman Poma: Writing and Resistance in Colonial Peru. (Latin American Monographs, No. 68). Austin: University of Texas Press.

————. 1989. Cronista y príncipe. La obra de don Felipe Guaman Poma de Ayala. Lima: Pontificia Universidad Católica del Perú.

————, ed. 1982. From Oral to Written Expression: Native Andean Chronicles of the Early Colonial Period. Syracuse, N.Y.: Syracuse University, Maxwell School of Citizenship and Public Affairs.

Aijmer, Göran. 1987. The cultural nature of ritual and myth. *In* Symbolic Textures: Studies in Cultural Meaning, ed. Göran Aijmer, pp. 1–22. Gothenburg Studies in Social Anthropology, 10. Gothenburg: University of Gothenburg.

Alberti, Giorgio, and Enrique Mayer. 1974. Reciprocidad e intercambio en los Andes peruanos. Lima: Instituto de Estudios Peruanos.

Allen, Catherine J. 1982. Body and soul in Quechua thought. Journal of Latin American Lore 8(2): 179–96.

————. 1983. Of bear-men and he-men: Bear metaphors and male self-perception in a Peruvian community. Latin American Indian Literatures Journal 7(1): 38–51.

————. 1984. Patterned time: The mythic history of a Peruvian community. Journal of Latin American Lore 10(2): 151–74.

————. 1988. The Hold Life Has: Coca and Cultural Identity in an Andean Community. Washington, D.C.: Smithsonian Institution Press.

Anderson, Arthur J.O., Frances Berdan, and James Lockhart, eds. 1976. Beyond the Codices: A Nahua View of the Colonial World. Berkeley–Los Angeles: University of California Press.

Anderson, Benedict. 1983. Imagined Communities: Reflections on the Origin and Spread of Nationalism. London: Verso.

Anderson, Lloyd B. 1986 [1982]. Evidentials, paths of change and mental maps: Typologically irregular asymmetries. *In* Evidentiality: The Linguistic Coding of Epistemology, ed. Wallace Chafe and Joanna Nichols, pp. 273–312 (Advances in Discourse Processes, vol. 20). Norwood, N.J.: Ablex Publishing.

Aranguren Paz, Angelica. 1975. Las creencias y ritos mágicos-religiosos de los pastores puneños. Allpanchis 8: 103–132.

Arguedas, José María. 1941. Yawar Fiesta. Lima: Editorial Horizonte.

————. 1955. Taki parwa y la poesía quechua de la república. Letras Peruanas 12(8): 73–75.

————. 1978 [1956]. Deep Rivers. tr. Frances Horning Barraclough. Austin: University of Texas Press. Originally published as Los Ríos Profundos. Buenos Aires: Editorial Losada.

Arnold, Denise Y. 1988. Matrilineal practice in a patrilineal setting: Ritual and metaphors of kinship in an Andean ayllu. Ph.D. thesis. University of London.

————. 1992a. La casa de adobes y piedras del Inka: género, memoria y cosmos en Qaqachaka. *In* Hacia un orden andino de las cosas: Tres vistas de los Andes meridionales, ed. Denise Arnold, Domingo Jimínez, and Juan de Dios Yapita, pp. 31–108. La Paz: HISBOL/ILCA.

————. 1992b. At the heart of the woven dance-floor: The wayñu in Qaqachaka. Iberoamericana 16(3/4): 21–66. Special Issue: Literaturas autóctonas en América Latina, ed. M̃. Lienhard.

————. 1993. Adam and Eve and the red-trousered ant: History in the southern Andes. Travesía: Journal of Latin American Cultural Studies 2(1): 49–83.

————. 1994. The "flower in the corral": An Andean textile guide for interweaving worlds. *In* Fertility: Images and Icons, Rites and Rituals. Catalogue for the exhibition at the University Gallery, University of Essex, May 16-June 3, 1994, pp. 20–25.

————, and Juan de Dios Yapita. 1992. Fox talk: Addressing the wild beasts in the southern Andes. Latin American Indian Literatures Journal 8(1): 9–37.

————, and Juan de Dios Yapita. 1994. Traditional Maternity in Qaqachaka, Oruro, Bolivia. Preliminary Report to the European Community. La Paz: ILCA

————, and Juan de Dios Yapita with Cipriana Apaza M. In press. Mama trama y sus crías: Analogías de la producción de la papa en los textiles de Chukiñapi, Bolivia. *In* Mama Melliza y sus crías: Una antología de la papa, ed. Denise Y. Arnold and Juan de Dios Yapita. La Paz: HISBOL/ILCA.

————, Domingo Jiménez A., and Juan de Dios Yapita. 1991. Scattering the seeds: Shared thoughts on some songs to the food crops. Amerindia 16: 105–78.

————, Domingo Jiménez A., and Juan de Dios Yapita. 1992. Hacia un orden andino de las cosas: Tres vistas de los Andes meridionales. La Paz: HISBOL/ILCA.

Ascher, Marcia, and Robert Ascher. 1981. The Code of the Quipu. Ann Arbor: University of Michigan Press.

Aveni, Anthony F., ed. 1988. New Directions in American Archaeoastronomy: Proceedings of the 46th International Congress of Americanists (Amsterdam, Netherlands 1988), (BAR International Series 454). Oxford: BAR.

Barriga Barahona, Oscar. 1981. Colección de ponchos bolivianos. Exhibition leaflet. La Paz: MUSEF.

Barstow, Jean R. 1981. Marriage between human beings and animals: A structuralist discussion of two Aymara myths. Anthropology 5(1): 71–88.

Barthes, Roland. 1977. Rhetoric of the image. *In* Image, Music, Text, pp. 32–51. New York: Hill and Wang.

Bastien, Joseph W. 1987. Healers of the Andes: Kallawaya Herbalists and Their Medicinal Plants. Salt Lake City: University of Utah Press.

Benveniste, Emile. 1966. Les relations de temps dans le verbe français. Problèmes de linguistique générale, I, pp. 237–50. Paris: Gallimard.

Bergren, Anne. 1983. Language and the female in early Greek thought. Arethusa 16(1/2): 69–95.

Bernal Villa, Segundo. 1953. Aspectos de la cultura páez: Mitología y cuentos de la parcialidad de Calderas, Tierradentro. Revista Colombiana de Antropología 1(1): 279–309.

Bernales Ballesteros, Jorge, ed. 1969. Fray Calixto de San José Tupac Inca, procurador de indios y la 'Exclamación' reivindicacionista de 1750. Historia y Cultura 3: 5–35.

Bertonio, Ludovico. 1956 [1612]. Vocabulario de la lengua aymara. Facsimile edition. La Paz: Universidad Mayor de San Andrés.

————. 1984 [1612]. Vocabulario de la lengua aymara. Facsimile edition. Cochabamba, Bolivia: CERES/IFEA/MUSEF.

Beyersdorff, Margot. 1988. La adoración de los reyes magos: Vigencia del teatro religioso español en el Perú andino. Cusco: Centro Bartolomé de las Casas.

————, and Sabine Dedenbach-Salazar Sáenz, eds. 1994. Andean Oral Traditions: Discourse and Literature/Tradiciones orales andinas: Discurso y literatura (Bonner Amerikanistische Studien, 24). Bonn: Holos.

Bills, Garland D. 1972. The Quechua directional verbal suffix. Papers in Andean Linguistics 1(1): 1–15.

Bloch, Maurice. 1991. Language, anthropology and cognitive science. Man 26: 183–98.

Bourdieu, Pierre. 1977. Outline of a Theory of Practice. Cambridge: Cambridge University Press.

Bouysse-Cassagne, Thérèse. 1987. La identidad aymara: Aproximación histórica (Siglo XV, Siglo XVI). La Paz: HISBOL/IFEA.

———, and Olivia Harris. 1987. Pacha. En torno al pensamiento aymara. In Tres reflexiones sobre el pensamiento andino, ed. Thérèse Bouysse-Cassagne and Olivia Harris, Tristan Platt, and Verónica Cereceda, pp. 11–59. La Paz: HISBOL.

———, and Olivia Harris, Tristan Platt, and Verónica Cereceda. 1987. Tres reflexiones sobre el pensamiento andino. La Paz: HISBOL.

Bricker, Victoria Reifler. 1981. The Indian Christ, the Indian King. Austin: University of Texas Press.

———. 1989. El cristo indígena, el rey nativo. El substrato histórico de la mitología ritual de los mayas. Mexico: Fondo de Cultura Económica.

Briggs, Lucy. 1994. El k"arik"ari en dos textos de lengua aymara: Análisis morfosintáctico y del discurso. In Andean Oral Traditions: Discourse and Literature/Tradiciones orales andinas: Discurso y literatura, ed. Margot Beyersdorff and Sabine Dedenbach-Salazar Sáenz, pp. 161–97 (Bonner Amerikanistische Studien, 24). Bonn: Holos.

Brotherston, Gordon. 1979. Image of the New World: The American Continent Portrayed in Native Texts. London: Thames and Hudson.

Brown, Michael. 1986. Tsewa's Gift. Magic and Meaning in an Amazonian Society. Washington D. C.: Smithsonian Institution Press.

Burke, Kenneth. 1966. What are the signs of what? A theory of entitlement. In Language as Symbolic Action, pp. 359–79. Berkeley: University of California Press.

Calvo López, Julio-Alexis. 1994. Los evidenciales en las lenguas andinas y amazónicas. In Estudios de lengua y cultura amerindias I. ed. Julio Calvo Pérez, pp. 85–94. Valencia: Universidad de Valencia.

Cameron, Deborah, Elizabeth Frazer, Penelope Harvey, M.B.H. Rampton, and Kay Richardson. 1992. Researching Language: Issues of Power and Method. London: Routledge.

Carlson de Coombs, Heidi. 1975. La cláusula relativa en quechua de Cajamarca. Datos Etnolingüísticos no. 5. Lima: Instituto Lingüístico de Verano.

Castillo-Cárdenas, Gonzalo. 1987. Liberation Theology from Below: The Life and Thought of Manuel Quintín Lame. Maryknoll, N.Y.: Orbis.

Cereceda, Verónica. 1978. Sémiologie des tissus andins. Annales. E.S.C. 33(5–6): 1017–35.

———. 1986. The semiology of Andean textiles: The talegas of Isluga. In Anthropological History of Andean Polities, ed. John V. Murra, Nathan Wachtel, and Jacques Revel, pp. 149–73. Cambridge: Cambridge University Press.

———. 1987. Aproximaciones a una estética andina: De la belleza al tinku. In Tres reflexiones sobre el pensamiento andino, ed. Therese Bouysse-Cassagne et al., pp. 133–231. La Paz: HISBOL.

———. 1993. Cette étendue entre l'Altiplano et la mer...un mythe chipaya hors texte. In Mémoire de la tradition, ed. Aurore Becquelin, Antoinette Molinié, and Danielle Dehouve, pp. 227–84. Nanterre: Société d'Ethnologie.

Cerrón-Palomino, Rodolfo. 1987. Lingüística quechua. Cusco: Centro Bartolomé de las Casas.

Chafe, Wallace, and Joanna Nichols, eds. 1986. Evidentiality: The Linguistic Coding of Epistemology (Advances in Discourse Processes, Vol. 20) Norwood, N.J.: Ablex Publishing.

Clanchy, M. T. 1979. From Memory to Written Record, England 1066–1307. London: Edward Arnold.

Clifford, James, and George Marcus, eds. 1986. Writing Culture. The Poetics and Politics of Ethnography. Berkeley: University of California Press.

Cohen, Anthony P. 1985. The Symbolic Construction of Community. London: Tavistock.

Cole, Peter, Wayne Herbert, and Gabriella Hermon. 1982. Headless relative clauses in Quechua. International Journal of American Linguistics 48(2): 113–24.

Colombia, República de (Ministerio de Gobierno). 1983. Fuero indígena: Disposiciones legales del orden nacional, departamental y comisarial—jurisprudencia y conceptos. Bogotá: Presencia.

Condori Chura, Leandro, and Esteban Ticona Alejo. 1992. El escribano de los caciques apoderados/kasikinakan purirarunakan qillqiripa. La Paz: HISBOL/THOA.

Connerton, Paul. 1989. How Societies Remember. Cambridge: Cambridge University Press.

Costa, Rachel. 1972. A study of -sqa, -na, -y, and -q nominalizing suffixes in Quechua. Papers in Andean Linguistics 1(1): 29–77.

Crickmay, Lindsey. 1994. Ancestral spirit and Andean devil: Divergence of a single concept. Paper presented at the Institute of Amerindian Studies, University of St Andrews. Unpublished ms.

Cummins, Thomas B. F. 1988. Abstraction to Narration: Kero Imagery of Peru and the Colonial Alteration of Native Identity. Ph.D. dissertation. University of California—Los Angeles.

Cummins, Tom. In press. "Let me see"! Reading is for them: colonial Andean images and objects 'como es costumbre tener los caciques señores'. In Native Traditions in the Post-Conquest World, ed. Elizaeth H. Boone and Tom Cummins. Washington D.C.: Dumbarton Oaks Research Library and Collection.

De Certeau, Michel. 1984. The Practice of Everyday Life. Berkeley: University of California Press.

———. 1986. Heterologies: Discourse on the Other. Minneapolis: University of Minnesota Press.

Dedenbach, Sabine. 1982. Versuche zur Rekonstruktion der in den Quechua-Quellen verwendeten Dialekte. Appendix to: Zur Rekonstruktion des Ackerbauwortschatzes der Inkazeit. pp. 164–78. Unpublished German version of MA thesis. University of Bonn.

Dedenbach-Salazar Sáenz, Sabine. 1993. El desarrollo del sufijo -sqa a la luz de las fuentes quechuas del siglo XVIII. Paper presented at the "V Coloquio Internacional: El Siglo XVIII en los Andes", Paris, April 1993. Unpublished ms.

———. 1994. El arte verbal de los textos quechuas de Huarochirí (Perú, siglo XVII) reflejado en la organización del discurso y en los medios estilísticos. In Andean Oral Traditions: Discourse and Literature/Tradiciones orales andinas: Discurso y literatura, ed. Margot Beyersdorff and Sabine Dedenbach-Salazar Sáenz, pp. 21–49 (Bonner Amerikanistische Studien, 24). Bonn: Holos.

———, Utta von Gleich, Roswith Hartmann, Peter Masson, and Clodoaldo Soto Ruiz, tr. and ed. 1994. (3rd ed.) "Rimaykullayki". Unterrichtsmaterialien zum Quechua Ayacuchano. Based on Quechua—Manual de Enseñanza by Clodoaldo Soto Ruiz (Lima 1979). University of Bonn. Berlin: Reimer Verlag.

Deere, Carmen Diana. 1977. Changing social relations of production and Peruvian peasant women's work. Latin American Perspectives 4(12): 48–69.

Desrosiers, Sophie. 1988. Les techniques de tissage ont-elles un sens? Un mode de lecture des tissus andins. Techniques et Culture 12: 21–56.

Dorris, Michael. 1987. Indians on the shelf. In The American Indian and the Problem of History, ed. Calvin Martin, pp. 98–105. Oxford: Oxford University Press.

Douglas, Carrie. 1984. Toro muerto, vaca es: An interpretation of the Spanish bullfight. American Ethnologist 11: 242–58.

Dransart, Penny. 1988. Continuidad y cambio en la producción textil aymara tradicional. Hombre y Desierto: Una Perspectiva Cultural 2: 41–57.

———. 1991 Fibre to Fabric: The Role of Fibre in Camelid Economies in Pre-Hispanic and Contemporary Chile. D. Phil. thesis. University of Oxford.

Durand-Flórez, Luis, ed. 1980–82. Colección documental de bicentenario de la revolución emancipadora de Túpac Amaru: Vol. 1, Documentos varios del archivo general de Indias; vol. 2, Descargos del obispo del Cuzco; vols. 3–5, Los procesos a Túpac Amaru y sus compañeros. Lima: Comisión Nacional del Bicentenario de la Rebelión Emancipadora de Túpac Amaru.

Duranti, Alessandro, and Charles Goodwin. 1992. Rethinking Context: Language as an Interactive Phenomenon. Cambridge: Cambridge University Press.

Duviols, Pierre. 1979. Un symbolisme de l'occupation, de l'aménagement et de l'exploitation de l'espace: Le monolithe "huanca" et sa fonction dans les Andes préhispaniques. L'Homme 19(2): 7–31.

Duviols, Pierre, and César Itier, eds. 1993. Relación de antigüedades deste reyno del Piru. Edición facsimilar y transcripción paleográfica del códice de Madrid, pp. 127–78 (Travaux de l'IFEA/74; Archivos de Historia Andina/17). Lima and Cusco: Institut Français d'Etudes Andines/Centro Bartolomé de las Casas.

Earls, John, and Irene Silverblatt. 1976. La realidad física en la cosmología andina. Paris: Proceedings of the 42nd Congress of Americanists 4: 299–325.

Fabian, Johannes. 1983. Time and the Other: How Anthropology Makes its Object. New York: Columbia University Press.

Fairclough, Norman. 1989. Language and Power. London: Longmans.

———. 1992. Discourse and Social Change. Cambridge: Polity Press.

Fernandez, James. 1985. Exploded worlds—Text as a metaphor for ethnography (and vice versa). Dialectical Anthropology 10: 15–26.

Ferrell R., Marco A. 1994. La escritura incaica en Waman Puma. In II Congreso Nacional de Investigaciones Lingüístico-filológicas. Lima: Peru.

Flores Ochoa, Jorge. 1977a. Pastores de la puna: uywamichiq punarunakuna. Lima: Instituto de Estudios Peruanos.

———. 1977b. Enqa, enqaychu, illa y khuya rumi. In Pastores de la puna: uywamichiq punarunakuna, ed. Jorge Flores Ochoa, pp. 211–37. Lima: Instituto de Estudios Peruanos.

———. 1988. Llamichos y paqocheros: pastores de llamas y alpacas. Cusco: Centro Bartolomé de las Casas.

Floyd, Rick. 1994. The Wanka reportative as a radial category: A study in prototypes. In Language in the Andes, ed. Peter Cole, Gabriella Hermon, and Mario Daniel Martín, pp. 151–89. (Occasional Monographs in Latin American Studies, No. 4). Newark: University of Delaware, Latin American Studies Program.

Foley, John Miles. 1986. Introduction. In Oral Tradition in Literature: Interpretation in Context, ed. John Miles Foley, pp. 1–18. Columbia: University of Missouri Press.

Foucault, Michel. 1972. The Archaeology of Knowledge. London: Tavistock.

Fox, Richard, ed. 1990. Nationalist Ideologies and the Production of National Cultures. (American Ethnological Society Monograph Series, No. 2).

Franquemont, Edward M., Christine Franquemont, and Billie Jean Isbell. n.d. The unfolding of symmetries: The structuring of Andean cloth. Cornell University. Unpublished ms.

Fraser, Valerie. 1982. Hierarchies and rules of materials in building and representation. In The Other America: Native Artifacts from the New World, ed. Valerie Fraser and Gordon Brotherston, pp. 41–55. Colchester: University of Essex/Museum of Mankind.

Friedman, Jonathan. 1987. Beyond otherness or the spectacularization of anthropology. Telos 71: 161–70.

Garcilaso de la Vega, El Inca. 1963 [1609]. Los comentarios reales de los Incas. Biblioteca de Autores Españoles, vols. 133–35. Madrid: Atlas.

Gavilán V. Vivian, and Liliana Ulloa T. 1992. Proposiciones metodológicas para el estudio de los tejidos andinos. Revista Andina 10(1): 107–34.

Gee, James Paul. 1988. The legacies of literacy: From Plato to Freire through Harvey Graff. Harvard Educational Review 38(2): 195–234.

Geertz, Clifford. 1973. Thick description: Toward an interpretive theory of culture. *In* The Interpretation of Cultures: Selected Essays by Clifford Geertz. New York: Basic Books.

Getzels, Peter, and Harriet Gordon. 1985. In the Footsteps of Taytacha. Film. Watertown, Mass.: Documentary Educational Resources.

Getzels, Peter, Harriet Gordon, and Penelope Harvey. 1990. The Condor and the Bull: A Documentary Film. London: National Film and Television School.

Gillis, John, ed. 1994. Commemorations: The Politics of National Identity. Princeton, N.J.: Princeton University Press.

Gisbert, Teresa, Silvia Arze, and Martha Cajías. 1987. Arte textil y mundo andino. La Paz: Gisbert.

Gisbert, Teresa. 1980. Iconografía y mitos en el arte. La Paz: Gisbert.

Gonçález Holguín, Diego de. 1952 [1608]. Vocabulario de la lengua general de todo el Perú llamada Qquichua o del Inca. 2nd ed., ed. Raúl Porras Barrenechea. Lima: Universidad Nacional Mayor de San Marcos.

González Echevarría, Roberto. 1990. Myth and Archive: A Theory of Latin American Narrative. Cambridge: Cambridge University Press.

Goody, Jack. 1977. The Domestication of the Savage Mind. Cambridge: Cambridge University Press.

———. 1986. The Logic of Writing and the Organization of Society. Cambridge: Cambridge University Press.

———, and Watt, Ian P. 1963. The consequences of literacy. Comparative Studies in Society and History 5: 304–45.

Gose, Peter. 1986. Sacrifice and the commodity form in the Andes. Man 21: 296–310.

Gow, David. 1974. Taytacha Qoyllur Rit'i. Allpanchis 7: 47–100.

———. 1976. The Gods and Social Change in the High Andes. Ph.D. thesis. University of Wisconsin, Madison. Ann Arbor, Mich.: University Microfilms.

———, and Rosalind Gow. 1975. La alpaca en el mito y ritual. Allpanchis 8: 141–64.

Gow, David D. 1980. The roles of Christ and Inkarrí in Andean religion. Journal of Latin American Lore 6(2): 279–98.

Gow, Rosalind, and Bernabé Condori. 1982. Kay Pacha. Cusco: Centro Bartolomé de las Casas.

Graff, Harvey. 1979. The Literacy Myth: Literacy and Social Structure in the Nineteenth-Century City. New York: Academic Press.

Griffiths, Gareth. 1994. The myth of authenticity: Representation, discourse and social practice. *In* De-scribing Empire: Post-Colonialism and Textuality, ed. Chris Tiffin and Alan Lawson, pp. 70–85. London: Routledge.

Grosso, José Luis. 1995. La suerte de lo andino, sus saberes y poderes. Adivinación y mestizaje en el Norte de Potosí. Master's thesis. Universidad del Valle, Cali.

Gruzinski, Serge. 1985. La memoria mutilada: Construcción del pasado y mecanismos de la memoria en un grupo otomí de la mitad del siglo XVII. *In* La memoria y el olvido. Segundo Simposio de Historia de las Mentalidades, pp. 33–46. Mexico: Instituto Nacional de Antropología e Historia.

Guaman Poma de Ayala, Felipe. 1980 [1615]. El primer nueva corónica y buen gobierno, ed. John V. Murra and Rolena Adorno. Mexico: Siglo Veintiuno.

Gutmann, Margit. 1994. Vom Fuchs und vom Rebhuhn. Einige Merkmale des Erzählens in der Quechua-Kultur Perus. *In* Soziolinguistik und Sprachgeschichte: Querverbindungen, ed. Gabriele Berkenbusch and Christine Bierbach, pp. 147–74. Tübingen: Gunter Narr.

Hall, Stuart. 1993. Cultural identity and diaspora. *In* Colonial Discourse and Post-Colonial Theory: A Reader, ed. Patrick Williams and Laura Chrisman, pp. 392–403. New York: Harvester.

Hallpike, Christopher. 1979. The Foundations of Primitive Thought. Oxford: Clarendon.

Hanks, William. 1989. Text and textuality. Annual Review of Anthropology 18: 95–127.

Hanks, William F. 1993. Language and discourse in colonial Yucatán. Unpublished ms.

Harbsmeier, Michael. 1984. Early travels to Europe: Some remarks on the magic of writing. *In* Europe and Its Others, ed. Francis Barker et al., vol. 2, pp. 72–88. Colchester: University of Essex.

Hardman, Martha James. 1986. Data-source marking in the Jaqi languages. *In* Evidentiality: The Linguistic Coding of Epistemology, ed. Wallace Chafe and Joanna Nichols, pp. 113–36 (Advances in Discourse Processes, vol. 20). Norwood, N.J.: Ablex Publishing.

Harris, Olivia. 1982. The dead and the devils among the Bolivian Laymi. *In* Death and the Regeneration of Life, ed. Maurice Bloch and Jonathan P. Parry, pp. 45–73. Cambridge: Cambridge University Press.

———. 1986. From asymmetry to triangle: Symbolic transformations in Northern Potosí. *In* Anthropological History of Andean Polities, ed. John V. Murra, Nathan Wachtel, and Jacques Revel, pp. 260–79. Cambridge: Cambridge University Press.

———. 1994. Condor and bull: the ambiguities of masculinity in Northern Potosí. *In* Sex and Violence. Issues in Representation and Experience, ed. Penelope Harvey and Peter Gow, pp. 40–65. London: Routledge.

———. 1995. 'The coming of the white people': Reflections on the mythologisation of history in Latin America. Bulletin of Latin American Research 14(1): 9–24.

Harrison, Regina. 1989. Signs, Songs and Memory in the Andes: Translating Quechua Language and Culture. Austin: University of Texas Press.

Hartmann, Roswith, and Udo Oberem. 1981. Quito: Un centro de educación de indígenas en el siglo XVI. *In* Contribuções à antropologia em homenagem ao Profesor Egon Schaden, ed. Thekla Hartmann and Vera Penteado Coelho, pp. 105–27. São Paulo: Coleção Museo Paulista.

Harvey, Penelope. 1987. Language and the Power of History: The Discourse of Bilinguals in Ocongate (southern Peru). Ph.D. thesis, London School of Economics.

———. 1991. Drunken speech and the construction of meaning: Bilingual competence in the southern Peruvian Andes. Language in Society 20: 1–36.

———. 1992. Jugando por la identidad y la tradición. Las corridas de toros en el sur andino. *In* Tradición y modernidad en los Andes, ed. Henrique Urbano and Mirko Lauer, pp. 221–42. Cusco: Centro Bartolomé de las Casas.

———. 1994. Gender, community and confrontation: Power relations in drunkenness in Ocongate (southern Peru). *In* Gender, Drink and Drugs, ed. Maryon McDonald, ed. pp. 209–34. Oxford: Berg.

Hastrup, Kirsten, ed. 1992. Other Histories. London: Routledge.

Havelock, Eric. 1986. The Muse Learns to Write: Reflections on Orality and Literacy from Antiquity to the Present. New Haven, Conn.: Yale University Press.

Hillman, Grady. 1994. Aldeas sumergidas: Lot's wife and water rights. *In* Andean Oral Traditions: Discourse and Literature/Tradiciones orales andinas: Discurso y literatura, ed. Margot Beyersdorff and Sabine Dedenbach-Salazar Sáenz, pp. 83–116 (Bonner Amerikanistische Studien, 24). Bonn: Holos.

Howard-Malverde, Rosaleen. 1988. Talking about the past: Tense and testimonials in Quechua narrative discourse. Amerindia 13: 125–55.

———. 1989. Storytelling strategies in Quechua narrative performance. Journal of Latin American Lore 15(1): 3–71.

———. 1990. The Speaking of History: 'Willapaakushayki' or Quechua Ways of Telling the Past (Institute of Latin American Studies Research Papers, 21). London: University of London.

————. 1994. "La gente más bien hace guerra con los cuentos": Estrategias narrativas en una comunidad quechua del Perú central. *In* Andean Oral Traditions: Discourse and Literature/Tradiciones orales andinas: Discurso y literatura, ed. Margot Beyersdorff and Sabine Dedenbach-Salazar Sáenz, (Bonner Amerikanistische Studien, 24), pp. 117–35. Bonn: Holos.

Huanca, Tomás. 1989. El yatiri en la comunidad aymara. La Paz: Centro Andino de Desarrollo Agropecuario.

Husson, Jean-Philippe. 1984. L'art poétique quechua dans la chronique de Felipe Waman Puma de Ayala. Amerindia 9: 79–110.

————. 1985. La poésie quechua dans la chronique de Felipe Waman Puma de Ayala. De l'art lyrique de cour aux chants et danses populaires. Paris: L'Harmattan.

Ingold, Tim, ed. 1994. Debate on the Motion "The Past is a Foreign Country". Manchester: Group for Debates in Anthropological Theory.

Isbell, Billie Jean. 1978. To Defend Ourselves: Ecology and Ritual in an Andean Village. Austin: University of Texas Press.

————. 1982. Nature meets culture in the dialectical world of the tropics. Annals of the New York Academy of Sciences 1982: 353–63.

————, and Fredy Roncalla. 1977. The ontogenesis of metaphor: Riddle games among Quechua speakers seen as cognitive discovery procedures. Journal of Latin American Lore 3(1): 19–49.

Itier, César. 1991. Lengua general y comunicación escrita: Cinco cartas en quechua de Cotahuasi (1616). Revista Andina 17: 65–107.

————. 1993. Estudio lingüístico. *In* Relación de antigüedades deste reyno del Piru, ed. Pierre Duviols and César Itier, Edición facsimilar y transcripción paleográfica del códice de Madrid, pp. 127–78. (Travaux de l'IFEA/74; Archivos de Historia Andina/17). Lima and Cusco: Institut Français d'Études Andines/Centro Bartolomé de las Casas.

Ixtlilxochitl, Fernando de Alva. 1975 [1608]. Compendio histórico del reino de Texcoco. *In* Obras históricas. Vol. I, ed. Edmundo O'Gorman, pp. 415–521. Mexico City: UNAM.

Jackson, Jean. 1991. Being and becoming an indian in the Vaupés. *In* Nation States and Indians in Latin America, ed. Greg Urban and Joel Sherzer, pp. 131–55. Austin: University of Texas Press.

Jones, Linda K. 1992. In pursuit of discourse particles. *In* Language in Context: Essays for Robert E. Longacre, ed. Shin Ja J. Hwang and William R. Merrifield, pp. 127–36. (Publications in Linguistics, no. 107). Arlington: Summer Institute of Linguistics and The University of Texas.

Keesing, Roger. 1987. Anthropology as interpretive quest. Current Anthropology 28(2): 161–69.

Kemper Columbus, Claudette. 1990. Immortal eggs: A Peruvian geocracy; Pariaqaqa of Huarochirí. Journal of Latin American Lore 16(2): 175–98.

————. 1994. Curious confessions: Cristóbal Choquecaxa, informant and actor of Huarochirí. *In* Andean Oral Traditions: Discourse and Literature/Tradiciones orales andinas: Discurso y literatura, ed. Margot Beyersdorff and Sabine Dedenbach-Salazar Sáenz, pp. 51–82. (Bonner Amerikanistische Studien, 24). Bonn: Holos.

Kendon, Adam. 1992. The negotiation of context in face-to-face interaction. *In* Rethinking Context: Language as an Interactive Phenomenon, ed. Alessandro Duranti and Charles Goodwin, pp. 323–34. Cambridge: Cambridge University Press.

Kristeva, Julia. 1980. Desire in Language: A Semiotic Approach to Literature and Art, ed. Leon Samuel Roudiez, tr. T. Gora, A. Jardine, and L. S. Roudiez. New York: Columbia University Press.

Lame, Manuel Quintín. 1971 [1939]. En defensa de mi raza, ed. and with an introduction by Gonzalo Castillo-Cárdenas. Bogotá: Comité de Defensa del Indio. (English translation in Castillo-Cárdenas 1987).

Lanser, Susan Sniader. 1981. The Narrative Act: Point of View in Prose and Fiction. Princeton, N.J.: Princeton University Press.

Lapidus de Sager, Nejama. 1968. El significado de algunos ideogramas andinos. Contribución al estudio de la comunicación prehispánica. In Idiomas, cosmovisiones y cultura (Publication of Instituto de Antropología). Rosario, Argentina: Universidad Nacional del Litoral.

Laqueur, Thomas. 1994. Memory and naming in the Great War. In Commemorations: The Politics of National Identity, ed. John Gillis, pp.150–67. Princeton, N.J.: Princeton University Press.

Leach, Edmund R. 1976. Culture and Communication. The Logic by which Symbols Are Connected. Cambridge: Cambridge University Press.

Levinsohn, Stephen H. 1976. Progression and digression in Inca (Quechuan) discourse. Forum Linguisticum 1(2): 122–47.

Lévi-Strauss, Claude. 1966. The Savage Mind. Chicago: University of Chicago Press.

Lienhard, Martin. 1990. La voz y su huella. Escritura y conflicto étnico-social en América Latina, 1492–1988. Havana: Casa de las Américas; Hanover, N.H. (USA): Ediciones del Norte 1991, revised edition; Lima: Horizonte 1991, 3rd revised and expanded edition.

———. 1992. La voz y su huella. Lima: Editorial Horizonte.

Lofgren, Orvar. 1993. Materializing the nation in Sweden and America. Ethnos 3–4: 161–96.

Lowenthal, David. 1985. The Past is a Foreign Country. Cambridge: Cambridge University Press.

MacCormack, Sabine. 1991. Religion in the Andes: Vision and Imagination in Early Colonial Peru. Princeton, N.J.: Princeton University Press.

Mamani Mamani, Manuel. 1990. Myth and music in the livestock marking ritual of the Chilean Andes. Latinamericanist 25(2): 1–7.

Mannheim, Bruce. 1986a. Poetic form in Guaman Poma's Wariqsa Arawi. Amerindia 11: 41–57.

———. 1986b. The language of reciprocity in southern Peruvian Quechua. Anthropological Linguistics 28: 267–73.

———. 1991. The Language of the Inka since the European Invasion. Austin: Texas University Press.

Manrique, Nelson. 1981. Las guerrillas indígenas en la guerra con Chile [prologue by Pablo Macera]. Lima: Ital Perú/CIC.

March, Kathryn S. 1983. Weaving, writing, and gender. In Man (N.S.) 18: 729–44.

Martínez, Gabriel. 1976. El sistema de los Uywiris en Isluga. Anales de la Universidad del Norte (Homenaje al Dr Gustavo Le Paige S.J.) 10: 255–327.

Mateos, Francisco, ed. 1949. Cartas de indios cristianos del Paraguay. Missionalia Hispanica 6(18): 547–72.

Melo, Jorge Orlando. 1989. Etnia, región y nación: El fluctuante discurso de la identidad (notas para un debate). In Identidad: Memorias del simposio "Identidad étnica, identidad regional, identidad nacional", ed. Myriam Jimeno, Gloria Isabel Ocampo, and Miguelangel Roldán, pp. 27–48. Bogotá: ICFES.

Meneses, Teodoro L. 1983. Teatro Quechua colonial: Antología. Lima: Ediciones Edubanco.

Messick, Brinkley. 1987. Subordinate discourse: Women, weaving, and gender relations in North Africa. American Ethnologist 14(2): 210–25.

Mignolo, Walter D. 1994. Afterword: Writing and recording knowledge in colonial and postcolonial situations. In Writing without Words. Alternative literacies in Mesoamerica and the Andes, ed. Elizabeth Hill Boone and Walter D. Mignolo, pp. 292–313. Durham, N.C.: Duke University Press.

Millones, Luis. 1985. La familia endemoniada de Chupamarca. Temas sobre psiquiatría y psicología 1: 51–8.

————. 1989. En busca de Santa Rosa: Reflexiones en torno a una biografía duradera. Bulletin of the National Museum of Ethnography of Osaka 14(4): 891–905.

————. 1991. Los años oscuros de Santa Rosa y los sueños de Santa Rosa de Lima. *In* El umbral de los dioses, ed. Moisés Lemlij and Luis Millones, pp. 121–81. Lima: Sociedad Peruana de Psicoanálisis y Seminario Interdisciplinario de Estudios Andinos.

————. 1992. Actores de altura. Ensayos sobre el teatro popular andino. Lima: Editorial Horizonte.

Montoya, Rodrigo. 1993. Quechua theater: History, violence and hope. Indiana Journal of Hispanic Literatures 1(2): 53–77.

Moore, Henrietta. 1989. Paul Ricoeur: Action, meaning and text. *In* Reading Material Culture: Structuralism, Hermeneutics and Post-Structuralism, ed. Christopher Tilley, pp. 85–120. Oxford: Blackwell.

Moreno Proaño, A. 1979. Cronología de la vida de Fray Jodoco Ricke, fundador del convento de San Francisco de Quito (1498–1578). Boletín de la Academia Nacional de Historia 131–32: 173–90.

Morote Best, Efraín. 1957. El oso raptor. Archivos Venezolanos de Folklore 5(5): 157–78.

Munn, Nancy. 1990. Constructing regional worlds in experience: Kula exchange, witchcraft and Gawan local events. Man 25: 1–17.

Murra, John V. 1972. El "control vertical" de un máximo de pisos ecológicos en la economía de las sociedades andinas. *In* Visita de la provincia de León de Huánuco en 1552. Iñigo Ortiz de Zúniga, visitador, ed. John V. Murra, pp. 429–76. Huánuco: Universidad Hermilio Valdizán.

————. 1975a [1973]. Las etno-categorías de un *khipu* estatal. *In* Formaciones económicas y políticas del mundo andino, pp. 243–54. Lima: Instituto de Estudios Peruanos.

————. 1975b [1958]. La función del tejido en varios contextos sociales y políticos. *In* Formaciones económicas y políticas del mundo andino, pp. 145–70. Lima: Instituto de Estudios Peruanos.

————. 1982. The mit'a obligations of ethnic groups to the Inka state. *In* The Inca and Aztec States 1400–1800: Anthropology and History, ed. George Collier and Renato Rosaldo, pp. 237–62. London. Academic Press.

————. 1989 [1962]. Cloth and its function in the Inka state. *In* Cloth and Human Experience, ed. Annette B. Weiner and Jane Schneider, pp. 275–302. Washington D. C.: Smithsonian Institution Press.

————, Nathan Wachtel, and Jacques Revel, eds. 1986. Anthropological History of Andean Polities. Cambridge: Cambridge University Press.

Nash, June. 1979. We Eat the Mines and the Mines Eat Us. New York: Columbia University Press.

Niessen, Sandra. 1985. Motifs of life in Toba Batak texts and textiles. (Verhandelingen, van het koninklijk instituut voortaal-, land-en volkenkunde, 110). Dordrecht: Holland.

Nora, Pierre. 1984. Entre mémoire et histoire: La problématique des lieux. *In* Les lieux de mémoire, ed. Pierre Nora, vol. 1, pp. xv–xlii. Paris: Gallimard.

————. 1989. Between memory and history: Les lieux de mémoire. Representations 26: 7–25.

Núñez del Prado Béjar, Daisy. 1972. La reciprocidad como ethos de la cultura quechua. Allpanchis 4: 135–65.

Núñez del Prado Béjar, Juan. 1970. El mundo sobrenatural de los quechuas del sur del Perú a través de la comunidad de Qotabamba. Allpanchis 2: 57–119.

Nuñez del Prado, Oscar. 1973. Kuyo Chico: Applied Anthropology in an Indian Community, tr. Lucy Whyte Russo and Richard Russo. Chicago: University of Chicago Press.

Ong, Walter. 1982. Orality and Literacy: The Technologizing of the Word. New York: Methuen.

————. 1986. Text as interpretation, Mark and after. *In* Oral Tradition in Literature, ed. John Miles Foley, pp. 147–69. Columbia: University of Missouri Press.

Ortíz Rescaniere, Alejandro. 1973. De Adaneva a Inkarrí: Una visión indígena del Perú. Lima: Retablo de Papel.

Ossio, Juan, ed. 1973. Ideología mesiánica del mundo andino. Lima: Ignacio Prado Pastor.

Ossio, Juan M. 1985. Los retratos de los Incas en la crónica de Fray Martín de Morúa. Lima: COFIDE.

Oviedo y Herrera, Luis Antonio de. 1867. Santa Rosa de Lima, poema heroico. Lima: Administración del Perú Católico.

Oxford English Dictionary. 1971. The Compact Edition of the Oxford English Dictionary. New York: Oxford University Press.

———. 1989. 2nd edition. Oxford: Clarendon.

Pachacuti Yamqui Salcamaygua, Joan de Santacruz. 1968 [1613]. Relación de antigüedades deste reyno del Perú. In Crónicas peruanas de interés indígena, ed. Francisco Esteve Barba (BAE no. 209), pp. 279–319. Madrid: Atlas.

———. 1993 [1613]. Relación de antigüedades deste reyno del Perú. Estudio etnohistórico y lingüístico de Pierre Duviols y César Itier. Cusco: Centro Bartolomé de las Casas/Instituto Frances de Estudios Andinos.

Palma, Ricardo. 1983. Tradiciones peruanas. Barcelona: E. Cappelletti.

Pärssinen, Martti. 1992. Tawantinsuyu: The Inca State and its Political Organization. Helsinki: SHS.

Paso y Troncoso, Francisco de, ed. 1939–42. Epistolario de Nueva España. Antigua Librería Robredo de José Porrúa e hijos, 16 vols. Mexico: Biblioteca Histórica Mexicana de Obras Inéditas.

Perrin, Michel. 1986. 'Savage' points of view on writing. In Myth and the Imaginary in the New World, ed. Edmundo Magaña and Peter Mason, pp. 211–31. Amsterdam: CEDLA.

Perroud, Pedro C., and Juan M. Chouvenc. 1969? Diccionario Castellano Kechwa, Kechwa Castellano: Dialecto de Ayacucho. Santa Clara, Peru: Seminario…Padres Redentoristas.

Platt, Tristan. 1978. Symmétries en miroir: Le concept de yanantin chez les Macha de Bolivie. In Annales E.S.C. 33(5–6): 1081–1107.

———. 1982. Estado boliviano y ayllu andino: Tierra y tributo en el Norte de Potosí. Lima: Instituto de Estudios Peruanos.

———. 1983. Conciencia andina y conciencia proletaria: qhuya runa y ayllu en el Norte de Potosí. Lima: HISLA 2: 47–73.

———. 1986. Mirrors and maize: The concept of yanantin among the Macha of Bolivia. In Anthropological History of Andean Polities, ed. John V. Murra, Nathan Wachtel, and Jacques Revel, pp. 229–59. Cambridge: Cambridge University Press.

———. 1987. The Andean Soldiers of Christ: Confraternity organization, the Mass of the Sun and regenerative warfare (XVIII–XX centuries). Journal de la Société des Américanistes 83: 139–92

———. 1988. Cultos milagrosos y chamanismo en el cristianismo surandino. Iglesia, religión y sociedad en la historia latinoamericana. Actas del VIII Congreso de la Asociación de Historiadores Latinoamericanistas en Europa, pp. 119–37. Szeged: University of Szeged.

———. 1992. Writing, shamanism and identity, or voices from Abya-Yala. In History Workshop Journal 34: 132–47.

———, Thérèse Bouysse-Cassagne, Olivia Harris, and Thierry Saignes, eds. In press. Qaraqara/Charka: Fuentes para el estudio de una confederación Aymara (siglos XV–XVII). La Paz: CID/IFEA/HISBOL.

Poma de Ayala, Felipe Guaman. 1980 [c. 1615]. El primer nueva corónica y buen gobierno. 3 vols., ed. John V. Murra and Rolena Adorno. Mexico City: Siglo XXI.

Poole, Deborah. 1982. Temporal classification and transformation in Andean devotional dance. Manchester: XLIV International Congress of Americanists. Unpublished ms.

————. 1984. The choreography of history in Andean dance. Denver, Colo.: 83rd Annual Meeting of the American Anthropological Association, Unpublished ms.

Poole, Deborah A. 1990. Accommodation and resistance in Andean ritual dance. Drama Review 34(2): 98–126.

Proust, Marcel. 1987. Remembrance of Things Past. Harmondsworth: Penguin.

Purin, Sergio, ed. 1990. Inca—Peru 3000 ans d'histoire. Brussels: Musées Royaux d'Art et d'Histoire.

Ramírez, Juan Andrés. 1969. La novena al Señor de Qoyllur Rit'i. Allpanchis 1: 61–88.

Randall, Robert. 1982. Qoyllur Rit'i, an Inca fiesta of the pleiades. Bulletin de l'Institut Français d'Etudes Andines 11(1–2): 37–81.

————. 1990. The mythstory of Kuri Qoyllur: Sex, *seqes*, and sacrifice in Inka agricultural festivals. Journal of Latin American Lore 16(1): 3–46.

Rappaport, Joanne. 1980–81. El mesianismo y las transformaciones de símbolos mesiánicos en Tierradentro. Revista Colombiana de Antropologa 23: 365–413.

————. 1985. History, myth and the dynamics of territorial maintenance in Tierradentro, Colombia. American Ethnologist 12(1): 27–45.

————. 1988. La organización socio-territorial de los Pastos: Una hipótesis de trabajo. Revista de Antropología 4(2): 71–103.

————. 1990. The Politics of Memory: Native Historical Interpretation in the Colombian Andes. Cambridge: Cambridge University Press.

————. 1994. Cumbe Reborn: An Andean Ethnography of History. Chicago: University of Chicago Press.

Redford, Bruce. 1986. The Converse of the Pen: Acts of Intimacy in the Eighteenth Century Familiar Letter. Chicago: Chicago University Press.

Reina, Leticia. 1980. Las rebeliones campesinas en México, 1819–1906. México: Siglo XXI.

Ricoeur, Paul. 1971. The model of the text: Meaningful action considered as text. Social Research 11: 529–62.

————. 1981. Hermeneutics and the Human Sciences, ed. John B. Thompson. Cambridge: Cambridge University Press.

————. 1991. From Text to Action. Essays in Hermeneutics, II, tr. Kathleen Blamey and John B. Thompson. London: Athlone.

Rivera Cusicanqui, Silvia, and Equipo THOA. 1992. Ayllus y proyectos de desarrollo en el Norte de Potosí. La Paz: Ediciones Aruwiyiri.

Rodríguez, Rosario. 1994. Desde las prácticas textuales aymaras. Talk given at the presentation of the book, Jichha nä parlt'ä: Ahora les voy a narrar. E. Espejo Ayka, ed. Denise Y. Arnold and Juan de Dios Yapita. La Paz: UNICEF/Casa de las Américas.

Rosaldo, Renato. 1989. Imperialist nostalgia. Representations 26: 107–22.

Rostworowski de Diez Canseco, María. 1986. Estructuras andinas del poder, 2nd ed. Lima: Instituto de Estudios Peruanos.

————. 1988. Conflicts over coca fields in XVIth century Peru. (Memoirs of the Museum of Anthropology, 21). Ann Arbor: University of Michigan.

Sallnow, Michael. 1974. La peregrinación andina. Allpanchis 7: 101–42.

————. 1987. Pilgrims of the Andes: Regional Cults in Cusco. Washington D.C.: Smithsonian Institution Press.

Salomon, Frank. 1981. Killing the yumbo: A ritual drama of northern Quito. *In* Cultural Transformations and Ethnicity in Modern Ecuador, ed. Norman Whitten Jr., pp. 162–208. Urbana: University of Illinois Press.

————. 1991. Introductory essay: The Huarochirí manuscript. *In* The Huarochirí Manuscript: A Testament of Ancient and Colonial Andean Religion, tr. and ed. Frank Salomon and George L. Urioste, pp. 1–38. Austin: University of Texas Press.

————, and George Urioste, tr. and ed. 1991. The Huarochirí Manuscript: A Testament of Ancient and Colonial Andean Religion. Austin: University of Texas Press.

Sánchez, Luis Alberto. 1950–51. La literatura peruana. Buenos Aires: Editorial Guarania.

Santacruz Pachacuti Salcamaygua, Juan de. 1879 [1613]. Relación de antigüedades de este reyno del Perú. *In* Tres relaciones de antigüedades peruanos, ed. Marcos Jiménez de la Espada, pp. 229–328. Madrid: Atlas.

Schiffrin, Deborah. 1994. Approaches to Discourse. Oxford: Blackwell.

Segal, Daniel A. 1988. Nationalism, comparatively speaking. Journal of Historical Sociology 1: 301–21.

Segal, Daniel A., and Richard Handler. 1992. How European is Nationalism? Social Analysis 32: 1–15.

Sharon, Douglas. 1980. El Chamán de los Cuatro Vientos. Mexico City: Siglo Veintiuno Editores.

Sherbondy, Jeannette E. 1988. Mallki: Ancestros y cultivo de árboles en los Andes. *In* Sociedad andina pasado y presente. Contribuciones en homenaje a la memoria de César Fonseca Martel, ed. Ramiro Matos Mendieta, pp. 101–35. Lima: Fomciencias.

Shopes, Linda. 1986. Oral history and community involvement: The Baltimore Neighborhood Heritage Project. *In* Presenting the Past: Essays on History and the Public, ed. Susan Porter Benson, Stephen Brier, and Roy Rosenzweig, pp. 249–63. Philadelphia: Temple University Press.

Silverman-Proust, Gail P. 1988. Significado simbólico de las franjas multicolores tejidas en los wayakos de los Q'ero. Boletín de Lima 57(10): 37–44.

Simpson, D. P. 1973. Cassell's Latin-English Dictionary. 5th ed. London: Cassell.

Skar, Harald O. 1982. The Warm Valley People: Duality and Land Reform Among the Quechua Indians of Highland Peru. Oslo: Oslo University Press.

Skar, Sarah Lund. 1994. Lives Together Worlds Apart. Quechua Colonization in Jungle and City. Oslo: Scandinavian University Press.

Solá, Donald. 1969. Cuzco Quechua Language Materials. Ithaca, N.Y.: Cornell University Latin American Studies Program.

Sontag, Susan. 1977. On Photography. New York: Delta.

Spivak, Gayatri Chakravorty. 1988. In Other Worlds: Essays in Cultural Politics. London: Routledge.

————. 1993. Can the subaltern speak? *In* Colonial Discourse and Post-Colonial Theory: A Reader, ed. Patrick Williams and Laura Chrisman, pp. 66–111. New York: Harvester.

Stobart, Henry. 1987. Primeros datos sobre la música del norte de Potosí. Série Anales de la Reunión de Etnología no. 1, tomo III: 81–96. La Paz: MUSEF.

Strathern, Marilyn. 1987. Comment on Keesing, Roger 1987. Current Anthropology 28(2): 173–74.

————. 1992. After Nature: English Kinship in the Late Twentieth Century. Cambridge: Cambridge University Press.

Street, Brian V. 1993. Introduction: The new literacy studies. *In* Cross-Cultural Approaches to Literacy, ed. Brian V. Street, pp. 1–21. Cambridge: Cambridge University Press.

Sullivan, Lawrence. 1988. Icanchu's Drum: An Orientation to Meaning in South American Indian Religions. New York: Macmillan.

Sweeney, Amin. 1987 A Full Hearing: Orality and Literacy in the Malay World. Berkeley: University of California Press.

Szeminski, Jan. 1987. Un kuraka, un dios y una historia. (Serie: Antropología Social e Historia No. 2). San Salvador de Jujuy: Talleres Gráficos Gutenburg.

Taussig, Michael. 1990. Shamanism, Colonialism and the Wildman: A Study in Terror and Healing. Chicago: University of Chicago Press.

————. 1992. The Nervous System. London: Routledge.

Taylor, Gerald. 1980. Supay. Amerindia 5: 47–63.

————. 1987a. Ritos y tradiciones de Huarochirí. Manuscrito quechua de comienzos del siglo XVII. Versión paleográfica, interpretación fonológica y traducción al castellano. Lima: Instituto de Estudios Peruanos/Institut Français d'Études Andines.

————. 1987b. Introducción. In Ritos y Tradiciones de Huarochirí, pp. 15–37. Lima: Instituto de Estudios Peruanos/Institut Français d'Etudes Andines.

————. 1990. Le dialecte quechua de Laraos, Yauyos: Étude morphologique. Bulletin de l'Institut Français d'Etudes Andines 19(2): 293–325.

————. 1994. Estudios de dialectología quechua (chachapoyas, ferreñafe, yauyos). Lima: Universidad Nacional de Educación.

Tedlock, Barbara, and Dennis Tedlock. 1985. Text and textile: Language and technology in the arts of the Quiché Maya. Journal of Anthropological Research 41(2): 121–46.

Terdiman, Richard. 1989. The mnemonics of Musset's confession. Representations 26: 26–48.

Theweleit, Klaus. 1989. Male Fantasies. Minneapolis: University of Minnesota Press.

Thompson, John B. 1990. Ideology and Modern Culture. Cambridge: Polity Press.

Tiffin, Chris and Alan Lawson, eds. 1994. De-scribing Empire: Post-Colonialism and Textuality. London: Routledge.

Todorov, Tzvetan. 1984. The Conquest of America: The Question of the Other. New York: Harper and Row.

Tomoeda, Hiroyasu. 1988. "La llama es mi chacra": El mundo metafórico del pastor andino. In Llamichos y paqocheros: Pastores de llamas y alpacas, ed. Jorge Flores Ochoa, pp. 225–36. Cusco: Centro Bartolomé de las Casas.

Tonkin, Elizabeth, Maryon McDonald and M. Chapman, eds. 1989. History and Ethnicity. London: Routledge.

Torero, Alfredo. 1964. Los dialectos quechuas. Anales Científicos de la Universidad Agraria (Lima) 2: 446–78.

Torrico, Cassandra. 1989. Living weavings: The symbolism of Bolivian herders' sacks. Sucre: HISBOL/Archivo Nacional de Bolivia. Mimeograph.

Trimborn, Hermann. 1967. Einleitung. In Francisco de Avila, ed. Hermann Trimborn and Antje Kelm, pp. 1–15. (Quellenwerke zur alten Geschichte Amerikas aufgezeichnet in den Sprachen der Eingeborenen, 8). Berlin: Gebrüder Mann Verlag.

Urbano, Henrique O. 1980. Dios Yaya, Dios Churi, Dios Espíritu. Journal of Latin American Lore 6: 111–27.

Urioste, George L. 1973. Chay Simire Caymi: The Language of the Manuscript of Huarochirí (Latin American Studies Series, no. 79). Ithaca, N.Y.: Cornell University.

Urton, Gary. 1981. At the Crossroads of the Earth and the Sky: An Andean Cosmology. Austin: University of Texas Press.

Valderrama, Ricardo, and Carmen Escalante. 1988. Del Tata Mallku a la Mama Pacha: Riego, sociedad y ritos en los Andes peruanos. Lima: DESCO, Centro de Estudios y Promoción del Desarrollo.

Van de Kerke, Simon, and Pieter Muysken. 1990. Quechua mu and the perspective of the speaker. In Unity in Diversity: Papers Presented to Simon C. Dik on His 50th Birthday, ed. Harm Pinkster and Inge Genee, pp. 151–63. Dordrecht: Foris.

Van Gennep, Arnold. 1960. The Rites of Passage. London: Routledge and Kegan Paul.

Wachtel, Nathan. 1977. The Vision of the Vanquished: The Spanish Conquest of Peru through Indian Eyes, 1530–1570. Hassocks: Harvester Press.

Wagner, Roy. 1981. The Invention of Culture. Chicago: University of Chicago Press.

Watson-Franke, M-B. 1974. A woman's profession in Guajiro culture: Weaving. Anthropologica 37: 25–40.

Weber, David J. 1976. Bases para el estudio de la relativización con referencia al quechua. (Documento de Trabajo 10). Yarinacocha, Pucallpa: Instituto Lingüístico de Verano/Ministerio de Educación.

———. 1986. Information perspective, profile, and patterns in Quechua. *In* Evidentiality: The Linguistic Coding of Epistemology, ed. Wallace Chafe and Joanna Nichols, pp. 137–55. (Advances in Discourse Processes, vol. 20). Norwood, N.J.: Ablex Publishing.

———. 1989. A Grammar of Huallaga (Huánuco) Quechua. (University of California Publications in Linguistics, 112). Berkeley: University of California Press.

Wightman, Ann. 1990. Indigenous Migration and Social Change: The Forasteros of Cuzco, 1520–1720. Durham, N.C.: Duke University Press.

Williams, Brett. 1988. Upscaling Downtown: Stalled Gentrification in Washington, D.C. Ithaca, N.Y.: Cornell University Press.

Wölck, Wolfgang. 1979. The structure of discourse as an integral part of Quechua grammar. Paper presented at the International Congress of Americanists, Vancouver, 1979. Unpublished ms.

Yupangui (Yupanqui), Titu Cussi (Cusi). 1985 [1570]. Ynstruçion del Ynga don Diego de Castro Titu Cussi Yupangui, intro. Luis Millones. Lima: El Virrey.

Zorn, Elayne. 1986. Textiles in herders' ritual bundles of Macusani, Peru. *In* The Junius B. Bird Second Conference on Andean textiles, ed. Ann P. Rowe, pp. 289–307. Washington D.C.: Textile Museum.

Zuidema, R. Tom. 1980. El ushnu. Revista de la Universidad Complutense 2(117): 317–62.

———. 1986. La civilization inca au Cuzco. Paris: Presses Universitaires de France.

———. 1988. The two pillars of Cuzco: Which two dates of sunset did they define? *In* New Directions in American Archaeoastronomy: Proceedings of the 46th International Congress of Americanists (Amsterdam, Netherlands 1988), ed. Anthony F. Aveni, pp. 143–89. (BAR International Series 454). Oxford: BAR.

———. 1989. Burocracia y conocimiento sistemático en la sociedad andina. *In* Reyes y guerreros: Ensayos de cultura andina, pp. 488–535. Peru: Fomciencias.

Index